Unveiling the French Republic

Studies in Critical Research on Religion

Haymarket Books is proud to be working with Brill Academic Publishers (www.brill.nl) to republish the *Studies in Critical Research on Religion* book series in paperback editions. This peer-reviewed book series offers insights into our current reality by exploring the content and consequences of power relationships under capitalism, and by considering the spaces of opposition and resistance to these changes that have been defining our new age. Our full catalog of *SCRR* volumes can be viewed at https://www.haymarketbooks.org/series_collections/6-studies-in-critical-research-in-religion.

Series Editor
Warren S. Goldstein, Center for Critical Research on Religion (U.S.A.)

Editorial Board
Christopher Craig Brittain, University of Aberdeen (U.K.)
Heather Eaton, Saint Paul University (Canada)
Titus Hjelm, University College London (U.K.)
Darlene Juschka, University of Regina (Canada)
Lauren Langman, Loyola University Chicago (U.S.A.)
George Lundskow, Grand Valley State University (U.S.A.)
Kenneth G. MacKendrick, University of Manitoba (Canada)
Andrew M. McKinnon, University of Aberdeen (U.K.)
Sara Pike, California State University, Chico (U.S.A)
Dana Sawchuk, Wilfrid Laurier University (Canada)

Advisory Board
William Arnal, University of Regina (Canada)
Roland Boer, University of Newcastle (Australia)
Jonathan Boyarin, Cornell University (U.S.A.)
Jay Geller, Vanderbilt University (U.S.A.)
Marsha Hewitt, University of Toronto (Canada)
Michael Löwy, Centre National de la Recherche Scientifique (France)
Eduardo Mendieta, Penn State University (U.S.A.)
Rudolf J. Siebert, Western Michigan University (U.S.A.)
Rhys H. Williams, Loyola University Chicago (U.S.A.)

Unveiling the French Republic

National Identity, Secularism, and Islam in Contemporary France

Per-Erik Nilsson

Haymarket Books
Chicago, IL

First published in 2017 by Brill Academic Publishers, The Netherlands.
© 2017 Koninklijke Brill NV, Leiden, The Netherlands

Published in paperback in 2018 by
Haymarket Books
P.O. Box 180165
Chicago, IL 60618
773-583-7884
www.haymarketbooks.org

ISBN: 978-1-60846-177-6

Trade distribution:
In the U.S. through Consortium Book Sales, www.cbsd.com
In the UK, Turnaround Publisher Services, www.turnaround-uk.com
In Canada, Publishers Group Canada, www.pgcbooks.ca
All other countries, Ingram Publisher Services International, intlsales@perseusbooks.com

Cover design by Jamie Kerry of Belle Étoile Studios.
Cover photo: Rett Rossi (Godafoss, Iceland)

This book was published with the generous support of Lannan Foundation and the Wallace Action Fund.

Printed in the United States.

10 9 8 7 6 5 4 3 2 1

Library of Congress Cataloging-in-Publication Data is available.

Contents

Series Editor's Preface   IX
Acknowledgements   X
Abbreviations   XII

Introduction: Everybody Welcome to France   1

PART I
Approaching French Secularism

1 (French) Secularism   13
   Secularization, the Secular, and Secularism   14
   Secularism(s)   17
   Critique   24
      Incongruities   24
      Contradictions   26
      A Western Gaze?   29
   Previous Research on the Islamic Veil Affairs and Secularism   31
   Analyzing Secularism   37
      A Critical Approach to Secularism   39
      Secularism as Governmentality   40
      Secularism as Discourse   42

2 A Shield Against Alterity   45
   The Islamic Veil Affairs   46
      1989   47
      2003–2004   50
      2007–2011   55
   State Feminism and the Other-Woman   61
   Alterity and Communitarianism   65
   Nation, Assimilation   72

PART II
The First Islamic Veil Affair

3 Ideological Battle Flags   79
   A New and Unwanted Situation   79

Post-Christian Islamic Challenges   80
A Question of Integration?   81
Manipulation   83
Islamic Communitarianism   84
A Glocalized World   85
Particular Versus National Law   85
Discrimination and Violence   87
Over T/here   90
Attacking Secularism   91
Behind the Veil   95
What Does It Represent?   96
Why Do They Wear It?   98
Conclusion   105

4 **Inventing Secularism**   107
An Unruly March Towards Unity   108
From Clash to Atonement   108
Exceptionality   112
The Cornerstone of the Republic   115
(Forced) Liberty   115
Equality and Neutrality   117
Brotherhood, Integration and French Communitarianism   118
Legislation, Education   122
Consensus   123
Urgency   125
Legislative Pedagogy   126
An Anti-Islamic Law?   129
Conclusion   133

PART III
The Second Islamic Veil Affair

5 **The Tip of the Iceberg**   137
New Times, Old Threats   138
The Return of Religion   138
Over T/here   141
Stigmatization?   143

    Walking Coffins   146
        A Religious and/or Political Symbol   147
        An Attack on the Republic's Principles and the Dignity of Women   149
        Voluntary Submission   154
    Conclusion   158

6 (Re)Inventing Secularism   159
    The History of a Christian Civilization   159
        A Christian Nation   160
        Historical Emancipation   161
    The Motor of Limited Tolerance   163
        Respecting a Value, Respecting a Principle   163
        Diversity, Positive Secularism and Tolerance   164
        Faith, Hope, and Unity   167
    Legislate, Educate!   173
    Reaffirmation   173
        Legitimacy   176
        Securing Public Order   178
    Conclusion   181

   PART IV
Consequences

7 Social Contracts, National Borders and Illiberal Governmentality   185
    National Frontiers and Social Contracts   186
    Discursive Displacement and Liberal Faith   190
    Post-Political Expansion   193
    Romantic Ideals and Secularist Retaliation   195

   Bibliography   199
   Index   223

Series Editor's Preface

The Islamic Veil Affairs (2003–4 and 2009–2011), which led to the banning of Muslim girls wearing Islamic headscarves in French public schools and wearing full-face veils in public spaces, has raised serious concerns about the relationship between secularism and the freedom of religious expression. In this book, *Unveiling the French Republic*, Per-Erik Nilsson engages in a careful critical analysis of the Veil Affairs. His critique, for the most part, is not on the decision of Muslim women to wear the veil but rather on the misuse of secular ideology to justify religious intolerance and mask ethnic prejudice.

Warren S. Goldstein, Ph.D.
Center for Critical Research on Religion
www.criticaltheoryofreligion.org

Acknowledgements

> After Sartre, after Foucault, after Deleuze, one could have wished for an end to the exploitation of universal values.
>
> ÉRIC HAZAN, publisher and writer

This book is a rewritten version of my dissertation presented in 2012 at Uppsala University. I would not have written this book were it not for a number of people to whom I want to extend my immense gratitude. Running the risk of forgetting some by mentioning others, I would like to start with my supervisor Mattias Gardell, who I admire and cherish deeply. Thank you for the opportunity to write and do research, for believing in me, for the supervision, and finally for being a good friend. I would also like to thank all the people involved in the proofreading and commenting on the book in its various forms: Edda Manga, Martha Axnér, Mattias Martinsson, Grace Davie, Naomi Goldenberg, Timothy Fitzgerald, Izabella Borzecka, Kjell Ljungberg, Baden Pailthorpe, Madelene Sultan-Sjöqvist, Joan W. Scott, Ruth Ilman, and Ola Sigurdson. Also, Yann Guerin, Geoffrey Eekhout, Emir Mahieddin, Heather Owen, and Warren Goldstein, thank you for the help with translations and language-related issues.

I would also like to thank my co-workers at the Faculty of Theology and the researchers at the research program The Impact of Religion, both at Uppsala University. Moreover, the members of the Higher Seminar at the Department of History of Religion and the Tornrumsakademien at Uppsala University have provided forums for critical reflection and challenging intellectual thought. Also, I extend a thank you to the research group GSRL at the Ecole Pratique des Hautes Etudes for inviting me to Paris as a visiting scholar in 2008, the Swedish Institute in Stockholm, the Smålands nation in Uppsala, the Critical Religion Research Group based at Stirling University, the Swedish Research Institute in Istanbul, and the research laboratory *Croyances, Histoire, Espaces, Régulation Politique et Administrative* (CHERPA) at Sciences-Po Aix.

In France, a number of people have aided me and given me their time. Among them are Michel Fouchard, Jean-Paul Willaime, Bertrand Gaume, Jean-Paul Martin, Mohamed Ali-Adraoui, and Leyla Arslan.

During my years as a PhD candidate and post-doc, I have had the great honor of receiving a number of very generous scholarships that have made it possible for me to travel and carry out my research. These are the Swedish Research Council's International Post-doc, the Håkanssons resefond, Anna Maria Lundins resestipendium at Smålands Nation, Carl Gustaf och Carl Cervins forskningsstipendium at Smålands nation, Jubelfeststipendiet at the Faculty of

Theology, the Swedish Institute's Franska stipendium, and the Ograduerade forskares fond at the Faculty of Theology, all in Uppsala. Furthermore, the Critical Religion Research Group has contributed generous funding for travel and participation at conferences and seminars.

During my research, friends have stood by my side in times of need—for friendship, for support, as well as for shelter. Yoyo-ing between Paris and Stockholm has meant that I have not always had an apartment at my disposal. Thank you for being there, Johanna Leonsson, Fredrik Bjureström, BK, Karin Hansson, Per Arnborg, David Bajt, Yann Guerin, Izabella Borzecka, Vanda Tönnesen, Oskar Belani, Ida-Johanna Lundqvist, Ellen Swedenmark, BonYoung Gu, Nicolas Clerc, Daphné Bengoa, Nils Billing, Ingmarie Froman, Maija Krastina, Fixie, and many others.

I would also like to extend a thank you to my cycling friends: Niklas Jakobsen, Mats Wall, Ola Hansson, Özgur Nevres, Melih Deltaban, Muzaffer Kuvet, C.J Paulin, Andrew Sheyer, C-J Paulin, CK Valhall, and all the others I have had the opportunity to share the road with.

To my family: My mother Rose-Marie Englund and my bonus-dad Björn Smedsberg, my sister Anja Nilsson and my brother-in-law Pelle Wennerström, and my precious nieces Kajsa and Elsa. Also, to my deceased father Bengt I would like to say: you are in my thoughts.

Abbreviations

AKP	The Justice and Development Party (Turkish).
AN	*Assemblée nationale.*
ANAEM	*Agence nationale de l'accueil des étrangers et des migrations.*
BDS	*Movement Boycott Désinvestissement Sanctions.*
CAI	*Contrat d'accueil et d'intégration.*
CCIF	*Collectif contre l'islamiphobie en France.*
CESEDA	*Code de l'entrée et du séjour des étrangers et du droit d'asile.*
CFCM	*Conseil français du culte musulman*
CHP	The Republican People's Party (Turkish).
CNCDH	*Commission nationale consultative des droits de l'homme.*
CR	*Communistes et républicains.*
CRI	*Conseil de réflextion sur l'islam.*
DCRG	*Direction centrale des renseignements généraux.*
DCRI	*Direction centrale du renseignement interieur.*
DNI	*Députés non inscrits.*
DOM-TOM	*Départements et regions et collectivités d'outre-mèr.*
DSP	Democratic Left Party (Turkish).
ECHR	European Court of Human Rights.
ETA	the *Bascian Euskadi Ta Askatasuna*
FLNC	*Fronte di Liberazione Naziunale Corsu*
FN	*Front national.*
GDR	*Groupe gauche, démocratique et républicaine.*
GS	*Groupe socialiste et apparentés.*
HCI	*Haut conseil d'intégration.*
IHEDN	*Insititut des hautes études des défence nationale.*
IFOP	*Institut français d'opinion publique.*
INED	*Institut National d'Études Démographiques.*
INSEE	*Institut National de la Statistique et des Études Économiques.*
LDH	*Ligue des droits de l'homme.*
MIVILUDES	*Mission interministérielle de vigilance et de lutte contre les dérives sectaires*
MODEM	*Mouvement démocrate.*
MP	Member of parliament.
MRAP	*Mouvement contre le racisme et pour l'amitié entre les peuples.*
NC	*Novueau centre.*
NPNS	*Ni putes, ni soumises.*
OFII	*L'Office français de l'intégration et de l'immigration.*

ABBREVIATIONS

OFPRA	*Office français de protection des réfugiés et apatrides.*
PCD	*Parti chrétien-démocrate*
PCF	*Parti communiste français.*
PIR	*Parti des indigènes de la République*
PS	*Parti socialiste.*
RDSE	*Écologiste, Rassemblement démocratique et social européen.*
RI	*Républicains et indépendants*
RIS	*Républicains indépendants sociale.*
RL	*Riposte laïque.*
RPR	*Rassemblement pour la Rébublique.*
S	*Socialiste.*
SNPDEN	*Syndicat national des personnels de direction de l'éducation nationale.*
SRC	*Socialiste, radical, citoyen et divers gauche.*
SSAE	*Soutien, Solidarité et Actions en Faveur des Emigrants.*
TCN	Third country national.
UCDP	*Union centriste des démocrates de progrès.*
UDF	*Union pour la démocratie française.*
UDR	*Union des démocrates pour la République.*
UMP	*Union pour un mouvement populaire.*

Introduction: Everybody Welcome to France

In 2010, the French Minister of Integration and National Identity, Éric Besson, welcomed some one hundred African refugees, just flown in from Malta, to their new country of residence. Besson started by saying: "Everybody, welcome to France" (2010b).[1] Standing behind a podium in a cramped room at Roissy airport north of Paris, Besson continued to explain that, except for access to housing and employment, "your integration starts with learning French." Since only a few of the refugees spoke French, Besson assured that them "we will help you get integrated." Having said that, the minister was clear on one point: this was not a one-sided deal. He said, "on your side, you are expected to do your utmost to make your integration possible."

What did Besson expect of these refugees? "Besides the language learning," Besson said, "you will have to respect the values of the french [sic] Republic." Besson referred to "Liberty, equality and fraternity [that] are the motto [sic] of our Republic." It was an easily memorized motto that, as soon as the refugees entered the public space, they would be reminded of daily as it is engraved above the entrance of a vast number of the Republic's official buildings. The Minister was, however, adamant in pointing out that one of these values—equality—was not something one could tinker with. For the French, Besson informed them, "equality between men and women" is of "crucial" importance.

Besson had more to say: "in addition, I would like to underline the critical value of secularity in the Republic." The minister then went on to explain that, given the French multi-religious landscape, "secularity" functions as a value preserving "anybody from being imposed upon by any religion," as a negative right (i.e., freedom from religion). Just as republican integration was a give-and-take process, secularity came with its proper demands. Besson, addressing the refugees as "it," accordingly stated that even if "everybody is free to practi[c]e *its* religion and to express *its* faith,"[2] this freedom has to be carried out within the restraints "fixed by the law, in particular in public places." The example Besson gave of these restraints was that "girls can not be veiled in public schools," which was a "must know."

---

1 Official English data is used when available, as in this case. Data not available in English has been translated by the author. As a service to the reader, original language quotes are provided for in the footnotes.
2 Italics added.

Up to this point, Besson had informed the refugees that integration was conditioned and that freedom was not unlimited. But no need to worry, the Minister assured them, "France is a tolerant country." To affirm this statement, Besson explained that France "has been shaped by various cultures," and "originally by Greek and Latin ones!" With these words, Besson had given the newly arrived refugees a crash course in what the Republic offers and demands. He stated finally that the only thing the refugees had to do was to "take this chance" and "be part of our common future!"

Thus, for half of this brief welcoming crash course on France Besson explained what is and what is not allowed and how these refugees were to become *integrated* into France. Three things exemplified this: *you* need to learn French, accept French values, and *you* must know that *you* cannot wear veils in public schools. As soon as *you* live up to these standards, *you* will integrate into the tolerant French national-secular community where the Republic protects *you* (as veil-wearing women) from religion. Besides presenting a negative understanding of religious freedom, Besson seems to have suggested that the acceptance or non-acceptance of French values (liberty, equality, brotherhood and, in particular, secularism) constituted the foundation for access to French citizenship, as if merely following the law was not sufficient.

This speech ought to be understood in relation to the nationwide debates on secularism (*la laïcité*), national identity, and Islam that have been taking place in France since the end of the 1980s, particularly during the Islamic Veil Affairs in 2003–4 and 2009–11. This specific speech epitomizes these debates in how it seeks to construct political subjects worthy or unworthy of rights, and republican and liberal freedoms, where categories like *secularism, religion, culture, tradition,* and *values* appear as regulatory techniques in controlling, disciplining, and attributing national identity. This speech and the political practices it legitimizes are, as I will show in this book, part of an expanding French neo-republican hegemony and a new set of illiberal and post-political practices in France.

By neo-republican, I refer to the hegemonic discourse on the French Republic that emerged during the last decades of the twentieth century. As Emile Chabal (2015) has pointed out, it was a response to the proclaimed crisis of the French political system in the 1970s. The ideological foundations of the French political arena were at the time fading, the French colonial empire saw its end, and the Post-War Golden Age, *les Trente glorieuses*, seemed long gone. To quote Chabal: "It was at this point that some public figures began to talk about republicanism again—not as a historical passion confined to the pages of history books, but as a living political ideal that could offer real solutions to intractable socio-economic and political problems" (2015, 18). Even though the development of a republican ideal, a neo-republican discourse, was carried out mainly by leading left-centrist politicians and intellectuals like Maurice Agulhon, Jean-Pierre Chevènement, Alain Finkelkraut, and Régis Debray, republicanism had soon become an obligatory referent for the political mainstream which has still not seen its end. In 2015, Nicolas Sarkozy, the former President and current leader of the leading conservative party, changed the party's name from *Union pour un mouvement populaire* (UMP) to simply *les Républicains* (see Auffray 2015). This "semantic hold-up," as one journalist has put it (Auffray 2015), has even become common lingua in the Far Right populist party *Front national* (FN) (Alduy and Wahnich 2015). According to Chabal, neo-republicanism is charactarized by a teleological nostalgia for the Third Republic (1870–1940), its symbols, concepts, and realization of the national and secular school system (here referring to public schools freed from the clergy's influence), and strong Republican state (2015, 10). To quote Chabal (2015): "Put simply, neo-republicanism has become one of France's most significant languages of politics, replete with evocative and highly charged words and vivid political symbolism. It has built on a rich French political tradition, and has contributed to the reinterpretation of French history in a variety of imaginative ways" (8).

It is important to note that although the established political parties from the Far Right to the Far Left all seek to make a legitimate claim to speak for the French Republic, and although their rhetoric is painstakingly mimical, there are important differences between the political parties (see for example Howarth and Varouxakis 2014). My interest in this book, however, is not so much with differences between political parties as it is with how secularism, as a key moment in neo-republican discourse, has allowed for a consensus transcending left-right political divisions. This does not mean that the republican discourse on secularism is not without its divergences and internal incoherence; in fact, it is full of them, which I show in the analysis. However, classical political dichotomies are rarely sufficient to explain these cleavages.

By the term illiberal, I refer to French and European developments by nation states in expanding measures of security and control: disciplinary political practices that states are implementing in the guise of republican and liberal credos such as a tolerance, freedom of speech, and secularism (Berezin 2009; Bigo and Tsoukala 2008; Carrera, Groenendijk, and Guild 2009). One example of the logic in play in illiberal discourse is the supposed death of multiculturalism as a political practice, but its imagined continuation as a societal reality (Lentin and Titley 2011). Prominent European leaders such as Angela Merkel (Connolly 2010) and David Cameron (Doward 2011) have proclaimed this death. We are told that multicultural politics, acknowledging communities based on common identities, has failed, leading to societies based on a plethora of different identities that are not compatible with the values of the British or German nation.

Merkel's and Cameron's statements, in one way, then strengthen the French "Republican Model of Integration." In France, where Anglo-Saxon multiculturalism is largely seen as the opposite of the republican model of integration, the political elite, with the development of neo-republican thought, has articulated a profound fear for the development of a multicultural or communitarian society.[3] Leading republican spokespeople thus see a politics that acknowledges different cultures as a path leading to societal collapse. Hence, to them, multiculturalism still functions as a diagnostic of a distressing multicultural societal reality, where different religious and cultural communities are thought to be in a potential clash with each other as well as with the majoritarian national community. To resolve this potentially devastating state of society, calls have been made for the importance of strengthening national identity through different disciplining measures such as monitoring the behavior of certain social, cultural, and religious groups, language and national tests, tightened border controls, and extralegal detention systems, which are seen all over Europe. Moreover, demands have been made to re-articulate national identity, preferably by emphasizing Europe's Christian heritage. Notably, the Sarkozy Administration (2007–2012) sought a solution to the calamities associated with multiculturalism in French history, and especially French secularism (Jansen 2013). It was as if an essential part of the nation had been lost by too much multiculturalism, and the prime task of the leaders of the nation was to find it, restore a society in peril, and reroute it on its universal path.

This rerouting society, the articulation of a neo-republican unity, is a political technique that sits well within what I call *post-politics* (see Mouffe 2005; Rose 1999; Žižek 1999). Post-politics is the representation of contemporary (French) social and political life as the final phase of human development, the end of political struggles, and sometimes even as the end of history. The virtues of the liberal-democratic world, free market capitalism, and the French-Christian-European universal values are understood to have superseded European religious wars and quarrels, and subsequently Nazism, Fascism, Communism, and totalitarianism. It follows a messianic logic where history has become an objective progression of humanity. In this conception of historical progress, colonialism has become a preparation for the pre-modern world

---

3 Multiculturalism or *multiculturalisme* is not a common term in French political lingua. A related concept is used which, in French, is *communautarisme* or in English communitarianism. I will use *communautarisme*. For further discussion, see Chapter 2.

to enter modernity, feminism has yet to develop within patriarchal politics, and oppression, racism, eugenics, and genocide are simply effaced (Dahlstedt and Tesfahuney 2008, 12). The post-political condition is one portraying itself as post-ideological, as the victory of a neutral human conduct over history's ills and in which secularism appears as an entity untainted by the mischievousness of European history (Elmessiri 2000, 55). As the liberal intellectual François Furet proclaimed in 1991: "Two hundred years after the French Revolution, France and Europe have entered a new—and better—period in their history: fascism and communism have marked a century that ends as one of the most tragic and stupid in the realm of the political passions" (quoted in Chabal 2015, 168–169). Furet continues: "It is indisputable that, having just emerged from these nightmares, the peoples of Europe do not see any horizon other than that of liberal democracy."

Politics is presented as a matter of good governance, a technocratic machine where democracy is a matter of choosing the right bureaucrat for the right situation—a rational and reasoned way of steering society where the emblem of the Republic has become a unifying moment. As put by the former president François Mitterand: "We must avoid permanent political confusion [trouble] and self doubt, which seems to be a common affliction of the French ... a great country can only be great if it knows how to unify itself around important goals" (quoted in Chabal 2015, 59). According to Mitterand, the French thus had to "give way to a higher conception of the public interest, which begins with the Republic".

In this regard, a paragraph in the French education law is instructive. It states that public education is secular and independent from all political, economical, religious, or ideological concerns (Article L-141) (*Code de l'éducation*).[4] As will become clear in this book, being secular in neo-republican discourse on secularism, as in the above quotation, is not only understood as something non-ideological, it is seen as neutral and objective, as universal, creating an ambiguous relation to its attributed, specific and particular French history. To quote Pierre Bouretz, contemporary public spokespeople in France appear to have a curious passion for the universal: "In terms of the values inscribed at the head of its public buildings, they are convinced that France has invented them" (Bouretz 2000, 11). As several critics of the neo-republican take on universalism and neutrality noted, not even the alleged founder of the Republican secular school Jules Ferry was naïve enough to talk about an

---

4 "Le service public de l'enseignement supérieur est laïque et indépendant de toute emprise politique, économique, religieuse ou idéologique."

ideologically neutral Republican ideal (see Baudouin and Portier 2001, 22; Monod 2007, 128).

Another, and crucial, aspect of post-politics is how it allows certain articulations of distinctions of political friend and foe. In this, I set out from Carl Schmitt's writings where he argues that political speech and political practice create and maintain political identities based on distinctions between *us* and *them*, *friend* and *foe*. Assuming this distinction is, according to Schmitt (2007), central:

> "[The enemy] need not be morally evil or aesthetically ugly; he [or she] need not appear as an economic competitor, and it may even be advantageous to engage with him or her in business transactions. But he or she is nevertheless, the other, the stranger; and it is sufficient for his or her nature that he or she is, in a specially intense way, existentially something different and alien, so that in the extreme case conflicts with him or her are possible" (7).[5]

The specificity of the post-political enemy is that this subject's strangeness is turned into a perpetually defining moment of that very subject (Guénif-Souilamas and Macé 2005). This means that an enemy of the imagined universally transcendent moral good becomes, by definition, an enemy of society and humanity itself. In this logic, the presence of such an enemy is a grave danger to society and, in order to cleanse society from such a danger, exceptional measures are necessary (Agamben 1998; Appadurai 2006). Hence, the republican discourse on secularism articulates an ahistorical battle between the universal and secular good versus the religious and, as will become clear, an Islamic evil through which sovereignty reifies its power and a particular conception of society is hegemonized (see Asad 2005; Schmitt 2005, 5ff; Fitzgerald 2007, 6ff; Scott 2007; Selby 2012; Fernando 2015).

It might appear anachronistic to call French neo-republican discourse on secularism illiberal. Indeed, Cécile Laborde has criticized what she sees as an anthropological approach focusing on the strangeness of French political culture and its tendencies to be unable to see beyond discursive contextualization, or how French political speech routinely rejects what Laborde calls "linguistic categories" such as *liberalism*, *race*, and *ethnic minorities*. According to Laborde, this leads to a normative judgment and biased analysis, which treat French political culture as substantially illiberal, racist, and ethnocentric.

---

5 For further readings on republican friend-foe distinctions, see Dornel (2004).

Laborde (2005) concludes: "French discourses and practices are unconsciously measured against a particular linguistic and normative background, with little attempt made—paradoxically—to account for the actual meanings of the concepts used in French discourse and their effects on political and social practice" (5).

The approach envisaged in this book might appear to fall into this biased trap. However, I set out to analyze how discursive categories are contingent and locally articulated in political speech and how republican spokespeople articulate them in relation to discourse and power (I will return to this in the following chapter). The interest in and the reason for categorizing these measurements as illiberal are because republican spokespeople employ a liberal-republican-universal lingua. Laborde actually suggests that the fundamental aspects of French secularism coincide with the "the secular core" in liberalism (Laborde 2005, 306; 2008, 4; see also Asad 2005, 500; compare to Hulliung 2002, 19ff). According to Laborde (2008, 3), this means that "republicanism seems to incorporate central liberal intuitions, such as commitment to the impartiality of the state, the universal and egalitarian status of citizenship, the separation between public and private spheres, preference for individual over collective rights, commitment to individual autonomy, and a civic not ethnic mode of national identity".

In other words, in both republicanism and liberalism, liberty, equality and universality are core percepts. "But" as Laborde (2008) has put it, republicanism differs from liberalism by being "communitarian in its advocacy of a strong public identity transcending private preferences and identities" and in "its commitment to the unitary nation-state as the chief site of citizenship" (3). In this regard, this analysis of secularism is not so much an enterprise of describing, as Jean-Claude Monod puts it, the tension between republican and liberal sources of secularism (see Monod 2013, 131) but rather, how they converge, form, legitimize, reproduce, and reform various formations of proscriptive constellations of power.

Given the extensive literature that exists on the topic, one might wonder why a new book is necessary. For one thing, an overlooked aspect regarding the articulation(s) of contemporary French secularism has been the one taking place in Parliament during the Veil Affairs. The Affairs refers to the political, legislative, and news media debates that took place during the public deliberations of the two French laws that ban female Islamic attire in public schools (hijabs, ratified 2004) and in public space (full-face veils, ratified 2010).[6] In

---

6   In order of appearance: Loi n°2004-228 du 15 mars 2004; Loi n°2010-1192 du 11 octobre 2010 interdisant la dissimulation du visage dans l'espace public.

addition, as I try to show, many writings on secularism theory contain both minor and serious issues regarding incongruities and contradictions. The aim of the following analysis is, then, to map and analyze the intersections of what I have been referring to as the neo-republican discourse on secularism, and the institutionalization of certain illiberal and post-political practices during the parliamentary deliberations and political interventions during the Islamic Veil Affairs in 2003–2004 and 2009–2011.

I hope to contribute to this field through my detailed analysis of how secular-religious distinctions are negotiated, construed, and performed through a will to know the "religious other" in contemporary French political speech (i.e., parliamentarian debates) and legislative text (the recent laws on secularism). The analysis shows how secularism, an essentially empty category, as a mode of national identity and as a governmental technique has legitimized expanding disciplinary measures to counter a perceived growth in identity politics and multiculturalist demands. Moreover, the analysis highlights how secularism during the period under analysis has been part of legitimizing illiberal political practices in France. Finally, I show how republican spokespeople employed the neo-republican discourse on secularism from 1989 onwards to create a hegemonic national image of France. This discourse drew heavily on various ideological and discursive techniques that articulate Islam and Muslims as the constitutive outside of neo-republican discourse on secularism. As I argue, without Islam and Muslims, secularism and republicanism would look quite different.

The structure of the book is as follows. The first chapter is a critical presentation of research and theories on secularism, the secular, and secularization. In particular, I focus on scholarly accounts of the history of French secularism and how the Republic employed the century-old secular laws in the French colonies, most notably in Algeria. I do this through a critical discussion of seminal works in the field where I show some theoretical and empirical shortcomings as well as some ideological problems—for example, that influential scholars of secularism, like José Casanova and Charles Taylor, conceptualize secularism through quite normative understandings of what secularism and religion entail. I discuss how to understand analytically French secularism in relation to secularism in other nation-states, notably Turkey, and the United States. After this theoretical and empirical introduction, I present previous research on French secularism and the Veil Affairs. I end the chapter with a presentation of my analytical approach to the study of secularism.

The second chapter provides background for the analysis. Here I contextualize the Veil Affairs in relation to French colonialism and, especially, colonial discourses on Muslim women, the post-Cold War discourse on Islam as the

INTRODUCTION: EVERYBODY WELCOME TO FRANCE

new emerging global threat to the West, French politics of integration, and the emergence of the "Muslim Problem" in the 1970s. The chapter draws on previous research but, here, I also bring in new empirical material such as articles and broadcasts from the news media as well as political speeches.

In the third chapter, I set out to analyze how the Muslim-other was constructed during the parliamentarian debates preceding the Law of 2004. Here I show how knowledge about the Muslim-other, and especially about young Muslim women, was constructed in Parliament. My argument is that a self-referential discourse developed constructed on hearsay and pseudo-theological readings of Islamic sources. For example, although the law targeted young, veiled Muslim women, the parliamentarian commissions interviewed only one such woman. Instead of problematizing and contextualizing the wearing of the veil in France, republican spokespeople understood it as a link to a subverting Orient threatening France.

Chapter Four analyzes how republican spokespeople articulated secularism during the parliamentarian debates preceding the Law of 2004. I focus on republican spokespeople engaged in writing a teleological history of secularism to portray the secular Republic as a universal and emancipatory entity. I highlight how republican spokespeople negotiated contested meanings of secularism and, finally, how they reached a sort of consensus about the need to enforce French secularism through legislation as a means of fighting back against the imagined Islamization of France.

The fifth chapter follows the same structure as Chapter Three in that I analyze the construction of the subject for the Law of 2010. While the contents of the argument changed slightly from the debates in 2004, a similar image of the Muslim-other emerged. The change mainly concerns an elevated focus on the security risk and the potential terrorist threat that the fully veiled Muslim woman came to embody. During these deliberations, the republican spokespeople did not hear any testimony from French Muslim woman wearing the *niqab*. News media and "the Orient" (Afghanistan, Saudi Arabia, and Iran as well as the medieval era) instead constituted the sources and references in the creation of an image of Islam and the fully veiled Muslim woman.

In Chapter Six, I once again turn to the articulation of secularism as a response to the *problem* symbolized by the full-face veil (*niqab*). The important difference between this debate and the one in 2004 is that the proponents of the law eventually abandoned secularism as the legal response to the full-face veil. Republican spokespeople suddenly seemed to become aware of freedom of conscience and realized that they could not legitimize a veil-ban on secular-religious grounds, and thus they reframed the full-face veil as a danger to the security of the Republic. Secularism became principally a fundamental value or spirit that oriented the overall understanding of the law. As such, a particular sense of being French was articulated in relation to the full-face veil: a bare face was understood as the mirror of the soul, a receipt of honesty, and a veiled face the opposite.

In the final chapter, having summarized the analysis of the republican discourse on secularism, I move on to discuss it more broadly in relation to post-political and illiberal developments in France up to 2011. In particular, I relate the two laws banning Islamic veils to French immigration laws and how secularism has been institutionalized as a prerequisite not only for being considered French but also for obtaining French citizenship. I also discuss the expanding legal reach for secularism in contemporary France to finally discuss the recent developments of the French populist Far Right vis-à-vis secularism. I end the chapter and the book with a brief conclusion.

PART I

Approaching French Secularism

∴

CHAPTER 1

(French) Secularism

In this book, I aim to analyze the intersections of republican, illiberal, and post-political discourse on secularism in France during the period 2003–2011. The overarching research question is how republican spokespeople have construed the French Republic as secular in mainstream political speech (parliament and government) and how it has been institutionalized in law. My main argument is that political mainstream conceptions of French secularism were articulated in close relation to stereotypical and imaginary conceptions of Islam and Muslims, making possible a re-articulation of French secularism as a hegemonic national identity and a technique of governance. Christian Joppke (2009) has suggested that "at a deeper level" the Islamic veil in France "functions as a mirror of identity that forces Europeans to see who they are and to rethink the kinds of public institutions and societies they wish to have" (2). While I am sympathetic to Joppke's argument, I believe it to be problematic as it suggests that "Europeans" are subjects that can actually see who they are—that Europeans or the French pre-exist as already-established political subjects (see Ardizzoni 2004).

Instead, I will point to the co-dependency of political identities and how secularism as discourse not only needs the idea of religion as a negative mirror but also how secularism creates certain notions of religion, especially Islam (see Roy 2005, 167). Several scholars have presented the basis of this argument before (e.g., Asad 2005; Barras 2010; Jansen 2013; Scott 2007; Silverman). Moreover, drawing on the work of scholars like Gil Anidjar (2003), Joseph Massad (2015), and Tomoko Masuzawa (2005), I argue that, in this fashion, Islam and Muslims become the simultaneous discursive outside and inside of secularism, as constitutive others for a secular self-identification. That is, in republican discourse on secularism (2003–2011), republican spokespeople articulated Islam into a premodern temporality on which they could project all sorts of self-serving imaginary creations while they reduced to a minimum any kind of self-reflective gaze (see Butler 2009, 100). Similar to how the figure of the Jew was entangled with European nationalist self-understandings (Sanos 2012; Sartre 1946, 35), the Muslim of today has become an ever-present negative marker of identification in French political speech, as elsewhere (Allen 2010; Gardell 2011; Geisser 2003). This analysis is thus a matter of understanding how a French secularist self-understanding has been parasitically clinging on to imaginary conceptions of Islam and Muslims. The way to achieve this deconstruction is not to reveal who the French or the Muslims really are. In the words of Slavoj Žižek (1989, 48): "It is not enough to say that we must liberate ourselves of so-called 'anti-Semitic prejudices' and learn to see Jews as they really are—in this way we will certainly remain victims of these so-called prejudices. We must confront ourselves with how the ideological figure of the 'Jew' is invested with our unconscious desire, with how we have constructed this figure to escape a certain deadlock of our desire" (24). Thus, my interest in secularism relies on how it has fueled the notion of a particular secular French identity, how it has reinvented it, and how it has been reinvested in it through the appropriation of a Muslim-other with illiberal and post-political techniques.

In this chapter, I walk through central theoretical points of departure in my approach to French secularism while highlighting what I see as core problems in many of the most influential writings on theories of secularism. To achieve this, it is necessary to consider central moments in secularism theory as well as describe some central aspects of secular countries and regimes. Throughout this chapter, I present foundational writings on French secularism and dedicate a specific section to earlier writings on the Islamic Veil Affairs.

Secularization, the Secular, and Secularism

The interest in theories of secularization has been on the rise for the last few decades (Berger 1967; Gauchet 1985; Martin 1979). There has also been increasing interest in the secular and in secularism. The reasons for this can be explained by the realization that, contrary to modernist and secularist proclamations, *religion* has not only retained a grip on human daily life around the globe but also could be a force for political action, with 9/11 often taken as emblematic evidence. For example, Robert Keohane suggests that "the attacks of September 11 reveal that all mainstream theories of world politics are relentlessly secular with respect to motivation. They ignore the impact of religion, despite the fact that world-shaking political movements have so often been fueled by religious fervor" (quoted in Calhoun, Juergensmeyer and VanAntwerpen 2011, 4). Following Keohane's line of argument, the tendency to neglect religion as a social and political force is explained by the hegemony of the secularization thesis in the humanities and social sciences (religion is, for example, still a non-existent subject in many social science departments in European and American universities) (see Kuru 2009, 1).

In introductions to theories of secularization, the secular, and secularism, it is commonplace to state that the validity of what were once hegemonic theories have, since the 1990s, been called into question (e.g., Asad 2003, 1;

Göle 2010, 44). One of the most influential voices writing in English on secularization and secularism is José Casanova (2011) who argues for an analytical distinction between the trinity of secularization-secular-secularism, suggesting that secularization is an "analytical conceptualization of modern world-historical processes," the secular a modern "epistemic category," and secularism a "worldview and ideology" (54).

Casanova seeks to break out of certain biases that he argues are built into the theory of secularization—for example, its Eurocentrism and the circular claim that a society is modern because it is secularized and secularized because it is modern. He seeks to rebut these biases by re-reading the theory of secularization. Casanova suggests that the theory draws on three historical claims (1994, 20ff). First, that a differentiation of society took place in the shift from the *ancien régime* to modern society (i.e., separation of religion from politics, economy, culture, etc.). Secondly, that modernity has brought about a decline in religion and religious practice. Finally, that these changes have resulted in the privatization of religion and religious practice. Casanova argues that this theory is so intrinsically interwoven with all the theories of the modern world and with the self-understanding of modernity that one cannot simply discard the theory of secularization without putting into question the entire web, including much of the self-understanding of the social sciences. He even suggests that the assumption that secularization is a historical fact attained a "truly paradigmatic status within the social sciences" from the nineteenth century onward, and that it was during the latter half of the twentieth century that theories of secularization were first developed into more comprehensive systems of thought (1994, 18). According to him, the theory is not entirely false; the first claim is correct but the other two are wrong. This leads him to argue that "the core of the [secularization] thesis, namely, the understanding of secularization as a single process of functional differentiation of the various secular institutional spheres of modern societies from religion, remains relatively uncontested" (2011, 61). He believes there are plenty of examples around the globe where religion plays an active, public, and non-private role in liberal-democratic states governed by law (i.e., Poland and the US). In other words, religion and modern society are not mutually exclusive; one might actually benefit from the other. Casanova, however, gives examples of where religion plays a more destructive role, where religion and modernity seem to clash (i.e., Egypt and Iran). The core of the thesis thus only holds for certain religions.

The secular is conceptually closely related to secularization but while the latter is seen by Casanova as a historical process, the former is, as previously noted, a modern epistemic category. By this, he means a modern category that seeks to designate a realm or reality separated from religion. He however stresses that the secular and the religious are "always and everywhere" mutually constructed (2011, 54). He identifies three different ways of being secular in the modern world. The first one he calls *mere secularity,* which is "the phenomenological experience of living in a secular world and in a secular age, where being religious may be a normal viable option" (60). The second is called *self-sufficient and exclusive* secularity and refers to the "the phenomenological experience of living without religion as a normal, quasi-natural, taken-for-granted condition" (60). The last is *secularist secularity*, which is "a phenomenological experience not only of being passively free but also actually of having been liberated from 'religion' as a condition for human autonomy and human flourishing" (60). Thus, according to him, secularism can be a consciuous normative project or an unconscious structure guiding action:

> "[S]ecularism refers more broadly to a whole range of modern secular worldviews and ideologies which may be consciously held and explicitly elaborated into philosophies of history and normative-ideological state projects, into projects of modernity and cultural programs, or, alternatively, it may be viewed as an epistemic knowledge regime that can be he held unreflexively [sic] or be assumed phenomenologically as the taken-for-granted normal structure of modern reality, as a modern doxa or an "unthought." (55)

Casanova sees one fundamental problem with secularism. It is its tendency to render "the particular Western Christian mode of secularization into a universal teleological process of human development from belief to unbelief, from primitive to irrational or metaphysical religion to modern rational postmetaphysical secular consciousness" (59). Instead, he suggests, we should acknowledge secularization "for what it truly was, namely a particular Christian and post-Christian historical process, and not, as Europeans like to think, a general or universal process of human or societal development" (64).

To qualify the analysis of secularism, Casanova suggests one should make an analytical distinction between secularism as statecraft and secularism as ideology. He understands secularism as statescraft as a basic principle of separation between "the religious and political authority" (66). This separation does not need to build on any particular theory of religion, whether negative or positive. However, he argues that when a particular state professes a particular understanding of what religion is or does, the state ventures into to the realm of ideology.

The influential theorist of secularism Charles Taylor articulates a theoretical stance of secularism as statecraft. He defines the core of secularism as a separation between church and state. He has, furthermore, argued for a secular society to deal with the pluralism of the modern world it "requires some kind of neutrality" in relation to religion, and that it does "not favor one [religion] over the other" (2008, xi). According to him, secularism involves a "complex requirement" based on the three categories of the French Revolutionary trinity (liberty, equality, and fraternity) (xi). He explains that religious liberty refers to the right to believe or not to believe and suggests "the domain of religion, or basic belief" should be free from coercion (xi). Moreover, Taylor suggests that there must be equality between people of different faiths, where no religious Weltanschauung can enjoy a privileged status. Finally, he says, all spiritual families must have the same and equal possibility to make their opinions known, which relates to fraternity. This, he argues, is a "neat schema" to which he is attached (xii).

The main interest of this book, as stated earlier, is in theories of secularism, but it should be clear the theory of secularism does not stand alone; it is accompanied by particular conceptions of secularization, the secular, and religion. Nevertheless, before my comments on Casanova's and Taylor's theories of secularism, it is necessary to scrutinize some empirical attempts to analyze secularism.

Secularism(s)

Casanova's division of secularism into secularism as statecraft and as ideology and Taylor's conceptualization of secularism as a neutral doctrine for governing a multireligious society correlate broadly to Ahmet Kuru's division of secularism into *passive* and *assertive*, the former associated with the United States of America (USA) and the latter with Turkey and France. His writings synthesize mainstream scholars of secularism such as Casanova and Taylor and, in the case of France, Jean Baubérot and Henri Pena-Ruiz. I will thus use Kuru's writings to introduce the reader to different types of secular regimes, or to different types of secularisms (see Göle 2010). In this section, I will not however engage in a polemical discussion with him.

According to Kuru (2009), the USA, Turkey, and France are secular as their legislative and judicial apparatus is outside institutional religious control and, since they constitutionally declare neutrality toward religions, "they adapt neither an official religion nor atheism" (2000, 6). They differ significantly however in state-religion relations. The most mediatized contemporary issue concerns the wearing of Islamic veils in public institutions and public spaces. In the USA, no restrictions exist; in France, the veil (hijab) is prohibited in public schools and the full-face veils (niqab and burqa) are prohibited in public spaces; and, in Turkey, Islamic headscarves have until recently been banned from public institutions. Kuru (2009) states that passive secularism implies a more lenient stance on religion by allowing its public visibility, such as in the USA, whereas assertive secularism means that the state seeks to exclude religion from the "public sphere and confine it to the public domain," as with the prohibitions in Turkey and France (8). The former "prioritizes neutrality" and the latter is more "comprehensive" (8). His main explanation for this builds on path dependence theory where the existence or non-existence of an *ancien régime* is of crucial importance (Kuru 2009).[1] Accordingly, the similarities between Turkey and France are explained through the conflictual origin of secularism developed as an ideology against a conservative past: the Ottoman Empire in Turkey and the Catholic Church and monarchy in France. He contrasts this with the USA, where "the absence of an *ancien régime* led to the consensual basis of passive secularism" (Kuru 2009, 231).

Kuru suggests that if the lack of an *ancien régime* based on "monarchy and hegemonic religion" allowed the development of passive secularism in the USA (74), it does not mean that secularism is unchallenged. There has been and still is an ongoing clash between conservatives who wish for close state-religion relations and liberals who wish for a strict separation between the state and religion. In the USA, these debates have largely focused on how to interpret the founding documents of the country. The conservatives "point to the Declaration of Independence's references to God and Congress's tradition of having publicly funded chaplains for prayer before its sessions" (75). George Washington referred to "God and religion in his swearing-in, his declaration of a Thanksgiving Day, and his Farewell Address" (75). The liberals argue instead that the Framers of the Constitution laid out the foundations for a secular state, primarily since God was not included in the constitution. They also highlight that there was a strong tendency to not allow government-based financial assistance for religion, as it would constitute an establishment of religion and thus violate its free exercise (76). For the liberals, yet another important historical moment was the signing of the Treaty of Peace and Friendship with the ruler of Tripoli in 1796, later approved by the Senate. In it, one can read that the United State's government is not founded on Christianity and that it has nothing against Muslims or any particular Muslim nation (76).

---

1 Also see Kuru and Stepan (2012).

By portraying the history of secularism in the United States as a struggle between liberal and conservative interpretations of secularism, Kuru shows how, historically, one can understand secularism in the United States through both continuity and change, and, while passive secularism has been the dominant form, it has been challenged and refined in these struggles. Thus, "the historical pendulum has kept swinging between religious 'establishment' and 'disestablishment'" resulting in a "trend toward more state neutrality in regard to religions" (77).

Many students of contemporary American political speech remark on the conspicuous usage of religious discourse, especially the Pledge of Allegiance's "one nation, under God" and the national motto "In God We Trust." While certain liberals interpret this as a heritage from the McCarthy era's attempt to distinguish itself from the atheist Soviet Union (75), the conspicuous relationship between the Republican Party and Christian Right is striking. Kuru argues that Ronald Reagan's presidency consolidated and President George W. Bush reinforced this alliance (41), while the Democrats have been "cautious" not to lose religious voters to the Conservatives and have been reluctant to withdraw the "one nation, under God" in the pledge of allegiance (42). Kuru thinks that state-religion relations in the United States are complex and in some aspects stricter than in France or Turkey. For example, collected taxes cannot be used "directly to fund religious schools" in the US. Religious instruction is not permitted in schools, nor are prayers, even though recitations of the Pledge of Allegiance occur first thing every morning in the large majority of public schools (70). He concludes, however, that state policies towards religion have been more inclusionary in the United States than in France and Turkey, due to its passive secularism (cf. Jacoby 2004).

Regarding assertive secularism in Turkey, Kuru urges caution and the need to go beyond what he sees as the clichés of Turkey's "unique" secularism (Kuru and Stepan 2012, 4). His take on Turkish secularism starts with the late Ottoman era. According to Kuru (2009), it is important to understand that the Ottoman Empire was not a theocracy. First, Islamic law was not the only source of legislation and, second, "the Ottoman ulema were civil servants paid by the state and under the political control of the sultan" (202). As he points out, scholars of Turkish history have deliberated whether the emergence of the establishment of the Turkish Republic in 1923 was a rupture or an extension of the Ottoman Empire.[2] He believes it was both: an extension since it "inherited the secular institutions of the empire, such as schools,

---

2 Also see Atasoy (2005).

courts, and laws" and a rupture since "the republic represented a radical change because it eliminated the Islamic institutions left from the empire" (203). In this regard, he suggests, one should see the assertive secularism that became the leading ideology of the Turkish Republic as quite different from that of the Ottoman Empire, as well as being a result of the evolution within the empire itself: "The Otto*man ancien régime* based on the alliance between the sultan and hegemonic Islamic institutions originated the assertive secularist ideological dominance in the Turkish Republic." Against this background, Kuru argues that the "Westernist Turkish elite regarded Islam as a defender of traditionalism and a barrier against Westernization. Yet they wanted to modernize the country within an Islamic, not a Western, sociocultural and even political framework, by preserving the hegemonic position of Islam" (231).

The Kemalists during the newly emerged Turkish Republic sought to contain Islam and pursue a "policy to exclude Islam from the public sphere by confining it to the Diyanet-run mosques" (Kuru and Stepan, 2012, 96). Two important laws in this regard are the Hat Law of 1925, prohibiting the *fez* (a read headgear associated with the Ottoman Empire) and the turban for men, and the prohibition of giving the call for prayer, *ezan*, in Arabic. He also states that the golden era of assertive secularism was the period from 1933 to 1949, when neither schools nor universities taught Islam. This was also the period of Mustafa Kemal Atatürk's Republican People's Party's (CHP) single party rule, which ended in 1946.

The period following CHP's rule has been turbulent. Turkey has been, as Kuru argues, the arena for a cycle of democratic elections and the army's interventions. After elections where over-reactionary and over-Islamic political parties have come to power, the army has stepped in to rid the country of its supposed anti-modern and anti-secular rulers, as during coups from the 1960s to the 1990s (Kuru 2009, 231). The 1997 "soft coup" is one example, in which, taking tight control of the National Security Council, it put an end to PM Necmettin Erbakan's premiership and his pro-Islamic conservative Welfare Party (2009, 161). The army had declared that Erbakan's "reactionism" was equal to terrorism and thus posed a grave threat to the nation. Kuru highlights how the army's methods, backed up by the CHP, the Democratic Left Party (DSP), high-ranking members of the state apparatus, major news media, as well as civil society, involved a cleanup of the state apparatus. They did this by getting rid of bureaucrats affiliated with Islamism, shutting down Quran courses and Imam-Hatip schools (secondary schools for the education of imams and *hatips*), imposing severe restrictions on corporations run by conservative Muslims, banning headscarves in all educational institutions, placing new restrictions on mosque construction and an even stricter control of existing mosques, and a five-year ban on Erbakan from the political arena. During this time, the current president, Reyep Tayip Erdoğan, was also sentenced to 10 months in prison for reciting a religious poem during a political rally.

Having served a six-month prison sentence, Erdoğan returned to politics and founded the Justice and Development Party (AKP) in 2001. Since 2002, the AKP has been a leading force in Turkish national politics and in the many democratizations implemented during the last decade to meet EU-standards. According to Kuru (2009), one of AKP's many objectives has been the implementation of a more passive secularism and democratic state apparatus (178). The AKP has also implemented changes to improve the conditions of non-Muslim minorities in Turkey. For example, the abolishment of the Subcommittee for Minorities in 2004, whose task it was to surveil non-Muslim citizens (180). The reformation in 2010 of the High Council of Judges and Prosecutors has led to the empowerment of civilian courts over the military, thus weakening the military's grip over society, and in the end, the Kemalists. "The developments in the judiciary and military" have revealed "that the Kemalist ideology is no longer preeminent in Turkey, although it still has powerful followers" (Kuru and Stepan, 2012, 10).

It should be noted that the situation in Turkey has changed drastically since Kuru published his thesis about Turkish secularism. Islam has since been ostensibly linked with state power. Erdoğan and the AKP have taken a tight control of the country and manage to eradicate oppositional voices. Two of the most important events in this regard are the Ergenekon Affair in 2007 and the *coup d'état* in 2016 which have lead to the imprisonment of journalists, polititicans, civil servants, and civilians in an unprecedent manner.

Kuru's other example of an assertive secularist regime is France. Kuru (2009) explores France's history with the Catholic Church, the close ties between it and the old monarchy (France as *la fille ainée* of the Church), and the Catholic Church as the dominant sociopolitical power in medieval times. This all changed with the revolution in 1789 and, in 1795, with the declaration of the first secular French state. He states that the "French *Lumières* was [sic] 'different' from the Enlightenment in the United States and in Britain where religion was not the exceptional enemy, as it came to be in France with the state's appropriation of the Church's land and the thousands of priests that were sent to the guillotine" (138). Since the Revolution, Kuru (2009) states, "the French progressive elite have [sic] preserved the idea that modernity and religion are incompatible and, therefore, the latter should be secluded from the public sphere" (138). He refers to two influential scholars on secularism in France. The first one is Jean Baubérot (1998), who has developed a theory of French secularism that explains its emergence and consolidation through two thresholds. Briefly put, the first threshold is the post-revolutionary period, 1789–1806, which resulted in the Napoleonic Concordat in 1801, with the re-establishment of the Catholic Church as the national church of France. The second threshold refers to the reforms brought about by the Third Republic's leaders from 1881 to 1905—most significantly the free and obligatory school system and the Law of 1905 separating church and state. In other writings, Baubérot (2004, 2008, 2012) talks about a third threshold that started with the first Islamic Veil Affair in 1989. In this regard, Baubérot's theory of French secularism revolves around continuity. As Kuru (2009) states, this idea has been criticized by Henri Pena-Ruiz, who stresses that the Napoleon Concordat of 1801 was a rupture with the Revolution just as the Law of 1905 was a rupture with the Republic's Catholic past. Kuru argues that from the perspective of assertive versus passive secularism, both perspectives have merit. He concludes: "While examining the ideological dominance of assertive secularism, I use the change-based approach and take the early Third Republic (1875–1905) as the critical juncture. Catholicism was influential in the French polity before the Third Republic, while assertive secularism became dominant afterward" (137).

Kuru elaborates his argument by stating that "the revolutionary period (1789–1801) constituted the ideological predecessor of secular state building in the early Third Republic" while "the establishment of assertive secularism did not mean the end of a two-century long debate on state-religion relations in France"; the "struggle between the anticlerical assertive secularists and conservative Catholics has continued" (136).

Since 1989 and the first Islamic Veil Affair, Kuru believes that the Republic's assertive secularism consolidated as the ideology of the state: "I argue that the headscarf ban and other exclusionary French policies toward Muslims are a reflection of the French state's restrictive attitude toward religion in general" (136). Except for the ban on Islamic veils in public schools, he states that that the French Republic has excluded religious symbols and discourses from the public sphere. There are no references to God or any placing of hands on the Bible in public institutions. As Kuru also mentions, the French state is quite hesitant in according freedom and religious autonomy to religious associations not judged to be mainstream religion. One case in point is the governmental institution *Mission interministérielle de vigilance et de lutte contre les dérives sectaires* (MIVILUDES) that surveils the more than one hundred sects deemed to be dangerous (109). He, however, states that the French public school system has, despite the dominance of assertive secularism, been quite accommodating to certain religious demands, like the financing of Catholic private schools, which constitute about 20 percent of French schools (see also Fabre 2007; Schwartz 2007; Weil 2007).[3] He moreover brings up a number of issues: the non-application of the Law of 1905 in Alsace-Moselle and in some overseas colonial departments (DOM-TOM); the financing of the over forty-five thousand churches in France; half-days in schools on Wednesdays with the possibility of having religious education; chaplains in public schools, hospitals and prisons (the majority were Christian but Muslim and Jewish chaplains are allowed); and the highly mediatized Catholic funeral of President Mitterand in 1996.[4] Besides these examples, it is the task of the *Bureau des cultes* (Bureau of Religions) to regulate the state's relationship with religious institutions. A number of informal advisors on religious affairs work in the Bureau, which is under the wing of the Minister of the Interior.[5] Since 1920, at the French Ministry of Foreign Affairs, there has been an official advisor on religious affairs (Champenois 1993; Guénois, Hoffner, and Senèze 2008).

These accommodating and controlling practices notwithstanding, Kuru is close to Baubérot in describing the historical unfolding of French secularism—from the Revolution, the Third Republic's reforms, and the Law of 1905 to the Law of 2004.

---

3 Exact numbers in 2011 were 16.9 percent of the students from kindergarten to high school and 21.3 percent of the students in junior high and high school attending a private institution. See, further, Ministère de l'Éducation nationale (2011). For a brief history on the French private school system, see Chadwick (1997).

4 In the case of Alsace-Moselle, it was ruled by the 1801 concordat and the Falloux Law from 1950 (concerning education) but when the region was lost to Germany in 1871 and later annexed by France through the Versailles Treaty in 1918, the 1905 legislation was never fully applied. This means that the curriculum contains obligatory classes in one of the four recognized religions: Catholicism, Lutheranism, Calvinism, and Judaism. The Dom-Toms, such as Wallis-et-Futuna, French Polynesia, Saint-Pierre-et-Miquelon, Mayotte, and New Caledonia, fall under article 74 in the Constitution, stipulating particular treatment of these departments and, in terms of secularist laws, these vary depending on the specific department. For example, in French Polynesia and Mayotte, it is stipulated that the weekly curriculum may not infringe on the parents' will to educate their children in religious teaching. See further Debré Report 2003a, 24ff and Baubérot and Regnault 2007.

5 Some seminal names of advisors are Charles Pasqua, Jean-Pierre Chevènement, and Alain Billon. See Liogier (2006, 39ff). The Bureau of Religion is situated at 11 rue des Saussaies in the 8th arrondissement in central Paris. An interview was conducted with the head of the Bureau, Bertrand Gaume, 12 December 2009. For a brief history of the Bureau, see Bernadette (2004).

Critique

In this section, I will discuss critically writings on secularism theory and secular regimes. As well as going through what I see as the most important critique of such defenders of the core of secularization theory like Casanova. I will present three aspects that I argue are the incongruities, contradictions, and ideological problems of secularism theory.

Talal Asad (2003) has pointed to both merits and problems with Casanova's critical reading and simultaneous defense of the "core" of the theory. Asad cherishes Casanova's attempt to break out of the theory's Eurocentric and modernist foundations. Notwithstanding, he argues that Casanova's critical reading and defense of theory is still founded on particular and normative conceptions of religion: "I begin by examining *the kind* of religion that enlightenment intellectuals like Casanova see as compatible with modernity ... Only religions that have accepted the assumption of liberal discourse are being commended, in which tolerance is sought on the basis of a distinctive relation between law and morality" (183).

By taking Casanova's defense of the theory seriously, as Asad does, it still appears incoherent. Asad (2003) wonders on what ground Casanova's secularization theory, based on differentiation, is tenable if religion, that is, modern and liberal religion, is given an active role in society. First of all, Asad argues that the very moment religion becomes a viable member and subject in public debate, the idea of separation of religion from the other public spheres, its differentiation, becomes untenable. Differentiation appears as but another liberal ideological claim of separation and the masking of power relations in society, similar to that of the separation between economics and politics. As he states: "Liberal politicians don't merely engage in public talk for the sake of 'enriching' it" (187). Second, if religion becomes a viable part of public debate and a normative voice on political conduct, ethics, norms, economics, and so on, decline of social influence cannot be restricted to measuring church attendance (182). Since the third claim is false, he summarizes: "It seems that nothing retrievable remains of the secularization thesis" (183).[6]

Incongruities

Indeed, if Casanova's defense of the core of the theory of secularization does not hold for the type of critical scrutiny provided by Asad, there should be

---

6 Casanova has rebutted Asad's critique and Asad has in his turn responded to Casanova's defense. See Casanova and Asad in Scott and Hirschkind (2006).

caution regarding his writings on the relation between secularization, the secular, and secularism. As I will try to show, the relation between these categories is far from self-evident and contains warranting incongruities. If the *secular* is a modern "epistemic category," and *secularization* an "analytical conceptualization of modern world-historical processes," I wonder what separates these two categories from *secularism* (an "epistemic knowledge regime" and a "philosophy of history"). If secularism is such a potent *something* that it enters into our "unthought," if it is an epistemic knowledge regime creating a philosophy of history, is it not pertinent to ask how secularism produces notions of secularization as a historical process and the secular as an epistemic category in the first place?

It seems to me that Casanova takes for granted that *secularization* and the *secular* have an independent meaning outside of *secularism* and that it is secularism that somewhat perverts their true meaning. The problem with secularism, according to Casanova (2011), is that it renders "the particular Western Christian mode of secularization into a universal teleological process of human development from belief to unbelief, from primitive to irrational or metaphysical religion to modern rational postmetaphysical secular consciousness" (70). Instead, he suggests, one should acknowledge secularization "for what it truly was, namely a particular Christian and post-Christian historical process, and not, as Europeans like to think, a general or universal process of human or societal development" (64).

While I believe Casanova is right in the assumption that one fundamental problem with secularism is how it seeks to universalize the theory of secularization, I am not so sure that a) secularization is a historical European fact and b) that "Europeans" disagree on Europe's particular Christian roots. One of the ideological problems, to use Casanova's lingua, is that, irrespective of whether the secularization thesis is taken to be applicable to the entire globe or only Europe, it still feeds into a liberal-modernist imaginary where Europe becomes the only successfully developed, secular, universal civilization, which is exceptionally developed and/or exceptionally unique (Fitzgerald 2007; Masuzawa 2005).

Moreover, I am quite hesitant about Casanova's distinction between secularism as "state-craft" and secularism as "ideology." If secularism as statecraft is simply the separation of the religious and the political authority, how is this separation done without the state deciding where and how to make this separation by deciding what *religion* is and does? I cannot see how a non-ideological secularism could be constructed at all. Even the simple separation of the *religious* and *political authority* is a performative act entangled with power and ideology (Fitzgerald 2015). I argue that this will to separate religion from politics and ideology from statecraft not only supports Asad's argument of a liberal and power-negligent bias in Casanova's writings but also demonstrates theoretical inadequacies and shortcomings, which I will address in the last segment of this subsection.

Moreover, if we take Taylor's (2008, 2011) theorization of secularism seriously, it is hardly applicable to the French case. Taylor states that secularism requires "state-neutrality" vis-à-vis a certain world-outlook and a separation between state and church. These close ties between the French state and religion make it difficult to sustain any image of a clearcut separation of church and state in France, either as a historical fact or as a prerequisite for secularism as a political doctrine. They also call into question the state's required neutrality or indifference in the promotion of one religion over another (see Liogier 2010). This is especially clear in relation to the Republic's promotion of a secular morality. Jules Ferry, one of secularism's alleged founding fathers, argued that secular morality was the "good old morale of our fathers" (as cited in Rochefort 2007, 66)—a morale arguably promoting a particular world-outlook.

Contradictions

Here I will comment on three contradictory and interrelated aspects of secularism theory. The aspects revolve around the ideal types: assertive and passive secularism, their supposed historical continuity, and the problems of using them as analytical categories on contemporary French secularism.

As Baubérot and many other scholars have pointed out, the Republic applied the famous Secularism Law of 1905 separating the church from the state unequally in the French colonial empire (see Frégosi 2008; Shakman Hurd 2008). In French Algeria, its non-application to the Muslim population led to a state-gallican model, or a tutelage role of the state in relation to Muslims and the practice of Islam, meaning that the state could keep Algerian mosques on a tight leash (see Schiappa 2005). The Republic, moreover, denied Muslims the status of full citizens and deemed them incapable of being secular. Not only did this contribute to making *Muslim* into an ethnic marker, it also rendered the *secular* into a marker for Christian Europeans. As stated by Elisabeth Shakman Hurd (2008):

> In French interventions in the Middle East and North Africa, the expulsion of religion from politics was identified with progress and civilization, while Islam was associated with Oriental despotism. By appropriating Islam as a regressive and even transgressive nemesis, as a stumbling block to be overcome on the road leading to the French (theoretical though

never actual) ideal of assimilation, French thinkers, writers, and colonial administrators contributed to the consolidation of republican identity and state authority as *laic*. (55)

The developments in Algeria led to the demand by Algerian leaders for a separation between religion and state. Ferhat Abbas, the founder of *L'Union démocratique du manifeste algérien*, saw in secularism a measure to fight the colonial order (Baubérot 2012, loc. 1099).

In this regard, Kuru's path dependent analysis of secularism is blind to the colonial power relations of the era when secularism developed into a comprehensive "state-ideology," to use Kuru's terminology. Far from being a marginal concern, the application of the Law of 1905 in the colonies was discussed in the National Assembly during the legislative deliberations on 30 June and third July 1905 (see Schiappa 2005). The point is that, by not taking seriously the impact of French colonialism, it is all too easy to argue on insufficient premises that the Law of 2004 is simply a continuation of the Third Republic's secular laws. The Laws of 1905 and 2004 might be regarded as commensurate if one takes into account how the separation of church and state was used to legitimize control and surveillance of Muslim colonial subjects deemed incapable of separating religion from politics, as white Christian French were said to be able to do (see Achi 2007; Conklin 1997; Monod 2007, 142). Moreover, if Islam is the new Christianity, there is a clear dissonance in how republican spokespeople of the Third Republic related to Christianity and how they relate to it today. As pointed out by Chabal (2015), "few nineteenth-century republicans were as thoroughgoing anti-clericals as neo-republican historiography would have us believe" (15). For example, former leader of the socialist party, Jean Jaurès, had a vision of a secular society that is far from any strict separation between the temporal and the spiritual world. He urged on the contrary for their fusion: "Long gone are the days when humanity idealized the separation between the spiritual and the temporal world; it is their fusion that should be desired" (quoted in Mathiez 2005).[7] Moreover, the Third Republic's secular school kept *God* as a reference for a good public moral standard up until 1923 (Monod 2007, 120), and since 1959, the French Republic indirectly supports the economic financing of religious groups through various forms of economic sanctions (Baudouin and Portier 2001, 32).

---

7 "Bien loin que l'humanité tende comme à un idéal à la séparation du spirituel et du temporel, c'est leur fusion, au contraire, qu'elle doit desirer."

Today, French white Christian politicians can conspicuously identify with Catholicism without losing their political legitimacy. A few examples of this are Charles de Gaulle's appraisals of Catholicism (Bardy 2011), Nicolas Sarkozy's public confessions of his love for Catholicism and the Republic's essentially Christian roots (examples will follow in this book), Christine Boutin and her Christian democratic party *Parti chrétien-démocrate* (PCD), and the massive Catholic anti-LGBT rallies in 2013 (Le Devin and Mouillard 2013 Non-Christian religious voices are, however, routinely delegitimated by reference to the strict separation of religion and politics necessitated by secularism to safeguard democracy in the Republic (see Amiraux 2009; Lévy 2010). If Kuru's analytical categories of assertive and passive secularism, as either-or ideologies for the state, are to answer this question, one would either have to argue that assertive secularism holds a tight grip on French state-religion relations and, thus, does not take into account the public visibility of Christianity (which is far more extended than just Mitterand's funeral), or state that there has been a shift to a passive secularism favoring a more public and visible role for Christianity. Kuru's path dependent analysis does not seem able to cope with these different and conspicuously contradictory articulations of secularism. Another answer would of course be to state that the two types of secularism work differently on different political subjects: passively on white Christians and assertively on non-white Muslims.

Shakman Hurd has certainly taken into account French colonialism in her analysis of French secularism. Although I am very much in line with Shakman Hurd, the distinction she makes between Judeo-Christian secularism and laicism, which is similar to Kuru's, bewilders me. Shakman Hurd understands laicism as a political doctrine seeking to "force" religion out of politics (Shakman Hurd 2008, 23) and to "confine religion to the private sphere" (38). She understands Judeo-Christian secularism as "a discursive tradition that aspires to negotiate the modern relationship between religion and politics" (38). Shakman Hurd stresses that these two secularisms are not "mutually exclusive," that there is "no strong or necessary dividing line between them" (23) but that the difference between them is that laicism "claims to have superseded religion and religious origins altogether" (27), whereas Judeo-Christian secularism "is associated with attempts to claim and reinforce the 'secular' as a unique Western achievement that both distills and expresses the essence of Euro-American history, civilization, and culture" (23). As will become clear in this book, if all the disparate articulations of French secularism by leading republican spokespeople are considered, laicism as described by Shakman Hurd is not applicable to contemporary French secularism during the period 2003–2011. Rather, it comes close to the Judeo-Christian version of secularism but with a republican twist. Not only do many republican spokespeople see secularism as uniquely Christian and uniquely Western, they see it as the final stage of Christianity while also being originally and essentially French (see also Milner 2009). I do not believe that this necessarily invalidates Shakman Hurd's historical analysis of French secularism or laicism. My argument is that it nonetheless points to specific problems associated with using ideal types of secularism for understanding its contemporary articulations.

A Western Gaze?

It should be clear at this point that theories of secularization and secularism have for a long time been developed with Eurocentric epistemology and a Christian bias, as argued by, for example, Casanova and Kuru. However, as I have tried to underline, Casanova's theory also builds on particular conceptions of religion: one that is compatible with modernity and one that is not. Another tacit bias in the articulations of secularism theory is the usage of Islam or the imaginary Orient as an objective backdrop to highlight or pinpoint certain aspects of the imaginary West. Ian Almond (2007), for example, has shown how certain postmodern thinkers have a tendency to "resort to Islam and Islamic cultures as a means of obtaining some kind of critical distance from one's own society [which has] become a familiar gesture, if expressed in a number of different ways" (2007, 2). In this regard, although not being a postmodern writer, Taylor's writings on secularism are emblematic. In *A Secular Age* (2007), Taylor has provided an extensive exposé of secularization and the development of secularism in Christian Europe. Taylor's argument, or, at least one of them, is that, in Christian societies, secularism has rendered religion into a free choice. Religion is no longer a part of the hegemonic Weltanshauung, as he puts it. In order to contrast and to validate this argument, Taylor turns to "Muslim societies":

> The shift to secularity in this sense consists, among other things, of a move from a society where belief in God is unchallenged and indeed, unproblematic, to one in which it is understood to be one option among others ... In this meaning ... the United States are secularized ... Clear contrast cases today would be the majority of Muslim societies ... Nevertheless, it seems to me evident that there are big differences between these societies in *what it is to believe*, stemming in part from the fact that belief is an option, and in some sense an embattled option in the Christian (or in the post-Christian) society, and not (or not yet) in the Muslim ones. (3)

The Muslim society here functions as the instinctive contrast to the secular society. In the over eight hundred page exposé on secularism, based on the statement above statement, he thinks that Islam is a monolithic entity and consequently does not provide analysis to substantiate the claim that belief is not optional in Muslim societies, (see Masuzawa 2008).

In other writings, Taylor has commented on the Law of 2004. According to him, "the recent legislation in France against wearing the hijab in schools" points to the problems of finding a common value base in a multi-religious society (2008, xiii). He identifies a perceived problem and explains that Muslims in Europe need to adapt to their new host countries' laws and regulations. Meanwhile, as they are invited to partake in the making of their new home country, "the host country is often forced to send a double message. (i) you can't do that here (kill Salman Rushdie, practice female genital process), and (ii) we invite you to be part of our consensus-building process" (xiii). These are indeed unexpected statements since they have nothing to do with the issue of wearing veils in school. Moreover, the usage of the term "host country" seems misplaced since the Veil Affair in 2004 was a concern for French citizens born and raised in France. Furthermore, in 2004, French law clearly prohibited murder and female genital mutilation but not wearing the veil in schools.

Elaborating on the dangers in modern societies, Taylor suggests that the real problem is one of failed politics of integration and the rise of counter identities. In addition, concerning the latter, Taylor (2008) adds:

> Of course ... in the Muslim case ... the building of a counter-identity is further encouraged by the global backlash that we now see in many Muslim countries, and which focuses in general on the West as an enemy. It is tempting for disoriented young people, frustrated in their ambitions for themselves, to draw on, sometimes partly and provisionally, sometimes with deadly intent, these 'Islamic' counter-identities, which grab so much attention and headlines everywhere. (xiv)

Here, he portrays the West as prey for a global backlash with deadly intent carried out by Muslims. However, there is hope; with an appropriate secular framework, Taylor (2008) suggests that "Muslim communities might develop in a similar manner as Catholicism has done" (xii). In other words, Christianity becomes the norm, and secularism is judged to be in need of revision due to a challenge named the "integration of Islam"—an integration that seems to hinge on statements of the obvious, for example that Muslims ought to follow the law.

Categories like secular, secularization, and secularism have for centuries been harbingers of anti-Muslim thought, legitimizing a sort of *bellum contra barbarus* discourse, *bellum* being Christian-Secular Europe, and *barbarus* the Turks (Keane 2000, 35; Mastnak 2002). The distinction between Christianity and secularism that is today commonplace overshadows how republican anti-clerical theoreticians and politicians of colonialism depended on their Catholic enemies to carry out the civilizing mission during the height of French imperialism (Daughton 2006, 6). To reflexively fall back on this discourse is to re-articulate a neglect of the more than two hundred year history of theorization on secularism by Islamic theologians and reformists. Imagined universal ideas and virtues ascribed to Europe were, and are, not alien to Islamic political thought. During the twentieth century there are many examples of where various forms of secularism have been welcomed by traditionalist and conservative Islamic groups, which might appear as a paradox to some Western scholars (see for example Esposito and Tammimi 2000).

In terms of what is commonly identified as anti-Western currents of thought among Islamic intellectuals, it is important not to ignore that they have "emerged to counter what they saw as a colonial design against Islam and the Muslims in the form of an intellectual and political onslaught aimed at westernizing the Muslims and stripping them of their cultural identity," as Azzam Tamimi (2000,13) has put it (see also Sayyid 2003, 2009). The disregard of colonial history and the employment of the Muslim-other or the Orient as an objective backdrop in the story of the West is also a question of political legitimacy in the sense that the West is attributed with the voice of universalism, and the Muslim, the Islamic and Islam are portrayed as essentially foreign to the universal—to democracy and reason (see Said 1985; Hosford and Wojtkowski 2010). This is one of the core problems with how the Islamic Veil Affairs played out in public debate.

Previous Research on the Islamic Veil Affairs and Secularism

Scholars have spilt a lot of ink over the Veil Affairs and French secularism. In this section, I will summarize some of the most important contributions on the issues written in English. I focus on how these studies relate to my own study by discussing how they have analyzed secularism and its relation to Islam in France. In the wake of the Affair in 2004–2005, a number of books were published on the topic. With *Why the French don't like Headscarves* (2007), John Bowen has written an anthropological account of the First Affair. Bowen asks why a law was thought of as important, given "that relatively few disputes over scarf-wearing ever went beyond the classroom and that virtually no one accused the scarf-wearing girls of presenting a danger to French society" (1–2). Bowen concludes that the veil "had become a symbol of mounting Islamism and decaying social life" (242) and that "banning the *voile* [veil] was the only way to show that politicians of the sensible center [were] responding to France's new enemies" (243).[8] Bowen points to how the law was part of a republican tradition where political thinkers and actors seek to "teach the French people moral lessons" (243). Secularism, Bowen states is an "essentially contested concept," but he adds that narratives "about *laïcité* give to these elements both a temporal continuity and a historical telos or purpose" (20). The point is that this has allowed public spokespeople to speak "as if there is a historical object called '*laïcité*'" (32). Bowen goes on to show how laïcité became a prerequisite value for accessing public speech, and how a secularist or laïciste identity became a marker in the attack on the wearing of the veil (229). However, apart from some key speeches by state officials and the recounting of scholarly accounts on secularism, Bowen does not engage in a systematic analysis of how the state apparatus articulated secularism during the First Affair. Bowen's study does however stand out since it is the only one that fuses anthropological fieldwork with a textual analysis of the media, political speech, and legislative text. As such, it is one of the most important studies on the topic.

In *Hijab and the Republic* (2008), Bronwyn Winter explicitly distances herself from Bowen. According to Winter, Bowen is "a specialist on Indonesia who has recently turned his attention to France" and who does not write from a "feminist perspective" (4). Winter has analyzed the developments from 1989 to 2005 and the stated aim "is to provide a more detailed feminist analysis of the many complexities and contradictions of the current political debate and its history than is, at the time of writing, available in English" (14). Winter seeks to provide a bridge, or "hearing aid," between French feminists who see their American counterparts as "cultural relativists" and American feminists who see their French counterparts as "assimilationist" and "imperialistically universalist" (14). After a long deliberation on the nature of the veil and what she calls the "new veiling" in late modernity in the "Muslim world" (19), Winter quotes some passages in the Quran and draws a general conclusion regarding women in Islam: "Women are the danger, they must be contained, controlled, covered" (44). Winter goes on to state that the question that concerns her "is less of diverse individual motivations of hijab [veil] wearers than the wider political manipulation of hijabization" (52). As I will show, this is one of the

---

8 Italics added.

themes running through the French state apparatus' knowledge production on women wearing the veil. Everybody knows that it is a highly complex issue. Still, it seems sufficient to glance at the Orient and some ancient texts to determine what really drives these women or, rather, see that they are tools of an "Islamist manipulation" of France (Winter 2008, 346). Agency is denied to these women. Of course, from a Foucauldian perspective, where power relations are thought of as omnipresent, unrestrained agency becomes problematic to maintain as an analytical category. But this is not the concern of Winter, who concludes that "it is at best naïve and at worst intellectually and politically dishonest to seek some 'feminist' justification of any women's pro-religion activism in the name of 'agency', anticolonialism, or whatever" (45). Winter's assessment that the young women who got caught in the media spotlight were enacting their "own personal Star Academy, Muslim style" (253) is as denigrating as it is empirically weak.

Regarding secularism, Winter describes the official take on its history where she traces the "true formal beginning of secularism" to "the creation of the first Republic in 1792" (2008, 63). She, moreover, identifies four contradictions within French secularism. First, she argues that since the birth of secularism coincided with that of universalism, which was constructed in a specific national French framework, secularism has been tightly connected with particular understandings of the universal and the nation. This particular French take on the universal is, according to her, the first contradiction (67). The second contradiction is that the exercise of freedom of conscience "is only acquired at the price of submission to the authority of the state." The third is that the liberation of the public school from Christian morality led to its replacement by a secular one, leading to the creation of a "Republican catechism." The last one is that secularism finds itself in "a permanent dialectic with the main institutional manifestation" of the transcendence it was thought to fight, "namely, the Catholic Church" (68). Exactly how secularism was articulated and what role it played in the 2004 law is, however, hard to read from her analysis. It seems to me that Winter in fact reproduces many of the unproblematized assumptions made by French secularists, that the "prohibition of religious signs in schools and in the public sector is crucial to preserve the neutrality of public space" (345). However, if universality is bound with particularism, as she seems to suggest, are not conceptions of neutrality equally so? Nonetheless, in the end, Winter accuses the French state of not "fully [applying] the principles of secularism that it claims to defend" (347).

Joan W. Scott differs from Bowen and Winter in her theoretical approach. In *The Politics of the Veil* (2007), Scott's main argument is that the overarching discursive articulation of the headscarf controversies was that of a French clash of civilizations with roots in the Republic's colonial era. During the Affair, specific discursive constructions of culture were used as distinguishing markers between *us* and *them*, a "mythologizing of France as a universal and enduring 'republic'" and "the objectification of Muslims as a fixed 'culture'" (7). This led to a deadlock—into an imaginary *Kulturkampf*, where the only solution for the other was to succumb to the dominant culture. According to Scott, the "choice was clear ... only by giving up all signs of belonging to the Islamic faith could these people [immigrants] become 'fully French'" (83). This statement helps us to highlight a crucial aspect that Winter seems to miss, that the state is not an a-cultural machine. Instead, republican spokespeople argued according to logic similar to that of colonial times that resulted in there being "no need to tolerate Islam" (102). Scott suggests that by emphasizing the imaginary cultural boundaries, secularism versus (fundamentalist) Islam, and portraying them as a national "crisis," French politicians could divert attention from far more real and important social issues, such as gender inequalities and "how to improve the lot of an impoverished, marginalized 'immigrant' population, and, more generally, how to recognize the difference in social and political terms" (120).

Although Scott spends one chapter on the topic of secularism in *The Politics of the Veil*, I believe she makes her strongest contribution in a text called "Sexularism" (2009). Here, Scott calls into question the modernist evolutionary emancipatory narrative of secularism and the displacement of unachieved universal credos on unacceptable religious others (1). Scott argues that there is no necessary connection between secularism and gender equality, as republican spokespeople and liberal-republican scholars suggest. Instead, Scott shows how the "public/private demarcation so crucial to the secular/religious divide rests on a vision of sexual difference that legitimizes the political and social inequality of women and men" (4).

Scott is not alone in this assessment. Florence Rochefort (2007) has shown how the 1905 law did little for equality between men and women. Rochefort concludes: "The representation of the feminine and femininity are still heavily attached to a sex-based dichotomy of qualities and values; to men, reason and power; to women, intuition and sentiments. And intelligence? Yes, sometimes, but at home!" (65). "The republican majority that supported secularization [*laïcisation*]" as Rochefort has put it, "did not want to hear about any reforms of the Civil Code [changing the status of women] ... not even partially, equating them with children, madmen, and criminals" (65).

Given that secularism did not bring about a gender-equal society, it should be troublesome to maintain the idealized view of secularism's neutral emancipatory qualities. Actually, as Scott suggests, secularism seems to do more to obscure and even maintain the very inequalities it is said to fight. Indeed, if inequalities persist, does "it matter if God or nature or culture is the foundation on which explanation rests [sic]?" (2009, 9). This brings Scott to a discussion about agency. Instead of religion denying religious agency, Scott (2009) argues that "It follows that religious belief does not in itself deny agency; rather, it creates particular forms of agency whose meanings and history are not transparently signaled by the wearing of a veil. If one of those meanings has to do with the idea that women are subordinate to men ... this is not a problem confined to Islam" (12). During the Affair, republican spokespeople wanted to make believe that, except for Muslim communities, France was a gender-equal society. As Christine Délphy (2008) has put it: "In a newsletter from *La ligue de droits de l'Homme* (LDH) one could read that 'the veil tears a hole in the equality between the sexes.' This was how I learned that equality between the sexes existed in France" (154).

Another important study of French secularism is Laborde's *Critical Republicanism* (2008). It is a critical analysis of contemporary republicanism and a defense of what she sees as its core principles. She has elaborated on the ideas of freedom and agency in relation to secularism and stated that "laïcistes [secularists] are liberal perfectionists" since they "believe that the state should promote worthwhile forms of life, and that worthwhile forms of life are those that exhibit a high degree of individual autonomy" (102). The point is that, in secularist-republican logic, "one is not free when one mindlessly follows the opinions, ideals, goals, and values of others" and "they [secularists] go on to lay stress on the need for rationality to direct the autonomous person's behavior" (103). As such, she argues that French secularism on the one hand "contains both an institutional doctrine of separation, which outlines what separation means for governmental institutions" and, on the other, functions as "a doctrine of conscience, which prescribes norms of conduct both for religious organizations and for individual citizens" (31). In the concluding remarks, Laborde states that the republican ideal as expressed by the republican elite during the First Affair indeed "proved to have exclusionary effects on minorities such as Muslims and youth of immigrant origin" (255). "Yet" she continues, "this is not because (as some multiculturalists would claim) republican citizenship is an intrinsically exclusionary ideal. It is rather because, in public discourse, the ideal of republicanism has functioned as a social ideology that purports to describe, and thereby legitimizes, existing arrangements in actual society. Thus, official republicans implicitly assume that French society already meets republican standards, and then urge members of minorities to comply with them" (255). Whether or not republican citizenship is an intrinsically exclusionary ideal, it leads us to a quest to inquire into the real essence of this citizenship.

Yet, another important book on the matter is Jennifer Selby's *Questioning French Secularism* (2012). Selby's book builds on ethnographical fieldwork conducted in Parisian suburbs during the Veil Affairs. She argues first of all that "secularism in the Republic today is given weight and importance as a way to secure women's equal rights" (7). She further suggests that: "African colonialism and the migration of Maghrebians to France—particularly visibly Muslim women—have changed the way in which the strict separation of religion and state is publicly rationalized" (7). Selby then sets out to "show how headscarves in particular have come to symbolize a threat to a largely unarticulated but marked equation between democracy, nationhood and the secular public sphere" (7). These are important questions indeed; I am however not certain about how to interpret them. First, as my analysis and others show (e.g., Scott 2007; Fernando 2014), the debates about Islam and secularism were to a large degree debates about women's rights. Selby is not clear if republican spokespeople employed the category of women's rights to legitimize the laws or whether they were really secured, and, in that case, the rights of which women? Second, to suggest that colonialism and migration have challenged the "strict separation" is problematic for two reasons. As I have argued, it is difficult to talk about a strict separation in the first place. Thus, the question of who challenged what needs to be further problematized. Third, that republican spokespeople portrayed veiled women as a threat is beyond doubt, but that they were a threat to an "unarticulated" equation between democracy, nationhood, and the secular public sphere was not the case in the parliamentarian debates preceding the Laws of 2004 and 2010. Notwithstanding, Selby's problematizing approach to French secularism is instructive (2012, 72ff). First, drawing on Schmitt, she suggests that one should understand secularism as political theology and stresses the importance of understanding the theological underpinnings of the secular state in order not to be blind to the implicit power structures inherent in the secular state. Second, she argues that Muslims were judged incompatible with secularism, based on the normative dichotomic discourse of public private, religion-politics, religion-secular. Third, she argues that secularism is a tautological term and suggests that secularism is not nearly as neutral as republican spokespeople like to believe.

Mayanthi Fernando (2014) has made a similar approach to French secularism. She describes secularism as governmentality and seeks to understand how the French state (via secularism) controls, disciplines, and excludes, yet also includes, the Muslim French, and how they respond to these techniques of governmentality (20). This is a clear break from republican accounts of secularism and, as Fernando says, is a story about the "imbrication of religion and politics rather than their separation, and about the production of and regulation of religious subjects rather than simply the guarantee of their freedom" (20). In other words, Fernando's analysis focuses on the productive and regulative power of secularism as governmentality, where the regulation of religion is a crucial function (21). Most significantly for my analysis, Fernando's discussion is between "the continuities and discontinuities between colonial and postcolonial constructions of race and religion," where she shows "how racialization and secularization intersect to produce contemporary forms of alterity" (18). It is in this vein that I construct my analytical approach.

Analyzing Secularism

I base my analysis of the affairs on the qualitative methodology of discourse analysis, and more specifically its poststructural and/or postmodern branch (see Torfing 1999). In this section, I describe the method for analyzing and selecting the data. In the two following sections, I discuss the theoretical aspects of the analysis. At its most basic level, the discourse analysis I employ is a qualitative reading of the data. More specifically this means that, through inductive reading, I have identified key statements and categories in French political speech related to the Islamic Veil Affairs. As stated by David Howarth, Aletta Norval, and Yannis Stavrakakis (2000), discourse theorists "seek to articulate their concepts in each particular enactment of concrete research" instead of applying "preexisting theory on to a set of empirical objects" (4). I have moreover digitalized and structured the data in a searchable database, which has made possible cross-readings of the identified statements and categories in order to compare and contrast the initial reading.

The analyzed data comprises thousands of pages of political speeches, state reports, legislative text, interventions in the media, and three years of fieldwork, mainly in the Paris region. More specifically, I have analyzed speeches, interventions, and decrees by government officials, mainly presidents and ministers, gathered during the time of the Veil Affairs.[9] I have collected this material from the presidential and the ministries' archives, much of it digital, but also from the press and TV. I have analyzed debates in the National Assembly leading to the laws of 2004 and 2010—in 2004 the deliberations lasted

---

9 The government and parliament reports analyzed from the first *Affair* are *Laïcité et République: Commission de réflexion sur l'application du principe de laïcité dans la République, Rapport au Président de la République* by the Stasi Commission, appointed by Bernard Stasi on the command of President Chirac in 2003 (Stasi 2003); *Rapport fait au nom de la mission d'information sur la question du port des signes religieux à l'école* by the Debré Commission

three days in February and, in 2010, they lasted two days in July. The Senate's deliberations were not as long; in 2004, they took place over two days in March and, in 2010, one day in October.

When referring to statements in the material, I use the title, name, and political affiliation of the specific individual talking (i.e., President, Prime Minister, Member of Parliament (MP), and Senator). I employ the term republican spokespeople when referring to these figures in the plural. I also add the republican spokespeople's political party affiliations and/or group affiliation in Parliament.[10] The fieldwork in the Paris region has been dedicated to collecting data from archives and partaking in the daily debate through the media flow,

---

headed by the president of the national assembly Jean-Louis Debré (UMP) in 2003 (Debré 2003a, b and c); *Rapport fait au nom de la commission des lois constitutionnelles, de la législation et de l'administration générale de la République sur le projet de loi relatif à l'application du principe de laïcité dans les écoles, collèges et lycées publics* by the Clement Commission headed by depute Pascal Clement (UMP) in 2004 (Clément 2004); and finally *Rapport fait au nom de la commission des Affaires culturelles sur le projet de loi, adopté par l'Assemblée nationale, encadrant, en application du principe de laïcité, le port de signes ou de tenues manifestant une appartenance religieuse dans les écoles, collèges et lycées publics* by the Valade Commission in 2004 with senator Jacques Valade (UMP) as its president (Valade 2004). The specific reports for second Affair are *Rapport d'information fait en application de l'article 145 du règlement au nom de la mission d'information sur la pratique du port du voile intégral sur le territoire national* by the Gerin Commission in 2010 led by MP André Gerin (PCF) and MP Éric Raoult (UMP) in 2010 (Gerin 2010); the hearings by the Gerin Commission conducted in 2009; *Rapport d'information fait au nom de la délégation aux droits des femmes et à l'égalité des chances entre les hommes et les femmes sur le projet de loi, adopté par l'Assemblée nationale, interdisant la dissimulation du visage dans l'espace public* by the Hummel Commission headed by senator Christian Hummel (UMP) (Hummel 2010); as well as The Study of possible legal grounds for banning the full veil (original in English) by the Conseil d'État (2010).

10   The political parties are *Front national* (FN), *Parti communiste français* (PCF), *Mouvement démocrate* (MoDem), *Parti socialiste* (PS), *Union pour la démocratie française* (UDF), and *Union pour un mouvement populaire* (UMP). The groups in the national assembly are *Communistes et républicains* (CR), *Députés non inscrits*, non-affiliated MPs in Parliament (DNI), *Groupe gauche, démocratique et républicaine* (GDR), *Nouveau centre* (NC), *Rassemblement pour la République* (RPR), *Socialiste* (S), *Socialiste, radical, citoyen et divers gauche* (SRC), and *Union pour la majorité présidentielle* (UMP). In the Senat: *Communiste, républicain et citoyen* (CRC), *Écologiste, Rassemblement démocratique et social européen* (RDSE) *Socialiste* (S), *Union centriste des democrates de progès* (UCDP), *Républicains et indépendants* (RI), *Républicains indépendants sociale* (RIS), *Union des democrates pour la République* (UDR), *Rassemblement pour la République* (RPR), *Union pour un mouvement populaire* (UMP).

by attending meetings and demonstrations and by talking with state officials and spokespeople from religious and secularist organizations.

A Critical Approach to Secularism

My analytical approach to secularism sets out from the growing body of literature on Critical Religion Theory (CRT) (see Stack, Fitzgerald, and Goldenberg 2015). CRT is an interdisciplinary approach that is largely rooted in Foucauldian discourse analysis (i.e., genealogy) and poststructural discourse theory. Scholars in CRT seek to unpack "religion" and related categories (like "secularism") by analyzing them as discursive and contingent categories bound to the workings of contingency, power relations, and social antagonism. Asad's (1993) work captures this aspect of CRT: "My argument is that there cannot be a universal definition of religion, not only because its constituent elements and relationships are historically specific, but also because that definition is itself the historical product of discursive processes" (29).

Still, religion, just like secularism, is commonly perceived to be universal. One of the reasons for this hegemonic assumption is that since colonial times and through academic disciplines such as orientalism, anthropology, and philology, religion and secularism have been neutralized into objective categories for how the world is perceived (Masuzawa 2005). Moreover, as Timothy Fitzgerald (2007) has argued, any articulation of the religious and the secular is necessarily a political and parasitic articulation which is deeply bound up with how the contemporary social world is rendered meaningful. Articulations of religion and secularism create, shape, and reposition political identities and, most importantly, they delineate and set up borders for the included and excluded: good religion versus bad religion, the religious versus the non-religious, the moderate versus the fundamentalist, and, most important for this analysis, the secular versus the religious (Liogier 2010; Mamdani 2004).

In this regard Tomoko Masuzawa has forcefully shown that the "modern discourse on religion and religions was from the very beginning ... a discourse of secularization; at the same time, it was clearly a discourse of othering" (Masuzawa 2005, 20). Following Masuzawa, my interest resides with the co-related articulation of secularism and Islam. Hence, I focus on understanding the intersections of secularism and ruling conceptions of Islam and how secularism is negatively identified through Islam_that is, how secularism is constructed, construed, articulated, re-invented, and made real through different conceptions of Islam.

This is where I believe Shakman Hurd's work to be of great importance for my analysis. Although I see analytical problems associated with her distinction of Judeo-Christian secularism and laicism, I believe she is correct in pointing out that "one way in which these traditions of secularism and national identities with which they are intertwined have been consolidated is through the opposition to the idea and practice of Islam" (Shakman Hurd 2008, 44). If secularism is nothing without Islam, as Hurd suggests, not only would Islam be secularism's constitutive outside, secularism could not be without Islam. Ian Coller (2011) similarly suggests that "colonial Arab Paris was a play of mirrors in which French power and prestige were endlessly reflected, and peoples to be 'civilized' were brought to provide a spectacle of their own inferiority for the education of the 'civilizers'" (217).

My aim is that this analytical approach to contemporary French secularism will help to highlight how French republican discourse on secularism is negatively articulated and that the category of secularism is in itself utterly empty. One can thus not falsify or twist secularism because there is no single secularism to distort.[11] From this perspective there is a plethora of meanings retroactively articulated through the empty category whose meaning, content, and function are products of power relations and social antagonism.

Secularism as Governmentality

According to Asad (2005), one of the most important aspects in the analysis of secularism is not the prohibition of one religion (e.g., Islam in France or in Turkey), but the "installation of a single absolute power—the sovereign state—drawn from a single abstract source and facing a single political task: the worldly care of its population regardless of its beliefs" (499). As he argues, the state functions as "a transcendent as well as a representative agent" (499). For the state to practice its worldly care, "state power needs to define its proper place for the worldly well-being of its population in its care" (500). Thus, the state needs on the one hand to define governable and ungovernable subjects and on the other to designate the governable from the ungovernable. In this analysis, this means that I seek to understand the performativity of the religious-secular divide(s) by analyzing how state power defines the "religious" and "secular" in relation to government and identity (see Dressler and Mandair 2011).

To capture this aspect of performative state power and the reification of the sovereign state, I employ Foucault's theoretical-analytical neologism *governmentality*. I take governmentality to involve the state apparatus' will to govern (see Rose 1999, 5ff). He used governmentality to signify "state reason" (*gouverner*/govern and *rationalité*/rationality). "With government," Foucault

---

11   Compare with discussion on religion by Russel McCutcheon (2003, 8ff)

(1991) stated, "it is a question not of imposing laws on men, but of disposing things: that is to say, of employing tactics rather than laws, and even of using laws themselves as tactics—to arrange things in such a way that, through a certain number of means, such and such ends may be achieved" (95).

Rationality, to quote Foucault, refers to how "forms of rationality inscribe themselves in practices or systems of practices, and what role they play within them, because it is true that 'practices' don't exist without a certain regime of rationality" (79). Analytically, governmentality seeks to capture, as Xavier India (2005) has put it, "the conduct of conduct, all those more or less calculated and systematic ways of thinking and acting that aim to shape, regulate, or manage the comportment of others, whether they be workers in a factory, inmates in a prison, wards in a mental hospital, the inhabitants of a territory, or the members of a population" (1).

However, as India reminds us, for the state apparatus to govern, knowledge becomes crucial—to know what to govern and how (7). This suggests that "government is inherently a problematizing sphere of activity—one in which the responsibilities of administrative authorities tend to be framed in terms of problems that need to be addressed" (7).

The goal of governmental practice is, then, to articulate the nature of these problems and propose solutions to them (see Bacchi 1999). However, "modern political power not only manages populations and produces certain sorts of subjects," as Wendy Brown (2008) puts it; "it also reproduces and enlarges itself" (83). Brown continues: "A full account of governmentality then would attend not only to the production, organization, and mobilization of subjects by a variety of powers, but also to the problem of legitimizing these operations by the singularity accountable object in the field of political power: the state" (83).

I argue that a fundamental way, and perhaps the most important way, in how the state legitimizes the exercise of sovereign power and its governing of subjects is channeled through a certain conception of national identity. I understand identity, and specifically national identity, in line with scholars like Chantal Mouffe (2005), Ernesto Laclau (1994), Yannis Stavrakakis (1999), Jacob Torfing (1999), and Slavoj Žižek (1999, 2008) and see the category of nation as essentially empty where the role of nationalist discourse is to articulate its imagined content and to implement it through institutionalizing practices and techniques. As such, political and social actors can employ the category of nation in nationalist discourse to create a sense of societal unity for the nation's subjects based on specific inclusionary and exclusionary techniques and borders—its pure people and its true territory. In addition, they can use the category of people in several other classificatory explicit or implicit categories—ethnicity, language, culture, religion, class, and gender (see Anthias and Yuval-Davis 1992; Walby 1986). To quote Žižek (1990):

> A nation exists only as long as its specific enjoyment continues to be materialized in certain social practices, and transmitted in national myths that structure these practices. To emphasize, in a 'deconstructivist' mode, that the Nation is not a biological or transhistorical fact but a contingent discursive construction, an overdetermined result of textual practices, is thus misleading: it overlooks the role of a remainder of some real, non-discursive kernel of enjoyment which must be present for the Nation qua discursive-entity-effect to achieve its ontological consistency. (53)

The function of a nationalist discourse is thus to create a sense of societal closure, of boundaries demarcating those who are inside and those who are outside through discursive techniques like ethnicity, race, gender, culture, and religion. These boundaries are not merely imagined, they are constantly performed, materialized and institutionalized through everything from daily performances of national identity, like partaking in rallies, demonstrations, watching sports, citizenship, passports, customs, the police, the military, schools, and so on (see Breuilly 1996). Just as secularism needs its others to be articulated, I understand the articulation of nation in a similar manner: a national community can only be articulated in relation to a power outside of that society (Lefort 1986, 286). "That's why," as Žižek (2002, 109) has pointed out, "the political struggle concentrates on the production of a recognizable image" (162–163). This analysis of republican secularism is thus a way to inquire how national identity and secularism intersect and what kind of politics French republican secularism legitimizes.

Secularism as Discourse

Analytically, my critical approach to secularism as governmentality means that I analyze secularism as discourse, as a contingent and power-bound producer of religion, identity, and alterity (see Taira 2013). My approach to discourse is mainly genealogical. A genealogical analysis of secularism is not a pursuit of its essential origin, of the what-has-always-been. Instead, "the genealogist" says Foucault (1984), "needs history to dispel the chimeras of the origin" (80). My concern with history is to deconstruct the very idea of it. As Foucault explains, genealogy "does not pretend to go back in time to restore an unbroken continuity that operates beyond the dispersion of forgotten things, its duty is not to demonstrate that the past actively exists in the present" (81). A genealogical analysis of secularism is not a quest to reveal secularism's supposed real essence or how certain actors betray this supposed real essence in this or that historical period. Rather, it sets out to explore how secularism as discourse was made possible in the first place. This relates to what Foucault (2004) called "the politics of truth" where the role of the analyst, my role, is to analyze the effects of the knowledge regimes produced through struggle, confrontation, and combat, and lay bare the tactics of power that are the elements of these struggles (5).

Analyzing discourse means that I seek to understand: on what kinds of subjects and objects a certain discourse speaks (i.e., the religious, the secular, the fanatic, the terrorist); what are considered to be legitimate and truthful statements about these subjects and objects (i.e., by political leaders, intellectuals, religious leaders, witnesses) and from what speech-positions; what kinds of moments are involved in the articulation of these subjects and objects (i.e., secularism, republic, nation, freedom, liberty, brotherhood); what kinds of theories are developed through these statements (i.e., society needs to be purified of them, the abnormal, the bad, the unjust, the unlawful so that we, the normal, the good, the righteous, the lawful can prosper); how these theories are materialized (i.e., laws, regulations, institutionalization of norms, values, and identities through laws and regulations), and finally, what the discourse stipulates is to be done with these subjects and objects (see Foucault 1972). I give special attention to discursive techniques of othering as a means of bringing closure to "our" identity. This approach means that discourse is not merely words; it is material in the most concrete sense. As Faisal Devji (2008) has put it: "Humanity becomes embodied during the twentieth century, when it is given biological as well as juridical form in debates about the states of the unborn, the comatose, the criminal and the insane" (6).

Following Foucauldian writers, a discourse can be understood as whatever constrains as well as enables writing, speaking, and thinking within specific historical limitations (see McHoul and Grace 1993, 31). More specifically, I take discourse to be an assembly of a specific set of statements: "Sometimes as the general domain of all statements, sometimes as an individualized group of statements, and sometimes as a regulated practice that accounts for a certain number of statements" (Foucault 1972, 80; see also McHoul and Grace 1993, 34ff).

Ernest Laclau and Chantal Mouffe's writings on Discourse Theory are particularly useful for an analytical understanding of the articulation of statements. Laclau and Mouffe (2001) define discourse as "the structured totality resulting from the articulatory practice" (105). It comes close to Foucault's definition of discourse as a regulated practice for a number of statements. To allow an analytical distinction to delineate an articulated signifier in discourse and a not-yet-articulated signifier, Laclau and Mouffe calls the latter "element" and the former "moment" (2001, 105). I understand statements to articulate elements into moments. For example, secularism and democracy are attributed different meanings in statements made by the AKP and the CHP in Turkey, but the AKP statements may in certain regards come quite close to those of President Nicolas Sarkozy, as in the need for a public morality rooted in the nation's Christian or Islamic traditions. In this specific analysis, where my interest is on the co-related articulation of secularism and Islam, I focus on the intersections of secularism and ruling conceptions of Islam and how republican spokespeople negatively identify secularism through Islam. To conclude, I understand discourse as a contingent and performative articulation of a number of moments and statements that are united through their unique language. What drives a discourse is the inner emptiness of discourse and the will to bring closure to this emptiness. In other words, the contingency and emptiness of discourse is its constitutive lack (see Torfing 1999).

Here I want to stress that my analytical approach focuses exclusively on political speech and legislative text, thus I will not be able to analyze how the neo-republican discourse on secularism has been diffused and understood by the French population (see Breuilly 1996, 148). I also want to underline that, although I am not sympathetic with the neo-republican discourse on secularism, my aim is not to get into a polemical debate about its contents, its empirical facts, or the validity of its truth statements. Rather, I am interested in how knowledge about the objects and subjects of the discourse comes into being, what it builds on, how it is reasoned, and what the consequences are from this knowledge game. With that said, I aim to be as transparent as possible, to myself and to the reader. This is the purpose of the next chapter.

CHAPTER 2

A Shield Against Alterity

During the period analyzed in this book (2003–2011), it is the rightwing conservative *Union pour un mouvement populaire* (UMP) that occupied the major positions in the government and in parliament. This has of course made a mark on the articulation of the neo-republican discourse on secularism. Pierre Tévanian (2014), for example, has argued that the period saw a "conservative revolution" of French secularism. It was a revolution defined by "the transition from libertarian to 'securitiarian' secularism; the transition from democratic to totalitarian logic; and the transition from egalitarian to 'identitarian' secularism" (Tévanian 2014). As I will show, if it is correct to talk about a conservative revolution, this does not mean that UMP representatives were the only ones making their voices heard. Politicians from the leftwing parties *Parti socialiste* (PS) and *Parti communiste français* (PCF) have been active forces in this revolution. In fact, the very idea of what secularism entailed was about to be changed. The question of secularism was no longer merely designating the battle of the two schools, private versus Catholic, it expanded to incorporate a whole field of questions previously unknown to it (see Baudouin and Portier 2001, 15 ff; Monod 2007).

These evolutions have been taking place in a France where the Muslim-other has become the equivalent of an internal enemy—an enemy that needs to be neutralized either through expulsion or assimilation. According to a study by the national opinion poll institute IFOP conducted in 2010, 42 percent of the French see Islam as a threat "to the national identity of their country," with a strong dominance among the Right- and Far-Right voters (71 percent to 24 percent among the Left). Sixty-eight percent consider people of Muslim origin to be "not well integrated in France," out of which 61 percent perceive that the failed integration is a result of the "Muslim's refusal to integrate." The words and phrases mostly associated with Islam were "rejection of Western values" (31 percent), "fanaticism or intolerance" (18 percent), "submission" (17 percent), and "violence" (6 percent). Fifty-nine percent of the French are against the wearing of the veil in public space (*dans la rue*) (IFOP in *Le Monde* 2010). As stated by Abdellali Hajjat and Marwan Mohammed (2013), the number of anti-Islamic and anti-Muslim statements made by public spokespeople is today far beyond counting. For the last twenty years, participants in French public debate have been virtually obsessed by the so-called "Muslim Problem" and its supposed solution: secularism (also see Fernando 2014).

In this chapter, I introduce the reader to the events leading up to the Veil Affairs and discuss briefly how they were constructed in the news media. I also place these Affairs in a historical, socio-political, and analytical context, focusing on the central subjects and moments of, and the political techniques legitimized by, the republican discourse on secularism that I set out to analyze in this book. These central subjects and moments of the discourse are the *other-woman*, the *other-immigrant, the (white) French, Islam/Muslim,* and *Republican/French*. I discuss these subjects and moments in relation to the central political techniques legitimized by the discourse: *state feminism, nationalism, integration,* and *citizenship*.

The Islamic Veil Affairs

Scholars usually divide what I call the first Islamic Veil Affair into three phases (Nordmann 2004; see also McGoldrick 2006). The first was its eruption in 1989, when three students wearing veils were excluded from school. The second was in 1993–1994 when the Minister of Education, François Bayrou (1994), published a decree that sought to prohibit "conspicuous signs" and "proselytizing symbols" that "separate certain students from the school's common rules." The third phase was in 2003–2004 when the debate was resumed, which led to the ratification in Parliament of a law prohibiting Islamic veils in public schools. This period is what I henceforth refer to as the First Veil Affair. What I call the Second Veil Affair refers to 2009–2011 when the National Assembly launched a Commission to evaluate the possibilities of legislating against the wearing of a full-face veil (niqab or burqa). The affair was instigated when (MP) André Gerin from the French Communist Party (*Parti communiste français* or PCF) submitted a proposal for investigating a ban on the full veil in France (see Gerin 2010).

As has been well documented elsewhere (see previous chapter), these debates became a scene for public figures' confessions and avowals of their attachment to and love of the Republic. It is noteworthy that a number of public figures who had at first problematized the prohibition of the veil abruptly changed their opinion to speak in favor of a law proclaiming that young Muslim women were indeed the visible part of Islamic communitarianism.[1]

---

1 One case in point is Alain Touraine who, at the beginning of the Affair, first problematized the veil and defended the students' right to wear it and later argued that these students were markers of communitarianism. On this particular case, see Jansen (2013) and Baubérot (2009).

Here I sketch out the contours for my reading of these two Affairs. I start with the events of 1989 and continue by focusing on 2003–2004 and 2009–2011.

1989

The events leading up to the Veil Affair took place in Creil, a small city north of Paris, and they were the start of a long theatrical performance divided into its proper acts. Here I briefly recap how the news media construed and framed the affair.

At the beginning of the fall semester in 1989, three students arrived at Gabriel Havez, the public junior high school, wearing Islamic veils, or hijabs. Leaning on a regulatory decree from 1937, which says nothing about religious clothing,[2] the principal of the school, Ernest Chenière, declared that dressing in this way was a violation of the French principle of secularism.[3] Chenière and the school board proceeded by expelling the students. Anti-racist organizations like SOS *Racisme* and *Mouvement contre le racisme et pour l'amitié entre les peuples* (MRAP) appealed for the right of these students to access school. They argued that the students' choice of clothes was not the Republic's concern and that it was actually Chenière who was breaking the law by refusing these students access to school (see Hargreaves 2007, 112). Soon thereafter, the news media, politicians, and public spokespeople were entangled in what was to become a recurring (and seemingly never-ending) republican obsession with Muslim women and their choice of clothing.

In the news media, one republican spokesperson after another reproduced a discourse that articulated these students and their veils as the physical manifestation of the old/new enemy to the Christian secular West: Islam. For nearly four months, the Veil Affair made it to the front pages each week and journalists wrote about it on a daily basis in the national daily and weekly newspapers.

---

2 It was in fact a matter of two decrees. One published in 1936, saying nothing about confessional proselytism but which instead set out to prohibit political propaganda and recruitment by third-party members. It stated that "les écoles doivent rester l'asile inviolable ou les querelles des hommes ne pénètrent pas." In 1937, under the pressure of secularist groups, Zay added that confessional propaganda and proselytism also be prohibited. This law was however put into effect in an attempt to stop confrontations between right-wing groups and communists in school. For further reading see Loubes (2004).

3 The principle Ernest Chenière was also reported to be annoyed by some twenty Jewish students being absent on Saturdays. Chenière however thought it "impossible to search them in their homes and drag them to school." A law could thus be understood as a strategy on Chenière's behalf to address this issue. See Raphelle (1989).

The debate in the three major dailies (*Le Figaro, Le Monde,* and *Libération*) reached a feverish pitch where immigration and immigrants from North Africa were portrayed as a cause of the problems now facing France. Front pages of newspapers were covered with headlines like: "The War of the Chador" (*Le Figaro* 1989b); "Emotions are Rising" (*Le Figaro* 1989a); "French Schools Facing Islam" (*Le Monde* 1989a); "Three Headscarves and One Country" (*Le Monde* 1989c); "A Veiled Blow to Secularism" (*La Libération* 1989a); "Islam and Secularism: The Wearing of the Headscarf in School Poses a Problem to Integration" (*Le Monde* 1989b); "The Challenge of the Secular School" (*La Libération* 1989a).[4]

Articles in the journals followed suit. One in *Le Figaro* said that the three students, Leila, Fatima, and Samir, of Tunisian and Moroccan origin, "had demonstrated violently about their total subjugation to Islam, which petrified people in their surroundings" (Gallerey 1989).[5] In another article, Chenière, when interviewed, explained that these students and their headscarves, "symbols of islamic fundamentalism," had caused concern for a while among the staff (Miaro 1989).[6] The same article published a photo of the three students. The text accompanying the photo explained that their way of dressing, in headscarves and in sports-dresses, "showed their obvious submission" and how "they were ready for combat in the name of Allah" (Miaro 1989).[7] Another article quoted Chenière as saying that the students demonstrated a "delirious intransigence" (Gallerey 1989). In these articles, Chenière's statements were unchallenged and tacitly given the status of objective fact. In a similar fashion, teachers were reported to "recognize that there is a problem" with these young women, and veiled women in general (Miaro 1989). In the story about the students, these teachers became voices from within the institutions, testifying to an Islamic resurgence undermining French identity and culture.

French public intellectuals soon entered the debate to enlighten the situation from a historical-philosophical perspective. One seminal case in point was the jointly written article by five public intellectuals published

---

4   In order of appearance: "La guère du tchador"; "La montée des passions"; "Les écoles françaises face à l'islam"; "Trois foulards et un pays"; "Coup de voile sur la laïcité"; "Islam et laïcité: Le port du foulard à l'école pose le problème de l'intégration"; "Le défi de l'école laïque." Moreover, The 'secular' or "laïque" refers to the secular school system of Jules Ferry in the 1880s.

5   "[Elles ont manifesté leur foi] avec une violence qui avait pétrifié leurs interlocuteurs, leur attachement farouche et total à l'islam."

6   "On avait beaucoup parlé d'elles ... et de leur foulard, symbole d'intégrisme islamique."

7   "Vêtues d'un survêtement de sport ... coiffées du fameux foulard, leur soumission n'est qu'apparente. Au nom d'Allah, on sent bien qu'elles sont prêtes au combat."

in *Le Nouvel Observateur*. In the article *"Profs: Ne Capitulons pas!"* (Teachers: Let's not Give Up!), Catherine Kintzler, Élisabeth de Fontenay, Régis Debray, Alain Finkelkraut, and Élisabeth Badinter likened the situation to the Munich accord in 1938 when France and Britain succumbed to the demands of Germany's expansionist demands (Kintzler et al. 1989; see also Winter 2008, 136).[8] The five intellectuals said that France was facing a new occupation, like that of the Second World War. The journalist Max Clos (1989) explicitly stated that a "retribalization" was taking place, aimed at destroying what "the Republic and the French Kingdom" during centuries had been trying so hard to establish, namely "national identity."[9] The central question, as Clos put it, was whether, in the name of tolerance and respect of others, "we" were supposed to accept "excision and cannibalism on our soil." Clos continued to assess that "certain civilizations are compatible with each other because they are founded on the same roots and recognize the same values."[10] Others were not.

One cartoon among many in *Le Figaro* emphasized this sort of cultural and civilizational incompatibility by sketching a debate between a Muslim student and a non-Muslim teacher. In the cartoon the teacher asks the student about the date of the "victory," and then corrects herself to say, instead, "defeat" at Poitiers (Konk in Soustell 1989).[11] This cartoon suggests that teachers rewrote and reversed French history to the satisfaction of Muslim students, which could lead to a dangerous subversion of French society. In *Le Monde* the journalist Robert Solé (1989) proclaimed that, "in a secular society based on a Judeo-Christian culture, Islam could not have the same public role as it would have in a Muslim country." To deny this fact under "the pretext of tolerance and

---

8   "Profs: Ne Capitulons pas!"
9   "C'est à dire le contraire de ce que la royauté et la république, pendant des siècles, se sont efforcées de construire: l'identité nationale."
10 "La question est: au nom de la tolérance, au nom du respect des autres, devons-nous accepter sur notre sol l'excision et le cannibalisme? ... Certaines civilisations sont compatibles entre-elles parce que fondées sur les mêmes racines et reconnaissent les mêmes valeurs."
11 This refers to the battle at Tours-Poitiers in 732 when the Frankish King Charles the Hammer put an end to the northern expansion of Arab forces on the European continent. The intepretation of the battle varies greatly among historians. Some refer to it as the defining moment of Christian Europe and others as a largely overstated and ideological construction to support European and Christian supremacy (see Mastnak 2002, 99ff). Today the battle and Charles the Hammer have been turned into an icon in French anti-Muslim and ultra-nationalist circles (see Nilsson 2015).

generosity would," according to Solé, "be an immense hypocrisy burdened by consequences."[12]

One can of course say more about this particular period. For example, that the Minister of Education, Lionel Jospin, overturned Chenière's decision to expel the students (see Lombard 1989), or that two of the students decided to take off their veils a couple of months later (see *Le Monde* 1989d). In addition, the *Conseil d'Etat* (France's highest administrative court) published a legal judgment that led the Minister of National Education, Lionel Jospin, to publish a decree that a large number of commentators understood as supporting the students by allowing them to wear veils in schools.

The Decree from Jospin states that secularism is a constitutional principle of the Republic and one of the foundations of the public school. The decree further states that the wearing of religious signs by students was not by itself incompatible with the principle of secularism, insofar as it resulted from the exercise of freedom of expression and the manifestation of religious faith affirmed by the Constitution and the fundamental principles, ratified and recognized by the Republic. However, quoting the verdict, Jospin added that students were not permitted to display religious signs that by their conspicuous or provocative nature constituted an act of pressure, provocation, proselytism, or propaganda that could disturb the normal functioning of public order. Jospin subsequently urged that students should show caution in relation to all conspicuous symbols that seek to promote a religious faith. To this, he added that if any student did not respect this bill, a period of dialogue should precede any expulsion from the school (see Conseil d'Etat 1989; Jospin 1989). It is also worth noting that Chenière seemed to have laid the grounds for a political career with this Affair, and that in 1994, as an elected member of the department of Oise, he handed in a bill proposing a ban on conspicuous religious affiliations (see Scott 2007, 26).

2003–2004

Several of scholars argue that the first Islamic Veil Affair reached its peak in 2003–2004, after a public speech by the Minister of the Interior, Nicolas Sarkozy (see for example Bowen, 2007, 102–103; Keaton 2006, 180–181; Scott 2007, 29–30). During this speech, held at the annual meeting of the Islamic organization *l'Union des Organisations Islamiques de France* (UOIF)

---

12   "Il est clair en effet que, dans une société laique, nourrie de culture judéo-chrétienne, l'islam ne peut vivre et s'exprimer publiquement de la même manière que dans un pays musulman. Nier cette évidence, sous prétexte de tolérance ou de générosité, serait une immense hypocrisie lourde de conséquences."

in the north Parisian suburb of Le Bourget, Sarkozy evoked the question of identity cards and veils.[13] Sarkozy (2003a) stated that nothing justified a Muslim woman wearing a veil on her photo ID, especially since all women, "especially Catholic women," living in France already accepted this requirement. By all accounts, the audience booed and whistled, showing discontent with Sarkozy's statement (Dufay 2003; Revel 2003). This incident became national news. Muslims were portrayed as anti-republican, rude, and foreign with regard to French fundamental values. Instantly forgetting the French tradition of free speech and the public demonstrations of dissatisfaction with the republican elite, demands for a debate on secularism that clearly established the Republic's borders against what was perceived as a religious bulldozing of the Republic started to echo from seemingly all corners of the Hexagon (see AFP 2003).[14] In June 2003, the National Assembly's vice-president, François Baroin (UMP), handed the report *Pour une nouvelle laïcité* (For a New Secularism) to PM Jean-Pierre Raffarin. The report stated that secularism could be a principle and value of the right to fight against the left's alleged embracement of multiculturalism and laxism towards communitarianism. The report concluded with a dozen or so propositions, one of which implied that the Republic ought to prohibit the wearing of the veil in schools by adding that an ad hoc commission should engage in an extensive debate with the concerned student before any decision of exclusion from school. Here, the schema of what would be taking place during the following year was laid out, as well as the sensation of entering into an already-accomplished debate (Airiau 2005, 149).

The imagined last straw proving Islam's incompatibility with the Republic came during the start of the new school year when the sisters Lila and Alma Lévy's veils became national news. The students were expelled from the Henry Wallon High School in the north-Parisian suburb of Aubervilliers. According to Baroin, this was a "courageous decision" (France 2 2003). Five teachers from the school later demanded the students' reinstatement, arguing that "they were neither adverseries of the veil nor of secularism; they simply wanted to ensure

---

13 The UOIF, created in 1983, is a moderate conservative Islamic organization—often tainted with the image of fundamentalist or close to fundamentalist in the media—with its administrative headquarters in a desolate industrial area in the North-Parisian suburb La Courneuve. The well-visited Islamic conference in Le Bourget, a North-Parisian suburb, has since 1983 been organized by the UOIF and invites Muslims and non-Muslims to partake in lectures, visit bookstands, pray, eat, drink, and socialize.

14 The Hexagon, or *l'Héxagon*, is another name for Metropolitan France, i.e. the European parts. It refers to the six edged shape of the countries boarders.

the students' right to schooling" (*La Libération* 2003).[15] Regardless, these veiled students became the focal point of the media spotlight as questions arose: Who were they? Why did they choose to go public with their beliefs? Why the veil? According to a parliamentarian report, this sartorial practice "questioned French society in its totality" (Debré 2003a, 11).[16]

To come to terms with this conundrum, a large investigative operation that turned into a national preoccupation was instituted by the government and Parliament. Summing up the investigation, MP Pascal Clément (UMP) (2004) stated that in this particularly sensitive national debate concerning French national cohesion two proceedings were set in motion (5). The first was the presidentially appointed Stasi Commission, whose task was to evaluate secularism in the Republic, and the other was when the National Assembly appointed the Debré Commission to undertake an evaluation of the future of religious symbols in public schools. In addition to the reports from these two commissions (Stasi 2003; Debré 2003a, b and c), there were two other reports critical in the assessment of the situation. The Valade Commission's (2004) report from the Senate and the aforementioned Clément Report by MP Pascal Clement (2004) from the National Assembly both evaluated the work of the Stasi Commission and Debré Commission, as well as the subsequent bills for prohibiting religious symbols in school.

Based on the work of these reports, the government and the parliament set out to solve the problematic presence of religious symbols on republican soil. Just as for Catholics and Jews, it was now time for Muslims, and Muslim women in particular, to become full members of the secular-republican unity.

When President Chirac (2003a) announced the formation of the Stasi Commission in 2003, he claimed that evidence indicating a loosening of the standards of secularism was multiplying.[17] The President explained, moreover, that what was at stake today concerning secularism and its application in France was "our capacity to reconcile national unity and the Republic's neutrality with the recognition of diversity, and especially religious diversity."[18] Secularism

---

15 "Nous ne sommes ni militants du foulard ni adversaires de la laïcité, nous estimons seulement que tous les enfants ont droit à l'instruction"

16 "la question du port, par les élèves, des signes religieux à l'école, interroge aujourd'hui la société française dans son ensemble..."

17 "Jour après jour, les témoignages se multiplient, qui indiquent un relâchement de l'exigence de laïcité"

18 "[La] laïcité et son application dans la France d'aujourd'hui, c'est notre capacité à concilier l'unité nationale et la neutralité de la République avec la reconnaissance de la diversité, et notamment de la diversité religieuse"

here appeared as a political strategy to unite France and cope with its diverse population.

When the Stasi Commission was appointed, the number of students wearing the veil differed according to the sources. According to Minister of the Interior Nicolas Sarkozy, based on a study by the French intelligence service *Direction Centrale des Renseignements Généraux* (DCRG), the number was 1,256, of which twenty-two caused a problem and where four cases had lead to expulsion (in Bernard 2003). Given that this particularly sensitive national debate concerned such a microscopic number of French citizens, and that more than 250,000 Muslim female students did not wear veils in school, it is tempting to draw the conclusion that this was indeed a false debate. Said Bouamama (2004), for example, argues that republican spokespeople used the veiled students as scapegoats to divert attention from the socio-economic problems facing the Republic.

While the imminent law prohibiting the wearing of conspicuous religious symbols concerned schools, Chirac (2003a) made clear that it also related to the workplace and public sector, and that he wished that the Stasi Commission would provide the base for a "genuine public debate" that would "sustain and nurture" the principle of secularism in French society. Even though this genuine public debate oscillated between school and society, of the twenty-six suggestions proposed by the Commission only one made it into the legislative apparatus and paved the way for the 2004 law: the prohibition of conspicuous manifestations of religious clothing in public schools. Socialist MP Martime David (S) argued that the law was "a tool for the rehabilitation of secularism" and asked: "What could be more symbolic than to start with the school" (Assemblée Nationale (AN) 2004c, 1391)?[19]

In 2002, Nicolas Sarkozy, soon to be Minister of the Interior, stated that the French rules needed to be respected; if a small number of people choose not to respect the rules of the secular public school, they should be excluded (quoted in Geisser and Zemouri 2007, 67). A year later Sarkozy made a comparison between schools and mosques by stating that if he entered a Mosque, he would surely take off his shoes. If a young Muslim entered the school, "the student must surely take off her veil" (quoted in Tincq 2003).[20] The comparison is curious. It suggests that a private place of worship is equal to the obligatory republican public school. It also points to what became a recurring moment in

---

19 "[U]n outil de réhabilitation de la laïcité ... mais quoi de plus symbolique que de commencer par l'école?"
20 "Quand je rentre dans une mosquée, je retire mes chaussures. Quand une jeune musulmane entre à l'école, elle doit enlever son voile."

the Veil Affairs. The French Republic was sacralized as the school came to be replaced by an expanding conception of the public sphere, where not only sartorial customs but also the desires of individuals became objects for the state's controlling and disciplining apparatuses.

Given that Parliament ratified the law almost unanimously, 494 in favor and thirty-six against in the National Assembly and 277 in favor and twenty against in the Senate, one could be led to believe that a large consensus concerning secularism prevailed among the French political elite (see AN 2004g; Sénat 2004b). However, as I will show, even though republican spokespeople reduced the law to a dualist stance of either for or against the secular republic, this did not mean that the republican political elite agreed on the contents of secularism. It meant only that an agreement existed on the necessity for a law prohibiting conspicuous manifestations of religious clothing (see for example Airiau 2005, 148). In fact, the expressed urgency and consensus on the importance of enforcing secularism was hard to find. A poll conducted in December 2003 in a public high school in Drancy asked 125 students about what they saw as the most burning problems in school (Tévanian 2005, 37ff). While the news media and politicians were occupied with questions of national identity, security, immigration, and of course secularism and Islam, just three students mentioned violence and insecurity as burning issues and only one mentioned the Veil, and this is out of 375 answers. What preoccupied the students' minds, then? Well, things like the school schedule, work on weekends, transportation to school, lack of understanding in cases of lateness due to traffic problems, lack of attention from teachers, gaps between rich and poor, and so on.

How did the teachers respond? A commonly quoted poll published in *Le Monde* in February 2004 suggested that 74 percent of the teachers asked were in favor of a law. This led the journal to conclude that three out of four teachers wanted a prohibition of religious symbols. However, as pointed out by Tévanian, something was overlooked: the difference between *wanting* something and *consenting to* something. Out of thirteen problems troubling public schools, teachers ranked secularism at number eleven. Only 14 percent of the teachers declared that it was one of the most burning problems. Instead, they talked about issues such as relations with parents, authority, pensions, decentralization, educational plans, insecurity, and so on. Furthermore, 88 percent of the teachers prescribed to the idea that "we talk too much about veiled girls in the media." Fifty-nine percent agreed with the question: "Do you think that the debate about the veil is a way to overshadow real problems posed in schools?" Finally, given the professed urgency and imagined gravity of the situation, it might come as a surprise that 91 percent of teachers asked did not even come across veiled students in their present workplace and that

65 percent had never met a student wearing a veil. These polls notwithstanding, Tévanian points out that of the 100 persons heard by the Stasi Commission, the only teachers interviewed were those who, in March 2003, held a demonstration against a student wearing a bandana, and two other teachers from the city of Flers, where in 1999, two students were excluded from school (16ff).

However, the law finally stated that "in public schools, the wearing of religious symbols by which a student conspicuously displays religious affiliation is prohibited and that, following local regulations, any disciplinary action will be preceded by dialogue with the student" (Loi n°2004-228 du 15 mars 2004).[21] One may wee ask why the 1989 verdict or the 1989 bill were not sufficient as the 2004 law does not seem to add anything, except naming of the veil as "conspicuous."

2007–2011

After the ratification of the Law of 2004, the news media and republican spokespeople lost interest in Muslim women and in secularism. This, however, changed with the presidential election of 2007. When the newly appointed president Nicolas Sarkozy talked publicly for the first time about secularism in an official speech, it was elevated to a principle of exclusion. According to the President, "Those who do not respect the French way of secularism are not welcome on the territory of the French Republic. This is France" (Sarkozy 2007a).[22] To Sarkozy, secularism appeared to signify an identity (a prerequisite for being French), a conduct (respectful to all religions and beliefs), and a regulatory technique (expulsion from French territory).[23] France seemed to be so respectful (i.e., secular) that it could not respect that which did not respect (i.e., the

---

21 "Dans les écoles, les collèges et les lycées publics, le port de signes ou tenues par lesquels les élèves manifestent ostensiblement une appartenance religieuse est interdit. Le règlement intérieur rappelle que la mise en oeuvre d'une procédure disciplinaire est précédée d'un dialogue avec l'élève." On a related matter, in the aftermath of the law, two French journalists, Christian Chesnot and Georges Malbrunot, were kidnapped by the Islamic Army in Iraq in 2004. The kidnappers are reported to have demanded as a ransom the overturning of the law but, in interviews with the journalists, the motives of the kidnapping have been described as aiming at keeping the French out of Iraq (see BBC News 2004).

22 "Ceux qui ne respectent pas la laïcité à la française ne sont pas les bienvenus sur le territoire de la République française. C'est cela la France."

23 It should be mentioned that Sarkozy was criticizing what according to him is a narrow and negative perception of laïcité. The positive laïcité he has argued for is one that pays attention to France's Christian history and that acknowledge religion to be a positive societal force. For a good overview see Schlegel 2008 and a critical analysis see Baubérot 2008.

non-secular) the Republic, meaning that the national litmus test marking out the frontier between the tolerable-intolerable, the admissive-expulsive, was articulated through secularism.

In June 2009, American President Barack Obama visited President Sarkozy in France; a new French-American alliance was to be born. During a joint interview in Caen, the two presidents commemorated their hard work in leading the free world. The interviewer evoked Obama's globally echoed speech "A New Beginning" given in Cairo a week earlier. In the speech, Obama was adamant about women's right to wear veils (Obama 2009a). Questioned about whether that statement would perhaps clash with French legislation, Obama (2009b) responded: "And as I said in the speech, I think that freedom of religious expression is critical. That is part of our liberal tradition both in France and the United States, and that we should not have two standards for freedom of religious expression, one for Muslims and one for non-Muslims."

To the surprise of many, Sarkozy (2009b) declared that: "I totally agree with what President Obama said, including on headscarves and veils" and added:

> But let me simply say two things. In France, any young girl, any girl who wishes to wear a veil or a headscarf may do so; it's her free choice to do so. We simply set two limits because we are a secular state; that is that civil servants who are actually on duty must not have—must not show any sign of their religious belief ... Secondly, the fact that young girls may choose to wear a veil or a headscarf is not a problem as long as they have actually chosen to do so, as opposed to this being imposed upon them, be it by their families or by their environment."

Whether or not Sarkozy simply forgot the 2004 law or was too occupied with pleasing the world's most powerful man is of course impossible to establish. However, Sarkozy's words were contradicted as soon as Obama left French soil—with the second Islamic Veil Affair.

The Affair got its public inauguration when communist MP André Gerin, in June 2009, proposed creating a commission of inquiry on the practice of wearing the burqa and the niqab on national territory. Fifty-seven MPs from the parliamentarian left and the parliamentarian right signed the proposition (three PCF, seven PS, forty-three UMP, and two *Nouveau centre* (NC), and three wild cards). A couple of weeks later, the Gerin Commission was set up, with Gerin as the president and MP Éric Raoult (UMP) as the official reporter. In his role as the head of the Commission, Gerin stated that "the objective was to investigate the reality of fundamentalist, communitarian, and barbarian tendencies" that, according to him, "had been developing in France during the last fifteen years" (Gerin in AN 2009d, 9).[24] According to Éric Besson (UMP) (2010a), the Minister of Immigration, Integration and National Identity, the Affair was an "opportunity for the French to question themselves, individually and collectively, on what it was that united them in a common project, on what it was that molded their will to live together."[25]

At the beginning of the debate, different assessments of the number of women wearing the full veil circulated in the press and among the benches in Parliament—numbers that, as noted by Maryam Borghée (2012), journalists and republican spokespeople presented without any methodological transparency (23). Supposedly, between 350 and 2000 women wearing full veils were marching around on the streets of the Republic (see AFP 2009b; Gabizon 2009b). During the summer of 2009, headlines containing the words *burqa* and *niqab* and photos of Muslim women wearing full veils strolling around public space dominated the press and the televised evening news, creating a daily, oriental, and exotic exhibition of the Islamic other. In the news media, journalists reported daily doings carried out by veiled woman; this contributed to their mystification and awkwardness. For example, in *Libération,* a photo depicting a woman wearing a niqab in front of a book stand was accompanied with the text: "A young Muslim woman" (Robine and Equy 2009).[26] In *Le Figaro* one headline asked "Who are the women wearing the burqa in France" (Gabizon 2009a)?[27] In *Le Monde,* one headline stated that "the burqa was a sectarian and not a religious sign" (Bouzar 2009).[28] In *Libération,* one headline proclaimed that the burqa was an "ambulating prison" (Equy 2009) and another proclaimed that the burqa was "a pathology of the Muslim culture" (Bidar 2009).[29] *Agence France-Press* (AFP) reported concerns about a new "war of the veil" (quoted in Charles 2009).[30]

---

24 "La mission a pour tâche d'enquêter sur la réalité des dérives intégristes, communautaristes et, pour reprendre le terme employé par Jean Glavany, barbares, qui se produisent depuis quinze ou vingt ans sur certains territoires de notre pays."

25 "c'est l'occasion de s'interroger, individuellement et collectivement, sur le lien qui nous unit autour d'un projet commun, sur ce qui forge notre volonté de vivre ensemble."

26 "Une jeune femme musulmane." On colonial oriental exhibition of the daily life of veiled women (for example postcards depicting women wearing veils with explanations such as "The Arab Woman," "Egyptian Women," "Turkish costumes" and "Turkish women walking") see Eldem 2010, 145–148, and Hale 2008, 46ff.

27 "Qui sont les femmes qui portent la burqa en France?"

28 "La burqa, un signe sectaire et non religieux."

29 In order of apparence: "une prison ambulante"; "La burqa, une pathologie de la culture musulmane."

30 "guerre du voile."

This new Affair was a debate that reiterated the frames of its predecessor in many ways. It articulated a threat signified by Muslim women's clothing attacking the Republic and its precious secularism. The most striking difference was that while the outcome of the first Affair focused on veils in schools, the second one revolved around a prohibition of full-face veils (i.e. burqas and niqabs) in the public space. At the beginning of the second Affair, republican spokespeople and the media all spoke about the burqa but after the realization that burqas did not exist in France, the full veil came to refer mainly to the niqab (see Albertini 2009).

The Gerin Commission (2010) was clear on the need for banning the full-face veil. While the Commission had difficulties in assessing whether or not adults wore the veil through free will, the Commission stated that, "regarding minors and especially the youngest ones, wearing the full-face veil is intolerable" (99).[31] Let me note that, according to the Minister of the Interior Brice Hortefeux, 1 percent of women wearing the full veil were minors (in Gerin 2010, 99). If it were approximately 370 women who wore the full veil, 1 percent would be 3.7 minors and if it were 1500 women, 1 percent would be fifteen minors. The disproportionality of the matter notwithstanding, republican spokespeople and institutions cherished the Commission's work. The *Conseil d'Etat* referred to the Commission as a "fact finding mission ... engaged in a process of reflection and discussion of a very high quality, based on great many instructive hearings" (Conseil d'Etat 2010, 47). The Council stated further that the "report enables us to grasp the full extent of the phenomenon and consider its significance, while appreciating the legal complexity of the question" (47).

After six months, the Gerin Commission reached a conclusion and, soon after, the Commission handed a report to the National Assembly. A debate commenced on how to turn the report's conclusions into a proper bill prohibiting the unwanted Islamic piece of cloth. In January 2010, Jean-François Copé, the parliamentary leader of UMP, proposed a bill prohibiting the full veil in the public space. The work of the Commission and the bill were not without critics. Socialist MP Jean Glavany saw the debate as disproportional, and as a way to create fear among the public. Glavany stated that the French had more important things to think about than "national identity and the islamization of France," which, according to him, was nothing more than "fear of the other, the foreigner, the one that did

---

31 "Il est tout à fait clair que, pour les mineures qui portent le voile intégral, et en particulier les plus jeunes d'entre elles, de telles pratiques sont intolérables."

not think as the French (as *us*), the one that did not share all *our* values" (AN 2010a, 5373).[32]

In a similar vein, MP Noël Mamère from the green party, *Les Verts,* seemed to agree and accused the debate of being pre-determined, stigmatizing, and guided by an Islamophobic theme: "In June 2009, when André Gerin asked for a parliamentary commission inquiring on the wearing of the burqa or niqab, it seemed clear that the match had already been played even before the pretended debate had taken place ... And what better than a debate that divides, that opposes, that stigmatizes, and that makes us, by its hubbub, forget social and ecological questions" (AN 2010a, 5378–9).[33] Communist MP Pierre Gosnat added that the debate about the law took place in a context of fearmongering about the dangers of immigration (AN 2010a, 5382).

The first article of the legislative text subsequently ratified by parliament stipulates that "nobody is allowed to wear a garment with the purpose of concealing one's face in public space."[34] Article three states that the punishment of not following this law would be a fee of 150€ and that a citizenship course can be added to the fee or can replace it (Law of 2010, Article 3). Article four states that anyone forcing another person to conceal their face in public space will be subjugated to a punishment of one year in prison and a fee of 30,000 € and if it concerned a minor, the punishment was to be doubled (Loi n°2010-1192 du 11 octobre 2010 interdisant la dissimulation du visage dans l'espace public).

If the Law of 2004 passed with impressive cohesion, the ratification of the Law of 2010 was more ambiguous. This was because a large majority of the parliamentary left abstained from voting. In the National Assembly (AN 2010d), 339 deputies out of 577 were present during the vote, 336 voted, 335 ratified the law, and one voted against it: the political wildcard Daniel Garrigue. UMP MPs applauded the legislative success.[35] In the Sénat (2010a),

---

[32] "ce soir, les Français qui sont chez eux ont mille autres choses en tête que le débat qui nous occupe ... sur l'identité nationale, la peur du minaret et celle de la burqa, ce qui n'est rien d'autre que la peur de l'autre, celui qui vient de l'étranger, celui qui ne pense pas comme nous, qui ne partage pas toutes nos valeurs."

[33] "Lorsque, le 17 juin 2009, André Gerin fit la demande d'une commission d'enquête parlementaire sur le port de la burqa ou du niqab, il semblait clair que les jeux étaient faits avant même que le prétendu débat n'ait lieu ... Rien de mieux, dans ces conditions, qu'un débat qui divise, qui oppose, qui stigmatise."

[34] "Nul ne peut, dans l'espace public, porter une tenue destinée à dissimuler son visage."

[35] The specific numbers were as follows: UMP, 313 MPs, 286 for, 1 absentee, 1 non-voting; SRC, 204 MPs, 18 for; GDR 26 MPs, 2 for; NC, 25 MPs, 23 for, 2 absentees; NI, 8 MPs, 6 for, 1 against.

247 senators out of 343 were present, 246 voted; 245 voted for the law, and one voted against it—Senator Anne-Marie Payet from the *Union Centriste* (UC). The absentees belonged mainly to the socialist group.[36] Given the large abstention from the parliamentary left, it would be tempting to draw the conclusion that they were against the law or at least some parts of it. To some extent, this seemed to be the case. However, as we are about to see, abstention was more about the formulation of the law than an outright rejection of it.

As I aim to show in my analysis, the Affair and the Law were partly about creating a common destiny for the Republic, which was what Minister of Justice Michèle Alliot-Marie suggested when acknowledging the work done by the Gerin Commission. Alliot-Marie praised the quality of the work. The debate had, according to the Minister, once again honored French democracy, especially as the will to live together depended on the French ability to assemble around common values and a shared destiny: "I salute the quality of the work effected by your commission and your reporter. The search for a general interest has prevailed over partisan considerations. The debate has once again honored our democracy. The will to live together depends on our ability to assemble around common values and a shared destiny" (AN 2010a, 5367; 2010c).[37]

If the Affairs articulated a common French destiny, they also came to articulate a discourse of threat, threatened, and defense. The threat was articulated by the categories of *veil, Islam, Moroccan, Tunisian, Arab, Maghreb, violence, suburbs, ignorance, invasion, problem*, and *cannibalism*. This chain of signifiers constituted a threat to the interconnected signifiers of France or *us*, such as *tolerance, nation, identity*, and *secularism*. The last line of defense against the imagined Islamic resurgence was the Republic's secularism, the "indispensable shield of our identity" as one journalist put it (Soustelle 1989).[38] My suggestion as I argue throughout my analysis, is that secularism can be understood not only as the articulated identity bringing the French people together and as a populist political moment signifying an imagined oppressed French majority, but also as a political technique used to fight back against the imagined Islamic resurgence.

---

36 The specific numbers were as follows: UMP, 150 Senators, 147 for, 3 not voting; GUC, 29 Senators, 28 for, one against; S, 116 Senators, 46 for, 70 not voting; RDS, 17 Senators, 17 for; CRC, 24 Senators, 2 for, 22 not voting; NI 7, Senators, 6 for, 1 not voting.

37 "Je salue la qualité du travail effectué par votre commission et votre rapporteur. La recherche de l'intérêt général a prévalu sur les considérations partisanes. Le débat parlementaire a fait une nouvelle fois honneur à notre démocratie. La volonté de vivre ensemble dépend de notre capacité à nous rassembler autour des valeurs communes et d'un destin partagé."

38 "le bouclier indispensable de notre identité."

State Feminism and the Other-Woman

The Islamic Veil Affairs' focus on publicly de-veiling the Muslim woman has been far from restricted to these Affairs alone. To these one can also add a number of minor affairs concerning women's denial of access to public housing, accessability to French courses for foreigners and postgraduate education at the university, the banning of a woman wearing a full-face veil from driving a car, and even circulating freely in the public realm without being interrogated by the police—all due to these women's choice of clothes (see for example *Le Nouvel Observateur* 2009). Another case concerns a Moroccan woman who had applied for French citizenship. In 2008, the *Conseil d'État* permanently denied her application due to her "radical religious practice" (I return to this case in the final chapter). Fadela Amara, the Secretary of State and former leader of the organization *Ni Putes, Ni Soumises* (NPNS), deemed the verdict "excellent" (Reuters 2008). Another incident in 2008 concerned a court-approved request to cancel a marriage because the wife had lied to her husband about her virginity. The court explained that this was as an essential matter for the husband, but in the news media it was portrayed as yet another example of the essential backwardness of Muslims (see *Le Nouvel Observateur* 2008; AFP 2008). In 2011, the school board at the Auguste Blanqui high school in the Parisian suburb of Seine-Saint-Denis called a student into a discussion to evaluate her violation of the school's secular regulations: her skirt was too long (Gresh 2011).

It is remarkable that these debates have focused on Muslim women and their freedom. Through them, the Republic has sought to break these women's Islamic chains and, when the chains are deemed unbreakable, denying the women access to the Republic (see Abu-Lughod 2002). Now, by bringing this up, I do not intend to defend the patriarchal politics surrounding some of these affairs, nor do I wish to disregard the hard reality in which some young Muslim women live. As pointed out by Tricia Danielle Keaton (2006): "The proliferating cases of Muslim girls and women killed for violating codes of honor or for challenging masculinity seem almost surreal. In France this is clearly illustrated by the cases of Nazmiyé ... and Sohane ... Their stories, indeed their murders, serve as constant reminders of just how tragic life can be for some Muslim girls" (164).[39]

---

39 These cases refer to violence committed against Muslim girls and women in France. Nazmiyé, a 15-year-old girl, was killed by her brother in 1994. The brother was sanctioned by the family since, as they argued, the family's honor had been betrayed by Nazmiyé's Western life-style. Sohane, was a 17-year-old girl who was killed in 2002. The killer, a young man, burned her to death for being too independent. See Keaton, 2006, 164–165.

It goes without saying, patriarchal practices are unacceptable in any democratic society worthy of the name. The focus I am suggesting here, however, seeks to highlight the discursive and political mechanisms involved in the claims to save, liberate, and speak for women who are thought, by republican spokespeople, to be subjected to foreign patriarchal structures (see Mahmood 2005). In this perspective, it is important to remind oneself that the recent battles over women's clothes and religious customs have a long historical lineage dating back to the very birth of the French Republic.

After the French Revolution in 1789 one of the Republic's first laws in the 26th of Brumaire in the year IX, according to the Jacobin calendar, declared that all women wishing to dress as men should present themselves at the *Préfecture de police* to receive authorization. In 1892 and 1909, two decrees allowed women to wear pants providing that they were riding a bike or a horse (Kauder 2006). The veiled Catholic nun has been seen as conspicuously non-republican (Rochefort 2007). During the later part of the nineteenth century, the emerging Third Republic's (1870–1940) leaders not only considered the church as an archaic institution threatening the (self-avowed) modern and progressive France, it was also seen as a threat to women or, rather, republican men's control over women (see Ford 2005; Sowerwine 2009, 42). Whilst men enjoyed the fruits of public life (i.e., politics, cafés, boules, and men's clubs), the household and the church were places for women. The church in particular became a place, in the male imagination that is, where women could speak about their husband's sexual secrets thus revealing their husband's masculine shortcomings and weaknesses, as the historian Jules Michelet's *La Femme* nicely illustrates (see Michelet 2014).

In colonized Algeria, the republican spokespeople articulated the veil was as an ambiguously desired object and as key in the Republic's civilizing mission. The "subjugation of Algeria," as Scott (2007) has put it, was often "depicted by metaphors of disrobing, unveiling, and penetration" (55). One case in point was of the de-veiling of the Algerian women shown in a public demonstration held in Algiers on 16 May 1958. French generals organized the demonstration where the military led a number of Algerian women wearing veils to the generals' wives, representing the French woman. Once the Algerian women reached the French, the latter literarily de-veiled the former. Thousands of Algerian men and a few women, bussed in from nearby villages, attended. At the end of the demonstration, they all sang the *Marseillaise* (the French national anthem) (see Lazreg 1994, 135). Other acts in undermining and destroying the colonial subject's culture and political order were more brutal. The journalist Mouloud Feraoun reported from a village where "French soldiers behaved for three nights as if they were in a bordello ... One woman was forced to see her daughter and her daughter-in-law raped before her eyes" (as cited in El Guindi 2003, 170–171). In another village "one old man was forced to dance naked" while other villagers were ordered to "beat time, applaud and cry out 'Vive la France'" and women "who tried to hide their faces in shame had their shawls ripped from their faces" (171).

These historical accounts suffice to point out the Republic's recurring preoccupation with saving women from the foreign other and help to highlight what scholars like John Gaffney (2010) have argued: namely, the Republic's leadership, historically as well as during the current Fifth Republic's presidencies, has been and remains guided by a mythology cherishing patriarchal, chivalric and masculine conduct (161). During the Veil Affairs a particular type of concern for the other-woman emerged. This had its roots in French state-feminism during the 1980s (Allwood and Wadia 2002). The particularity of the state-feminism that emerged during the Affairs was its merging of paternalistic and patriarchal underpinnings with a racist gaze. As Sylvie Tissot has argued, feminism became a legitimizing moment in racist discourse (Tissot 2008). One significant part in the construction of French state-feminism during the first Affair was the feminist organization *Ni Putes, Ni Soumises* (NPNS). As suggested by Anna Kemp (2009), in this specific case the organization has contributed to the construction of an ideal Marianne of today, transferred onto young Arab-Muslim women in the suburbs. Kemp has brought attention to how Amara, the former president of NPNS and later Secretary of State, created in her 2003 manifesto a typology measuring "different groups of women's divergence from or conformity to an idealized model of 'French' femininity" (2009, 23). This idealized model was used to articulate women's emancipation solely in terms of sexual freedom, measured by women's way of dressing. Clothes such as jeans and beauty accessories like lipstick were associated with the external world and freedom, whereas the veil was seen as a manifestation of the internal world, the world of the household or the suburbs, and where these young women need to conform to a male gaze (Amara 2004, 44). "What emerged from Amara's discourse," Kemp (2009) writes, "is an injunction to assume one's 'femininity', but the essentialized notion of femininity that she describes is imagined above all in terms of sexual desirability" (24). According to Kemp, Amara's emancipatory path allows women only one kind of agency: to be desirable in the eyes of others, in a patriarchal, sexualizing gaze.

The 2003 NPNS campaign *Mariannes d'aujourd'hui: Hommage des femmes des cités á la République* (Mariannes of Today: Homage to the Women in the Republic's Housing Projects) shows the importance attributed to NPNS as a mediator of French femininity. During the campaign, 14 monumental photographs covered the facade of the National Assembly:

> Ten of the 13 women photographed are of North-African, Arab or African ethnic origin, and all of them wear variations on the bonnet phrygien, icon of the French Republic. The first striking feature of the exhibition is that all the women are young (in their twenties or early thirties), attractive and impeccably made-up. Many wear off-the-shoulder dresses in red white and blue and each poses for the camera, one blowing a kiss to the spectator, while another throws back her head and laughs, the overall impression reminding the viewer of an advertising campaign for Printemps [one of Paris' huge luxury shopping malls]. This soft eroticisation of the femmes '*des cités*' [housing projects] is accompanied by short texts in which each woman explains what Marianne—figurehead of the Republic and icon of French womanhood—means to her. (Kemp 2009, 25)

In these statements, Kemp has discerned a two-sided image of Marianne. First of all, she appears as the embodiment of republican values: she is "proud of being French and to be living in the Republic," she "realizes herself through the Republican ideal," and she is "determined to ensure the adherence [*faire respecter*] to republican values" (25). Second, she is, as Kemp puts it, "seen to possess the distinctly 'feminine' virtues of peace, tenderness and maternity, while displaying revulsion for power" (25).

Another example shows how the NPNS was given the role of a French feminist yardstick. Siham Andalouci, representative of *Le Collectif des Musulmans de France* (CMF) was invited to face the TV spotlight and to declare repeatedly that "I am a Muslim, I am wearing a veil, I am a French citizen, and I am a feminist," something that "might be contradictory to some" (France 5 2003a). However, the talk-show host did not seem to listen as Andalouci had to answer to a proper interrogation on what points she agreed upon in the NPNS program.

One of the core problems with this type of feminist discourse is that it has a built-in exclusionary function. As I will argue in this analysis, even the integrated Muslim woman is a legitimate voice only as long as she speaks as a Muslim-other; in the case of Amara, it is the successfully integrated Muslim-other. Another telling example is Chadhortt Djavann. Djavann is a journalist of Iranian descent to whom many hours on TV and many pages in print have been devoted. The place given to Djavann in public debate was as one of the experts and testimonies from within—the role of the successfully integrated Muslim as the voice of the veil's true meaning: "I have been wearing the veil for ten years. It was the veil or death. I know what I'm talking about" (quoted in Deltombe 2007, 351). I do not suggest that it was wrong to listen to these women. On the contrary. However, to make them into spokespeople for all women in the suburbs and the housing projects is highly problematic since it was still her otherness, as a former Muslim, that took precedence and legitimized her participation in public debate. Nacira Guénif-Souilamas (2006) has put it like this: "These women can only hope to be considered French, when they are condemned to exhibit a difference that constitutes their unique space of existence on the market of French identity" (111).

French republican spokespeople are not alone in their focus on women in constructing national identities. Floya Anthias and Nira Yval-Davis (1992) have shown how women play crucial strategic roles in the construction of national identity. Elisa Camiscioli (2009) has documented the articulation of "women as biological reproducers of the members of collectivities; women as reproducers of the boundaries of national groups (because of restrictions on sexual and marital relations); and women as active transmitters and producers of national culture" (5). Yuval-Davis and Anthias also highlight how women turned into symbols for a given nation. In France, "*la patrie* was a figure of woman giving birth to the nation in the French Revolution," and they add that this was "the same Revolution that limited its universal message to the *fraternité*—the brotherhood of men!" (Anthis and Yuval-Davis 1992, 20). One can thus understand the desire to control the other-woman as a way to police the future of the nation, its identity, its boundaries, and its nationals.

Alterity and Communitarianism

Napoleon Bonaparte's invasion of Egypt in 1798 was emblematic in the creation of Muslims as a "recognizable image" (Said 1985). Of course, France and Islam have a much longer history dating back to the eighth century (Telhine 2010; Lorcin and Sanders 2007; Mastnak 2002).[40] Notwithstanding, Napoleon's invasion took place in a post-revolutionary society when the foundations for the modern nation-state and citizenship had been laid out (see Brubaker 1992, 35ff). Of importance here is how the invasion was linked to the creation of a French national ethos in relation to the foreign Orient, thought to be in need of a civilizing mission. Thus, the fruits of the Enlightenment were to be given to the uncivilized others (Coller 2011; Shakman Hurd 2008, 52ff). In a proclamation to the expeditionary army, 22 June 1798, Napoleon is quoted as saying: "You are about to engage in a conquest whose effects on civilization ... are incalculable" (as cited in Micheau 2008, 67). Françoise Micheau concludes

---

40 Historical periods when the French-Islamic relation intensified were the Crusades (medieval period), the Barbary Pirates (early modern period), and during the colonial enterprises (modern period).

that, to Napoleon, civilization meant nothing other than the *Occident*, and the expeditionary mission was thus an occidentalization of Egypt (67). As the French historian Jules Michelet put it in the middle of the nineteenth century: "[France is] a glorious mother who is not ours alone and who must bring every nation to liberty!" (quoted in Brubaker 1992, 2).

Today in republican discourse, as during the colonial period in Algeria, the *Arab-Muslim* has been constructed as a socio-ethnic *enemy*: the *other* of the national *we*. Mathieu Rigouste (2009) has argued that, in the wake of the Algerian war in 1962, immigrants from the former colonies incarnated the notion of the danger represented by the "internal enemy," which is still a common idea amongst the elites of the French nation (6). As I will show in my analysis, and as others like Rigouste before me have pointed out, just as during the colonial period, the Muslim-other was not solely a negative and dangerous other. The Muslim-other and the land from where he or she came were sites for projected desires and dreams. This meant that the other could incorporate multiple and conflicting identities in republican discourse. During the Affairs, this is visible in republican discourse on integration. On the one hand, the Muslim-other was a desired subject and a target for republican integration. An integrated Muslim-other was a token of a successful and benevolent Republic. On the other hand, a failure to integrate the Muslim-other was not so much a result of the Republic's failed politics of integration as the other's unwillingness to integrate. The Muslim-other was articulated into a communitarian and fundamentalist, actively choosing to live a life not only in negation of the Republic but a life whose sole purpose was to politically subvert the Republic. The focus on the Muslim-other as an internal enemy on metropolitan soil has changed, making the French security agencies change focus. In a pre-cold-war period, targeted groups were the Far Left *Action Directe* and separatist organizations like the *Bascian Euskadi Ta Askatasuna* (ETA) and the *Corsican Fronte di Liberazione Naziunale Corsu* (FLNC). Today, the focus is on Islamic and Algerian "terrorism" (Rigouste 2009, 181). Given the feverish articulations during the Veil Affairs of the Muslim as terrorist, it is important not to disregard the actual statistics that exist on terrorism in Europe. According to Europol, the number of "Islamic terrorist attacks" during the analyzed period, in comparison to separatist left-wing, and right-wing terrorist attacks, is low.[41]

---

41 In 2006, a single attack was carried out by "Islamists," 424 by "Separatists," 55 by "Left-Wing" groups, 1 by "Right-Wing," and 17 by "Other/Not Specified" (Europol, 2007, p. 13). In 2010, the number of attacks was in the same order 3, 160, 45, 0, 40, and 1 from "Single-issue," a newly added category (Europol 2011, 36).

Notwithstanding, the presence of the Muslim-other is a disturbing picture for republican white national identity. This development relates to the evolving post-colonial condition, or what Michael Azar (2006) has called the "colonial boomerang effect." The boomerang effect refers to, on the one hand, immigration from the former colonies to the former colonial empire's center, and on the other, it denotes an imagined sociological experience and demographic change brought about by this immigration. The former colonial other, *they*, has become *our* neighbor. In the words of Sadri Khiari (2009): "Anticolonial struggles had been transferred to the very heart of the Hexagon and France was no longer white" (78).

One seminal event in the public visibility of post-colonial immigrants was the 1983 March for Equality and Against Racism (*la Marche pour l'égalité et contre le racism*), also called The Arab Marche (*Marche de beur(s)*). However, if post-colonial immigrants were coming out as a group claiming equal rights and an end to discrimination, their Islamic and Arab identities were used against them. When, for example, large segments of the working class during the 1970s and 1980s went on strike, especially in the automobile industry, the fact that many of these workers were Algerians and of Algerian descent opened up a symbolic potentiality in which the French state apparatus and the media sought an answer to these strikes in these workers' Muslim identity. Claire de Galembert (2008) has explained how Islam became the perceived motor in these conflicts and how Muslims were seen not only as a religious group but also as a tormenting social one, incompatible with French values.

A number of political speeches and state documents have institutionalized the Arab and the Muslim as a socio-ethnic enemy. For example, in 1991, Jacques Chirac, the then Mayor of Paris and a prominent member of the conservative political party *Rassemblement pour la République* (RPR), explained that immigration and immigrants in themselves were not a problem. However, if immigrants caused no problems in themselves, Chirac made it clear that too many immigrants of a certain sort indeed could:

"Our problem is not the immigrants, it is rather the overdose of them. Maybe it's true that there are not more immigrants today than in the post-war period, but it is not the same type of immigrants and that makes a difference. It is clear that having Spanish, Polish, or Portuguese immigrants working here causes fewer problems than having Muslims and Blacks" (quoted in Geisser and Zemouri 2007, 121).

In the 1994 Defense Report *Islam, un danger Potential* (Islam a Potential Danger) from the *Insititut des hautes études des défence nationale* (IHEDN), the conclusion was that Islam constituted a twofold danger, one internal and one external; the enemy from over there was here (see Rigouste 2009, 229). In a governmental report on sects published in 2002, socialist Alain Vivien, who wrote the introduction, proclaimed that a "new totalitarianism," a "new barbarity," and a "fundamentalist violence" were gaining ground (quoted in *Mission Interministérielle de Lutte Contre les Sects* 2002, 5).

A commonly repeated moment in republican anti-Muslim discourse is the supposed natural and cultural-biological propensity of Muslims towards anti-Semitism. As will become clear in this analysis, for many of the leading republican spokespeople, anti-Semitism in France appeared to be something that had been imported by Muslims to France and practiced by young Arabs and Blacks, and where white French anti-Semitism was disregarded either as a historical fluke, like the Dreyfus Affair and the Vichy Regime, or something practiced by the poorer classes. To disregard these issues is of course a grave misreading of history. To be clear, far from being a historical fluke, the Vichy Regime was the culmination of governmental policies that had been stigmatizing Jews for nearly a century. In this regard, the concentration camps that existed on French soil between the Dreyfus Affair and the Vichy Regime should be of some concern. Anti-Semitism in France at the end of the nineteenth century was certainly not the fault of the Muslims. It was a Franco-French racist discourse deeply rooted in French society. Gerard Noiriel (2007) has explained how anti-Semitism, stemming from Catholic, bourgeois, nationalist, and conservative circles, could not have taken hold were it not for the constant hammering in the press of Jews as a "problem" (288ff).[42]

Éric Hazan and Alain Badiou (2011) have argued that historical anti-Semitism and the violence manifested by young Black and Arab French towards Jews have almost nothing in common. Part of the problem is the misinformation that young people have about this matter. Since the Israeli state identifies itself as Jewish, one might understand violence conducted in its name as Jewish (e.g., a *Jewish* state oppressing Palestinians). One can also understand that criticism of the Israeli occupation of Gaza or Israeli state violence can take anti-Semitic forms. To solve problems of this sort we would expect the republican school to play an educational role. However, as Keaton (2006) reminds her readers, a number of French schoolbooks have been criticized for their decontextualized and violence-focused accounts of the Israel-Palestine conflict (201). In November 2003, the EU deputy François Zimeray wrote a letter to

---

42 For a more extensive account of incarceration camps in France during the time of World War II see Grunberg (2000).

President Chirac demanding the withdrawal of textbooks from the publishing house Delagrave because of their anti-Semitic messages. Other publishers, such as Hatier and Hachette, have been criticized for demonizing Arabs and Muslims. In short, these books actually seemed to discourage critical thinking about the conflict and to encourage anti-Muslim racism and anti-Semitic violence (Keaton 2006, 119ff). Moreover, the confusion between Judaism and the state of Israel is not restricted to young people in the segregated suburbs (on this issue see Wieviorka 2007); the state apparatus also seems to confuse the two (see Hazan and Badiou 2011). In 2009–2010, when demonstrations were held to end what was considered to be an illegal occupation of Gaza, a number of activists wearing t-shirts saying "Boycott Israel" were accused of anti-Semitic slander. In 2011, members of the *Movement Boycott Désinvestissement Sanctions* (BDS), who made a non-violent appeal to boycott trade with and investments in Israel, were convicted for "racist provocations and discrimination," as the Minister of Justice Michèle Alliot-Marie described it (see Grenoble 2011; Manac'h 2011). Here, I do not want to banalize the rise of anti-Semitism in France but, rather, to direct attention to how certain historical events and actions are read in a certain manner. One could, for example, understand as counterevidence to the Muslim's imagined anti-Semitic nature the period during the Second World War when the Paris Mosque, an iconic symbol of foreign Islamic influence in France, served as a refuge for Jews (Haski 2011).

Even though studies show that many Muslims are far more occupied with gaining acceptance in France than in pursuing an Islamist agenda (see Roy 2004, 143ff), discussions concerning French-Islamic incompatibility in French public debate continuously focus on Muslim women and articulate Muslims in general as the driving force in a two-sided incompatibility: on the one hand sociability and, on the other, norms and values. In terms of sociability, *they* choose their own segregation through their ways of dressing, attending mosques, and their seclusion in communities. In terms of norms and values, *they* refuse to accept the precepts of French secularism and universal values, especially democracy and equality between the sexes (Bowen 2010, 178ff).

In French political speech, republican spokespeople use the category of *communautarisme* to define this supposed will to create sub-societies within the republican unity. According to Tissot, the word first appeared in a French dictionary in 1997 and derives from the English communitarianism and relates broadly to the term multiculturalism (Tissot 2012; see also Jansen 2013). While I employ the direct English translation (i.e., communitarianism) I want to stress that I approach communitarianism as an element to be articulated in neo-republican discourse on secularism. There are many ways to define communitarianism and many public figures that seek to do so: scholars, politicians, activists, and journalists (Geisser 2003; Trigano 2005). In the neo-republican discourse on secularism, however, communitarianism comes close to one of the definitions given by Pierre-André Taguieff (2005), who states that it is often made to refer to "tribalism," "exclusivism," and "racism" where the defining identity and conduct of one community is used to stigmatize and treat outsiders as enemies. Taguieff concludes that communitarianism in this sense is both absolutely non-inclusive and unconditionally exclusive (84–85). During the Veil Affairs, communitarianism became an emblematic slogan to designate all those who, according to the republican spokespeople, did not fit the picture of republican unity (Tissot 2012). The specificity of the articulation of communitarianism during the Veil Affairs was that it came to signify an active withdrawal from society through the creation of specific laws for the imagined Islamic community located in the metropolitan suburbs. Besides being a religious affair, it also became racialized: the communitarian was a Muslim and an Arab.

In this analysis, I will highlight in particular three functions of this discourse of majorities versus minorities. The first one is how it came to legitimize stigmatization and exclusion of articulated communitarian minorities. To paraphrase Tissot, as the veil was understood as an essentially communitarian sign it could not be allowed, since it would infect French society. A veiled Muslim woman could thus pose a danger by her very proximity to the non-veiled French woman; she was the anti-republican spirit incarnate. In other words, it was in the name of anti-communitarianism (i.e., democracy, liberty, feminism) that certain citizens were refused access to the public space, thus sending these citizens back to their imagined community (Tissot 2008).

Second, in the prevailing logic, communitarians were not only by their very nature denied full access to the public space in the name of democracy, liberty, and feminism, they were also deprived of any legitimate political voice. There will be many examples of this throughout this book but one case in point is the affair between the then Minister of the Interior, Nicolas Sarkozy, and the rap group Sniper. The group was fervently critical of what it saw as inequalities in French society (France is a "bitch" and consists of "fascists"). It also took a clear stance against the state of Israel's politics in Palestine. Sarkozy sought to bring the group to court and sue them for anti-Semitism and racism (Gentleman 2003; see also Pecqueux 2003). Ultra-nationalist groups and parties like the *Bloc identitaire* have, for quite some time, been calling Sniper anti-white and been complaining that they spread anti-white racism. This particular understanding of the group's lyrics was controversial but it has slowly gained acceptance among certain republican spokespeople (Mouloud 2003).

Third, if supposed communitarians are brought to court for anti-white and anti-Republican racism, this is not only because of the republican spokespeople's wills to exercise sovereign power to mute critical voices, as I will argue, but is also because they identify themselves with a particular conception of the Republic that they see threatened: a French-white Republic. In Khiari's (2009) words: "The immigrant is never herself or himself. To the left the immigrant is a victim, a scapegoat, and the proof that the right is not good. For the right, the immigrant is a 'communalist,' an Islamist, an 'anti-white racist,' and what have you!" (13).

The tacit articulation of the Republic's legitimate political subjects as white is a way for the established sovereign power to legitimate itself and to endure. One discursive technique employed in sustaining this power is how white political subjects distance themselves, as Alfred J. Lopez (2005) puts it, temporally, representationally, and politically, from "both neo-Nazi and other white supremacist groups of the present moment and colonial histories and other past forms of 'extreme' whiteness. This allows whiteness to continue to work its hegemonic power as the invisible norm" (22–23). Richard Drier states clearly: "The claim to power is the claim to speak for the commonality of humanity. Raced people can't do that—they can only speak for their race" (quoted in Hawley 2005, 54). The discourse of the communitarian other epitomizes the illiberal strand in republican discourse on secularism. The prevailing discursive logic exemplified here is one where the other can be disqualified from being French simply for criticizing French politics and republican spokespeople. As Sarkozy appears to personally identify with the Republic, criticizing the Republic is to criticize and even discriminate against him.

Alternatives to the publicly distributed and recurring stereotypes of the Arab-Muslim exist in abundance. As shown in this analysis, vivid estimations of the number of Muslims living in France play an important role in the construction of Muslims as a foreign and fundamentalist mass. Even if the inflated estimates of the number of Muslims living in France (5 to 6 million) were accepted, the numbers in terms of practicing Muslims are far less impressive. Only 8 to 15 percent regularly attend religious services, less than 5 percent attend Friday prayers, and 70 percent support secularism. These are very similar statistics to that of French Catholics (Giry, 2006, 4). Resistance to the stereotypes is just as common and many anti-racist groups and organizations, intellectuals, activists, and average citizens work hard to counteract anti-Muslim racism and discrimination. Among the many organizations in France are the *Collectif contre l'islamophobie en France* (CCIF), *Islam et laïcité*, and the *Parti des indigènes de la République* (PIR). One interesting but lesser-known example is the gay-porn production company *Citébeur*. This company plays with the local racial and ethnic naming of Arabs in France as *beurs* (arabs). As pointed out by Maxime Cervulle and Nick Rees-Roberts (2008), while, as a porn-producing company, *Citébeur* entertains white middle-class voyeurism of the exotic other, it also seeks to provide for a "critical space for the formation of gay *beur/racaille* identities with a degree of independence from institutional gay culture" (206).[43] In other words, it seeks to break with the colonialist gaze still alive in contemporary porn by "balancing hard-core sex with knowing social critique" (206).

Nation, Assimilation

Considering French national identity, Ian Coller (2011) notes that from "Molière to the Revolution, from Napoleon to Jean Moulin, 'Frenchness' has been determined above all by an identification with the historical past, a powerful sense of the continuity of French identity over time" (viii). Specific conceptions about France and the Republic, as Coller highlights, have simultaneously "inspired many of those who resisted the Nazi occupation after 1940, but also worked to mask the realities of collaboration and anti-Semitism during the Vichy years. In the 1950s it served to legitimate the destructive wars to retain colonial control in Asia and North Africa, and after decolonization and independence it helped erase the memory of those violent struggles" (viii).

One question that strikes many observers of French politics is how the imaginary universal reach of the French Revolution can be maintained when the *immigrant* was systemically excluded from its very beginning (Scott 2005; Wahnich 1997). The Republic has a long history of selective attributions of citizenship, rights, and freedoms during its colonial and assimilationist enterprises (Noiriel 2007). In the proclamation of universal rights during the French Revolution, immigrants were excluded. Along with immigrants, women were also denied the rights and freedoms associated with citizenship. According to Camiscioli (2009), this draws "our attention to two perturbing categories generated by the hybrid logic of French Republicanism: the female citizen who lacked voting rights, and the colonial subject who possessed French nationality without access to citizenship status" (10). Of special concern for this analysis is the Republic's long tradition of Muslim governance. As shown by Vincent Geisser and Aziz Zemouri, among others, the application of the *Code de l'indigénat* (The Indigenous Code) in 1887 in colonized Algeria is one

---

43   Italics added.

case in point (Geisser and Zemouri 2007, 8). With it, the colonial power created a double citizenship, dividing the Algerian population into fully-fledged French citizens and subjugated indigenous Muslims and Jews (the status of Jews changed in 1870, placing them above the Muslims but below the French). Franck Frégosi (2008) reminds us that French colonial legislation stigmatized Muslims as fifth columnists by rendering Islam as a sort of a pathological socio-religious reality (196).

In post-war France before 1980, the Republic passed no laws on integration, although it practiced a repressive politics of immigration. According to Alec Hargreaves (2007), republican legislators passed no integration laws because of the Republic's need for foreign labor (165). At the end of the 1970s and the beginning of the 1980s things changed and, despite the fact that post-colonial immigrants were valued for their work in rebuilding the nation, their ethnic, cultural, and religious background became used as explanatory elements for the Republic's slow economic growth during the period. In relation to a growing concern about Muslims as intrusive foreign others, the answer from the French Republican political elite was either integration/assimilation or expulsion.

In terms of expulsions, any reader of the contemporary French press has become acquainted with reports of the police chasing down illegal immigrants: the *sans-papiers*. This falls under the politics of *aide au retour* (Assisted Return) and *coups de poings* (Lightening Raid) instituted during the 1970s under the control of Minister of the Interior Christian Bonnet (RI) and Minister of Justice Alain Peyrefitte (UDR-RPR). One can read this as a continuation of Valery Giscard d'Estaing's suspension of immigration in 1974, due partly to a perceived overflow of foreign workers. In 1977, the Raymond Barre government set the goal of annual deportations to 35,000 (Masquet 2006, 8). In 1979, the minister of Manual Labour and Immigration, Lionel Stoléru, became a symbolic name in the 1979 objective to repatriate 100,000 immigrants annually. Stoléru was also a driving force in the adoption of the Bonnet Law restricting the opportunities of entering and staying in France.

In the end, the parliament abandoned the proposals for massive deportations. With the symbolic regularization of 130,000 foreigners in 1981, the newly elected Mitterand Government put a hold on such restrictive and repressive politics of immigration (Masquet 2006, 13). The 1980s were not, however, a complete rupture with the previous decade. For example, long-term minister Michel Rocard announced tougher controls against illegal immigrants, and Prime Minister (PM) Laurent Fabius commented upon the success of the emerging Far-Right party *Front National* (FN) by stating that their leader, Jean-Marie Le Pen, was "asking the right questions but giving the wrong answers" (quoted in Hargreaves 2007, 131). President Mitterand proclaimed that "I need to protect French jobs ... it is the reality" (quoted in Masquet 2006, 14). This was a period when a number of institutions seeking to regulate immigration as a problem were born: the *Office français de protection des réfugiés et apatrides* (OFPRA), *Haut conseil d'intégration* (HCI), and *Conseil de réflextion sur l'islam* (CRI) (see Masquet 2006, 19). However, most important were the Pasqua Laws in 1986 and 1993 and a Politics of Zero Immigration, all attributed to Minister of the Interior Charles Pasqua. They further accentuated a "politics of integration, expulsion, and pacification," as Rigouste put it (2009, 238). In 1994 Pasqua put in place an apparatus for controlling national identity that was without precedence: 27,000 checks in two weeks (Rigouste 2009, 232). The police carried out the controls in the poor suburban metropolitan areas by targeting suspected enemies against the state, and the police are still practicing this today. The reason? "If you don't go fishing you don't catch any fish" (Pasqua quoted in Rigouste 2009, 232).

During Nicolas Sarkozy's time as Minister of the Interior (2002–2004, 2005–2007) and President (2007–2012) new laws were passed. The most significant were the Sarkozy Law of 26 November 2003, the *Code de l'entrée et du séjour des étrangers et du droit d'asile* (CESEDA) of 24 November 2004, and the Hortefeux Law of 20 November 2007. New institutions and measurements for integration were also created: the *Agence nationale de l'accueil des étrangers et des migrations* (ANAEM), the *Office de l'immigration nationale* (OMI), the *Soutien, Solidarité et Actions en Faveur des Emigrants* (SSAE), and the *Contrat d'acceuil d'intégration* (CAI). These developments were attempts at managing integration through an expanded surveillance and disciplinary apparatus. Seminal points are: the elaborations of biometric visas and DNA testing to assure family lineage; the control of the immigrant's compatibility with French values; the penalization for aiding an illegal immigrant (L.662-1 in the CESEDA stipulates a punishment of 30,000 euros and up to five years in prison); the extralegal waiting zones and deportation systems at national airports and harbors (Paris-Roissy, Paris-Orly, Lyon, Marseille, Calais to name a few) (De Loisy 2005, 188–191); and the rising expulsion objectives (from 10,000 in 2002 to 30,000 in 2011) (AFP 2010; Bellan 2011; *Secrétariat général du comité interministériel de contrôle de l'immigration* 2008). The national objective was to double the number of expulsions, as Sarkozy (2003b) explained. In a dubious contest, newly appointed Ministers of the Interior even appear to be seeking to expel more foreigners than their predecessors (Carrera 2009; Vincent 2012).

During Sarkozy's time as head of state, his administration institutionalized national identity and immigration in the Ministry of Immigration, Integration,

National Identity, and Solidarity Development (2007–2010).⁴⁴ According to Sergio Carrera (2009), the results of these latest changes in integration politics have "led to the emergence of a neo-republican integrationist doctrine" where integration has become a "mandatory condition for TCNs [third country nationals] to have access to rights and protection linked with the policy dimensions of admission, security of residence and family unification" (333). As will become clear, this neo-republican integrationist doctrine merged with neo-republican discourse on secularism, creating and legitimizing extraordinary treatment not only of third-country nationals but also of French citizens not deemed worthy of being French. This became clear during the deliberations of the Law of 2004 where the school was constructed as the instrument of molding a national sentiment and the place where desire and secular morality were formed and taught—the desire to belong to the Republic and the morality to do so in the correct manner. One underlying irony in these statements, however, as Scott (2007) has pointed out, was that faith in the republican school system in fact seemed quite weak, since the veiled students were ordered to take off their veils before entering school (88). Similarly, the confidence in the republican model of integration was low since it demanded proof of integration before entering France. Moreover, if the public school was the most sacred space of the Republic, exclusion from school was a symbolic expulsion from the Republic itself. Manifested here is an underlying exclusionary logic in the republican discourse on integration. As Borghée has stated, the problem with talking about integration in relation to the veil is that these women are in fact French, have been educated in republican schools, and have names like Borghée (2012, 204).

---

44   The Ministry was taken over by the Ministry of Integration in 2010. The plan went under the name Espoir Banlieues and Fadela Amara announced it on 22 January 2008. It was presented as a Marshall Plan for the citizens in the suburbs but in the end was absorbed by the credo *travailler plus pour gagner plus*. See, further, Equy (2008) and La Libération (2008).

PART II

The First Islamic Veil Affair

CHAPTER 3

Ideological Battle Flags

In this chapter, I will analyze how the Muslim-other was articulated in republican discourse on secularism during the deliberations for the Law of 2004 prohibiting the Islamic veil in schools. As previously discussed (Chapter Two), the Muslim-other was given a specific symbolic place in the republican discourse on secularism, but it also became a discourse in its own right. The analysis here focuses on the different discursive techniques in play when producing otherness and how these techniques of othering worked to produce a subject to govern. Here I show how the Muslim-other was construed as a postpolitical enemy—as a temporal, geographical, religious, national, and (partly) civilizational other. I argue that this enemy created a sense of exceptionality and urgency, justifying a directed state of exception aimed at neutralizing this imagined enemy. This is a first step in understanding how republican discourse on secularism depended on the discourse of the other to fulfill itself—to achieve an imagined closure.

I structure the chapter through four interrelated questions: What was the rationale for the reasoning underlying the deliberations for the Law of 2004? In what ways were Islamic female students and their veils understood to undermine the foundation of the French Republic? What kind of identity was ascribed to them? What kind of political techniques did their identities legitimize?

A New and Unwanted Situation

The First Islamic Veil Affair of 2003–2004 was the climax of a nearly fifteen-year-long preoccupation with secularism and Islam by the political mainstream. This preoccupation and the debate itself, however, was not anything that those elected had wished for, at least so the argument went. According to them, they were facing a new and challenging situation that forced them into a legislative debate. In fact, they described the debate as an inconvenient and involuntary debate in a twofold sense: It was thought of as a result of the Republic's failed politics of integration caused by previous governments, and as something imposed on the Republic by external and foreign forces, by Islamic fundamentalists and communitarians.

Post-Christian Islamic Challenges

Regarding the perceived novelty of the challenges posed by the veil, President Chirac (2003b) explained that young women wearing the veil broke a consensus based on "reasonable usages" of religious symbols that were respected "spontaneously." The Debré Commission subsequently proposed that in this "new context" the veil evoked a necessity to re-evaluate the "established balance between freedom of conscience and secularism" (Debré 2003b, 11).[1] The Stasi Commission (2003) drew a similar conclusion, suggesting that "the old foe of secularism, the Catholic Church, no longer posed a threat and that secularism now was an integral and central part of the republican pact" (17).[2] These statements lead to the conclusion that before the veil entered the picture there was a tacit balance between public expressions of religion and secularism, or between republican positive and negative religious freedom. According to these spokespeople, the veil now challenged this balance. But it was not only the balance that was challenged; since secularism was a central part of the republican pact, challenging the balance struck between religion and secularism was the equivalent to challenging republican unity. Here, it is important to note that a number of statements suggested that the existing legal framework from 1905 would normally have been sufficient to counter non-reasonable usages of religious symbols but that those who wore the veil seemed to have lacked a spontaneous ability to respect this reasonable equilibrium, which supposedly, others did. The Valade Commission (2004) was clear in its analysis. A "new challenge" had emerged which had to do with "communitarianism and radical Islamism with political ambitions" (10).[3]

In articulating this novelty, Islam was presented not only as a newcomer but also as the second biggest religion in France. This is significant since it captures the imagined activity of Islam in terms of its perceived rapid growth resulting in clashing with the legal tradition and customs of the Republic. In the words of MP Pierre Lellouche (UMP), "the Veil Affair was an opportunity for the French people to realize that Islam had become the second biggest religion

---

1 "la question du port de signes religieux se pose aujourd'hui dans un contexte nouveau qui remet en cause l'équilibre trouvé entre liberté de conscience et principe de laïcité."
2 "Par rapport au contexte de 1905, la société française a changé: l'emprise de l'Eglise catholique n'est plus perçue comme une menace. La laïcité se retrouve au cœur du pacte républicain en des termes nouveaux."
3 "[U]n défi nouveau, celui du repli communautaire, attisé notamment par l'émergence récente d'un islamisme radical à finalité politique."

in France in only one generation" (AN 2004d, 1413).[4] "Islam being the second biggest religion in France," was, according to MP Chantal Brunel (UMP), a disturbing fact (AN 2004e, 1436).

According to MP Jèrôme Rivière (UMP), it was important to be cautious regarding the development of Islam in France and to recognize that the Islamists who were "seducing young people" were not as numerous as "they" claimed (AN 2004e, 1452). The Debré Commission (2003a) had concluded that no more than 12 percent of France's Muslims were practicing their religion (67).

Thus, during these deliberations, republican spokespeople argued that the veil signified something broader than merely being a religious symbol. They saw women wearing veils as not being fully integrated into French society since the veil was seen as a refusal to integrate and as a rejection of French secularism. The idea of the new situation added fuel to the supposed need to integrate the other (i.e., Muslim) into French society as Islam was becoming a rapidly growing religion on a collision course with the Republic, while its growth was being largely exaggerated by the Islamists.

A Question of Integration?

During the deliberations in parliament and the preparatory work for the Law of 2004, it became clear quite early on that integration was an important aspect of the matter. Indeed, to the president, the commissions, some ministers, and a large number of the MPS, the veil indirectly signified a double aspect of integration: its failure and the need for it. In this respect, the Debré Commission (2003b) drew the conclusion that the veil asked a new question regarding freedom of conscience and practice. In 1905, being a Franco-white question, it was a matter of navigating these freedoms in relation to anticlerical tendencies in society. Today, however, the veil added *identity* to the calculation since it was a sign of an external identity "that challenged the republican model of integration" (11).[5] The Commission, moreover, stated that the practice of wearing the veil and the emergence of Islamism in France "was

---

4 "L'affaire du voile a été l'occasion pour une majorité de Français de prendre conscience que l'islam était devenu, en une génération à peine, la deuxième religion du pays."

5 "[E]n 1905, le juge devait assurer la garantie de la liberté de conscience et de sa libre expression face à des comportements anti-cléricaux, il est aujourd'hui confronté à des comportements identitaires de types divers qui remettent en cause le modèle républicain d'intégration."

fueled by economic and social frustrations and unacceptable discrimination" (2003b, 71).[6]

The Stasi Commission (2003) reasoned in a similar manner: "France is not alone in experiencing this difficult conjunction of two contemporary phenomena: the breakdown of social integration and the transformation of the religious and spiritual landscape" (35).[7] On the one hand, this led to a loss of faith in the Republic: "[Failed integration] can result in a situation where the victims of this failed model start to lose faith in the republican model and its values" (49).[8] On the other hand, it made it possible for extremist groups to push young citizens into rejecting the Republic: "Yes, extremist groups are currently operating in our country with the aim of testing the resistance against the Republic and to push the youth to reject France and its values" (7).[9]

The commissions thus saw a failed politics of integration and a changing religious landscape as the structural reasons for young women choosing to wear the veil. The President and the Parliament followed the same logic: failed integration led to a loss of faith in the Republic. President Chirac (2003b) stated that "a failed integration and the aggravation of inequalities turned equality into a lie that threatens republican unity."[10] Chirac also pondered how the Republic could ask certain of its inhabitants to recognize themselves in a nation and its values when they live in secluded and inhuman ghettos. MP Christian Vannest (UMP) supported Chirac in saying that discrimination created a humiliated identity easily tempted by an extremist communitarianism (AN 2004d, 14).[11]

Another take on the matter was demonstrated by MP Jacques Myard (UMP), who stated that "the challenge to secularism had less to do with socioeconomic frustrations than religious extremism; it was a matter of a subversive political vision, a Weltanschauung, proclaimed by active fundamentalists

---

6   "La pratique identitaire de la religion musulmane est ainsi le fruit de frustrations sociales et économiques et … de discriminations inacceptables."
7   "La France n'est pas seule à connaître cette conjonction difficile entre deux phénomènes simultanés: la panne de l'intégration sociale et la mutation du paysage religieux ou spiritual."
8   "peut conduire ceux qui en sont victimes à désespérer du modèle républicain et des valeurs qui lui sont liées."
9   "[O]ui, des groupes extrémistes sont à l'œuvre dans notre pays pour tester la résistance de la République et pour pousser certains jeunes à rejeter la France et ses valeurs."
10 "[L]a persistance voire l'aggravation des inégalités, ce fossé qui se creuse entre les quartiers difficiles et le reste du pays, font mentir le principe d'égalité des chances et menacent de déchirer notre pacte républicain."
11 "Une identité humiliée risque d'être une identité révoltée, sensible, comme on l'a vu récemment, aux appels extrémistes et sans doute tentée par le repli communautaire."

who were well integrated and had even achieved a high level of education" (AN 2004e, 1458).[12]

Manipulation

Those who held a failed politics of integration responsible for the emergence of the veil mainly described it as the result of the fundamentalists' successful manipulation of the subsequent debate due to certain republican spokesperson's gullible respect for the other, as the Minister of Education Luc Ferry (UMP) (2003) put it. According to the Debré Commission (2003a), "fundamentalist networks supported the students and used the media to create sympathy and solidarity for their cause as well as a sense of victimization in the immigrant young" (57).[13] MP Éric Raoult (UMP) saw the veils of the Lévy sisters (see Chapter Two) in this light, arguing that they were intentionally provoking a rupture of French society and were testing the Republic whilst the majority of Muslim female students had adapted to the Republic and its values (AN 2004c, 1379). MP Jean-Christophe Cambadélis (SOC) also believed "that a new offensive had been launched" against the Republic. The sisters were the sign of an attack with the aim of challenging the Republic in a manner that went well beyond the question of religious freedom—it was "a question of whether to adapt the Republic to Sharia Law" (AN 2004d, 1403).[14]

• • •

Even though there was no real consensus regarding the Republic's role in the emergence of the veil in France in relation to the supposed Islamists' and fundamentalists' aims and desires, connecting the question of integration to the contextual understanding of the veil as a novelty framed the Veil Affair as foreign and essentially non-French. In this logic, it was definitely *not* un-French to negotiate the boundaries of positive and negative religious freedom, but to do it from a position outside French white hegemony *was*. I will discuss this later on.

---

12 "Le radicalisme religieux ne trouve pas sa source dans les frustrations sociologiques et économiques, mais va bien au-delà car il met en cause une conception de la foi, une vision politique du monde, une Weltanschauung dont l'objectif est subversive."

13 "Les réseaux intégristes qui soutiennent très souvent les élèves utilisent les médias pour donner le maximum de retentissement à leur action et susciter un sentiment de solidarité et de victimisation chez les jeunes d'origine immigrée."

14 "[U]ne nouvelle offensive a été engagée pour tester les résistances de la République ... la foi de quelques adolescentes, mais bien le désir que la République s'adapte à l'islam."

The articulated manipulation of the debate by Islamic fundamentalists resulted in a rather twisted view of integration. While republican spokespeople acknowledged structural discrimination and socio-economic gaps, the problem with these social realities was the fundamentalists' appropriation of them. Whether or not the veil was a manifestation of a real fundamentalist desire to overthrow the Republic or a demonstration of discontent with the Republic, it was framed as a problem of *mere existence*. If one were to pursue this logic to its end, the conclusion would be that, in a perfect Republic, the veil or any visible manifestations of Islam would not exist. Furthermore, as pointed out by Rigouste (2005), when republican spokespeople claimed that integration was responsible for the problems associated with the veil, they suggested that the young women wearing the veil were not French, that they were still subjects up for integration. They were in other words articulated as subjects being geographically French but culturally, religiously, and nationally foreign. On the growing number of Muslims, often stated to be around four to five million, the Debré Commission had reached the conclusion that only 12 percent were practicing their religion and that it was the Islamists that sought to exaggerate their numbers. Still, the republican spokespeople continuously talked about four to five million Muslims. This could be understood as an attempt to delegitimize any success or popular support for the veil while maintaining that the veil was articulated as a symbol of a threat of a growing mass of intruders.

Islamic Communitarianism

How is it that republican spokespeople believed that Islamic fundamentalists were pushing young women into direct confrontation with the French Republic? What did they think these fundamentalists had accomplished, and why? In what way did they perceive Islamic fundamentalists as a threat to the Republic? Moreover, who did they argue the Islamic fundamentalists were in the first place? The main argument or narrative here was that what the world was facing was akin to Samuel Huntington's famous clash of civilization thesis (1996), where Islamists or bad Muslims were overtaking France by creating expanding religious sub-communities with the aim of overthrowing the existing legal order (see Mamdani 2004). They were thought of as a prolongation of a foreign, ancient, and inherently immoral Orient. The sort of Islam they promoted was a perverted one, leading to anti-Semitism, racism, and violence; it was an Islam creating a sense of a state of emergency calling for exceptional political measures from the Republic.

A Glocalized World

According to President Chirac (2003b), the beginning of the twenty-first century was a time of change. The old ideologies of the twentieth century were fading away and human interaction was both increasing and disintegrating. Chirac stated that globalization worries and destabilizes individuals, "sometimes it even makes them retreat from society" and to search for "a new common ground in fanaticism, as seen around the world."[15]

Chirac believed that the rise in fanaticism around the world affected France as well. The Stasi Commission (2003), in a similar vein, explained that a number of contemporary global events, especially the conflicts in the Middle East, directly affected French society in a negative sense since it could lead to intra-communitarian clashes (7). The Debré Commission (2003a) claimed that the 2001 Intifada, the Gulf War, 9/11, and the War in Iraq all had a direct correlation with incidents of a communitarian nature in schools "leading to a political-religious identity clash" (41).[16] One can argue that to have politically interested students taking part in world politics is a positive. However, to the Commission, these specific events were problematic; both extremists and students were mixing religion and politics, or "the temporal and spiritual powers," which was "in direct opposition to French secularism" (14).[17]

The articulated geo-political context described here suggested that global conflicts were being played out in the midst of the Republic, resulting in a breakdown of the republican secular boundaries between religion and politics.

Particular Versus National Law

A significant moment in the construction of Islamic communitarianism was the idea that globalization and the rise of fundamentalism could entrap individuals in enclosed communities and even trap the "the souls" of individuals,

---

15   "Bien que porteuse de chances nouvelles, la mondialisation inquiète, déstabilise les individus, les pousse parfois au repli ... Au moment où s'affaissent les grandes idéologies, l'obscurantisme et le fanatisme gagnent du terrain dans le monde."

16   "La transposition des conflits internationaux à l'école ... tend pourtant à s'étendre et l'espace scolaire est devenu le lieu d'un affrontement identitaire politico-religieux."

17   [À] l'exact opposé de l'ambition laïque de distinction des pouvoirs temporel et spirituel, a conduit au développement d'un fanatisme dont les attentats du 11 septembre 2001 contre les tours jumelles du World Trade Center de New York sont, en quelque sorte, le tragique aboutissement.

as the Valade Commission (2004) put it (23). According to President Chirac (2003b), this was leading to intolerance and egoism. The fading away of the "grand ideologies" was thought to have opened up for the ominous development of fundamentalist, violent, and political Islam and their embodiment in a communitarian withdrawal. To Chirac, communitarianism was an active "refusal of the Republic"; it threatened the stability of French society as well as common law by imposing its particular religious and ethnic identity on national identity: "The danger resides in the liberation of centrifugal forces, of the exaltation of the particularities that separate us ... to impose particular rules on common law."[18] To exemplify the risks with communitarianism, Chirac turned his eyes to Anglo-Saxon multiculturalism, where inequality reigned: "Look at what is happening elsewhere. Societies structured around communities are more often the victims of unacceptable inequalities."[19]

The Stasi Commission (2003) appears to have agreed with the President by suggesting that "a drift towards a communitarian sentiment in a community would lead to a fragmentation of contemporary society" (18).[20] The Debré Commission (2003a) saw the dangers of Islamic communitarianism in its aim to exercise a moral and political power over the individual (67). In a similar fashion, MP René Couanau (UMP) sought to remind his fellow MPS that the goal of Islamic communitarianism was to impose an Islamic legal and moral code incompatible with the Republic: "Dear colleagues, these identity-based claims also comprise an adherence, conscious or not, to social norms, to a conception of the relations between citizens, and the relations between religions and the state that are not those of the French Republic" (AN 2004d, 1407).[21]

To some, like MP Yves Bur (UMP), Islam was not in itself a problem but that fundamentalists wanted to test the Republic and impose their laws was (AN 2004b, 1312). To give in to the communitarians' demands was, according to MP Jean-Claude Guibal (UMP), to let theocracy take a hold on the Republic

---

18 "Le danger, c'est la libération de forces centrifuges, l'exaltation des particularismes qui séparent. Le danger, c'est de vouloir faire primer les règles particulières sur la loi commune."
19 "Regardons ce qui se passe ailleurs. Les sociétés structurées autour de communautés sont bien souvent la proie d'inégalités inacceptables."
20 "La dérive du sentiment communautaire vers un communautarisme figé menace de fragmentation nos sociétés contemporaines."
21 "[C]ette revendication identitaire ... comporte aussi une adhésion, consciente ou non, à un code juridique, à des normes sociales, à une conception des rapports entre le citoyen, les religions et l'Etat qui ne sont pas, mes chers collègues, ceux de la République française."

(AN 2004e, 1432). MP Bernard Carayon (UMP) stressed that to tolerate the veil today was to open a door for "excision, polygamy, or stoning" (AN 2004d, 1410).

These statements suggest that, on the one hand, communitarianism was dangerous as it preyed on the lost souls of the Republic and used them to create secluded Islamic communities; on the other hand, it was dangerous because it sought to impose particular law over national law, Sharia law over Republican law.

Discrimination and Violence

Whilst none of the analyzed documents and speeches denied that racism exists in France, the degree and target of it was not clear. To the Debré Commission (2003a), racism was indeed a problem, but it was a direct result of the transposition of global events to France and its schools. Racist violence in schools was thus seen as a form of communitarianism, as a fundamentalist act committed by the Muslim-other (68). Communitarian-based racism and violence were gaining ground in schools and there were two sorts in particular that preoccupied the republican electives. The first was anti-Semitic violence. The Stasi Commission (2003) stated that disrespect towards or even threats against secularism were often related to anti-Semitic acts (48). Images from the Israel-Palestine conflict created the supposed powder keg for such actions. According to the Commission, to publicly wear Jewish symbols like the Kippah could be dangerous. Quoting the testimony from one student, the Commission concluded that one could not wear the Kippah without running the risk of being "lynched" (Stasi 2003, 48). According to the Valade Commission (2004), the increase in veils worn in France coincided with the growth in "racist and antisemitic violence" (20; see also Debré 2003a, 71).

The reality described was a dark one. In relation to numbers, the Debré Commission (2003a), relying on Yves Bertrand, the central director of the *Direction Centrale des Renseignements Généraux* (DCRG), reported a net progression of anti-Semitic acts committed in schools since January 2002. In 2002, seventy-seven anti-Semitic acts had been registered compared to twenty-nine in 2001, and forty-two acts of the same nature had been reported for the first semester in 2003 (42). The Valade Commission (2004) reported an increase in anti-Semitic acts (20). The Stasi Commission (2003) also reported an increase in anti-Semitic acts, declaring that for the first time (in 2002) anti-Semitism was the major cause of recorded racist acts and threats in France (48).

The other type of racist violence that was brought up was directed against the white French majority. MP André Gerin (CR), while stating that communitarianism and fundamentalism was a political project that threatened the Republic, suggested that if any racism was to be taken seriously, it was an "antirepublican spirit" that had normalized "anti-French racism" (AN 2004b). He argued that this manifested itself in hostilities towards the representatives of the Republic (firemen, police officers, and the elected) and in disrespect towards the symbols of the Republic, like whistles during the singing of the *Marseillaise*. Gerin stated that this was anti-French racism created by "pseudo-religious groups and criminals" (AN 2004b, 1318).[22]

What did anti-Semitism and anti-French racism have in common? They were both driven by the Muslim- or Arab-other and had nothing to do with state power, at least so it seemed. One government report did nonetheless acknowledge that white French citizens could commit anti-Semitic acts. The Rufin Report, published in October 2004 by the Ministry of Interior, presented a detailed analysis of France's growing problem with anti-Semitism. As suggested by Joëlle Marelli (2006), if you were Arab or Muslim, your anti-Semitism manifested itself through Islamism, and if you were French and white, through neo-Nazism (71). The future of Europe once again depended on the containment of anti-Semitism and anti-Semites, in this case meaning the control of youth with an immigrant background living in poverty in the suburbs:

> The culture of poverty makes out a considerably favorable place for violence: the contemporary life on the margins of society (insecurity, torn family relations, alcohol, drugs) as well as criminality that dwells in this anomy. The identity-malaise that the culture of poverty brings with it renders its populations sensitive to extremist political representations that offer them a rereading of their cultural heritage through a radical, megalomaniac, and violent frame. Thus, according to their origin, radical Islamism—in its different forms—as neo-Nazi ideologies might prosper in this context. Antisemitic impulsions unfortunately being their common point.[23] (Rufin 2004, 16–17)

---

22 "Ce racisme anti-français est orienté, manipulé, cultivé par ces 'pseudo-religieux', qui utilisent la délinquance et les traffics."

23 "La culture de la pauvreté fait une place considérable à la violence: celle, quotidienne, de la vie sur les marges de la société (précarité, déchirements familiaux, alcool, drogue) et celle de la criminalité qui se loge dans cette anomie. Le malaise identitaire qu'installe la culture de la pauvreté rend ces populations sensibles aux représentations politiques extrémistes, qui leur proposent une relecture de leur héritage culturel sur un mode

Here, anti-Semitism is presented as an "impulse" and a "drive" culturally attached to origin—to poor and/or immigrant citizens deemed incapable of distinguishing good from bad, a particularly malevolent racism being their mode of expression. According to the Rufin Report, one type of anti-Semitism was of the worst sort: "imported anti-Semitism, which came from the countries where anti-Semitism is culturally banalized" (i.e., Islamic countries) (2004, 21).[24] Based on the writings of the respected researcher and specialist on Islam, Gilles Kepel, the report talked about a "Battle of Europe": "Either the youth with an immigrant background choose republican values and 'participate fully in citizen-life'... or they join different radical movements that preach war against the West and its values" (Rufin 2004, 24).[25]

Other government reports, however, problematize the rise of anti-Semitism in France as a result of the Muslim-other's culture. According to studies conducted during the 1990s by the *Commission nationale consultative des droits de l'homme* (CNCDH), the group most targeted by racist slander and violence was of North-African descent.[26] In 2000, the CNCDH concluded that 69 percent of the population considered themselves to be racist (in Keaton 2006, 50). In 2003, the CNCDH (2003a) reported a massive increase in racial threats and violence against people identified as "Arab-Muslims," "immigrants," "blacks," and "Jews" (85ff). Although the report described these threats as emanating from multiple sectors of society, it identified the main aggressors as members of the extreme right and ultra-nationalist groups. The Commission concluded that racist acts were committed on a daily basis and that the main targets were "Arabs." Through opinion polls, the Commission concluded that two common perceptions among the French were that "there are too many blacks in France" and that "Jews have too much power."

---

radical, mégalomane et violent. Ainsi selon leur origine et le hasard des rencontres, l'islamisme radical—dans ses différentes formes—comme les idéologies néonazies, peuvent prospérer sur ce terrain. Les pulsions antisémites sont hélas leur point commun."

24 "[U]n antisémitisme d'importation, notamment chez des jeunes issus de familles originaires de pays où l'antisémitisme est culturellement banalisé."

25 "[Soit les jeunes issus de l'immigration font le choix des valeurs républicaines et] participent pleinement à la vie citoyenne, à travers les instruments éducatifs et culturels, qui favorisent l'ascension sociale et accompagnent l'émergence de nouvelles élites."

26 During 1980–1993, North-African descendants represented less than 40 percent of the foreign population but accounted for 78 percent of all those injured and 92 percent of those killed in attacks classified as racist (CNCDH 1994, 23).

Over T/here

As I have shown so far, republican spokespeople argued that Islamism and communitarianism were on the verge of taking root at the heart of French society. The geographical location where this was taking place was quite specific and far away from the buildings in which the parliamentarian deliberations took place. It was in the poor and economically overlooked metropolitan suburbs and housing projects, *la banlieue* or *la cité*. In the parliamentarian deliberations and in several reports, these places were described as border areas where communitarian law ruled, where republican values were long gone, and where young women were prey to an Islamic, male, controlling, and desexualizing gaze. The Stasi Commission (2003) reported the situation as a "veritable drama." Quoting a woman they interviewed, the commission stated that the Republic did not protect its "children" any more: "Young women are finding themselves the victims of a sexist resurgence that is translated by diverse pressures and by verbal, psychological, and physical violence. Young people are forcing them to wear covering and asexual clothes, to lower their gaze when meeting a man; if they do not comply, they are stigmatized as 'whores'" (46).[27]

The Debré Commission (2003a) supported this statement and referred to an interview with Kaïna Benzaine, the sister of Sohane Benzaine who was burned alive in a horrific murder in Vitry-sur-Seine in March 2002. To explain the reasons underlying this murder and the reported situation in which young women lived in the suburbs, the Commission turned to Fadela Amara, the president of the feminist organization *Ni Putes, Ni Soumises* (NPNS): "The ghettos are a true mould that nourishes those forms of fundamentalism that reinforce the sentiment of injustice and exclusion perceived in the projects and that hinders some young people from fully inscribing themselves in what one calls 'the sentiment of national belonging'" (76).[28] She suggests that the ghettos (suburbs) enforce the feelings of injustice and exclusion which fuel fundamentalist desires and imprison young women in Islamic communities.

---

27 "Les jeunes femmes se retrouvent victimes d'une résurgence du sexisme qui se traduit par diverses pressions et par des violences verbales, psychologiques ou physiques. Des jeunes gens leur imposent de porter des tenues couvrantes et asexuées, de baisser le regard à la vue d'un homme; à défaut de s'y conformer, elles sont stigmatisées comme 'putes'."

28 "Selon elle [Fadela Amara], les dérives des ghettos sont un véritable terreau qui nourrit toutes les formes d'intégrisme, qui renforce le sentiment d'injustice et d'exclusion perçu dans les cités et qui empêche une partie de la jeunesse de s'inscrire notamment dans ce que l'on appelle "le sentiment d'appartenance à la nation."

Accordingly, this hindered a large part of the youth from partaking in the feeling of belonging to a nation.

One of the supposed dangers in letting the religion of Islam become political resided in its temporal backwardness. MP Jacques Myard (UMP) suggested that fundamentalists have a literal reading of the Quran, meaning that, for fundamentalists, progress does not exist (AN 2004e, 1457). Dating a potential modern reform of Islam to the twelfth century, Myard concluded that, historically, fundamentalists had impeded all attempts to modernize Islam: "Fundamentalism is not new on Islamic territory. It is even recurrent there. It has put an end to every initiative by modern Muslims that wished to renew the Quranic message by measuring it against the yardstick of reason and the progress of civilization" (AN 2004e, 1457).[29] Myard was far from being alone in bringing up the supposedly retarded development of Islam for which fundamentalists, Islamists, and communitarians were responsible. MP Alain Néri (S), for example, referred to the threat as a "lethal poison" (AN 2004e, 1436). The suburb here emerges as a geographically distant but also very close location that is marked by a pre-modern temporality—Islam.

Attacking Secularism

Even if the imagined communitarian deviance was confined to the metropolitan outskirts, the concrete attacks occurred mainly in two parts of the public sphere: in the republican school and in the public sector (see Debré, 2003a, 11).[30]

Attacking the schools was, cccording to MP Bernard Carayon (UMP), a strategic move: "It is no coincidence that Muslim fundamentalists have chosen schools for their provocations and confrontations. In fact, the school is the republican melting pot of equal opportunity par excellence, the natural place of formation of all modernities and the acquisition of emancipation" (AN 2004d, 1410).[31]

---

29 "Le fondamentalisme n'est pas nouveau en terre d'islam. Il y est même récurrent. Il a mis un terme à chaque tentative des modernes—modernes musulmans—qui souhaitaient rénover le message coranique en le passant à l'aune de la raison et des progrès de la civilisation."

30 Also see MP Daniel Mach (UMP) (AN 2004f, 1481).

31 "Ce n'est pas un hasard si les intégristes musulmans ont choisi l'école comme terrain de provocations et d'affrontements. Elle est en effet, par excellence, le creuset républicain de l'égalité des chances, le lieu naturel d'éclosion de toutes les modernités et d'apprentissage des émancipations."

By attacking the schools, the fundamentalists would supposedly prohibit the Republic's emancipatory mission. Young women, the Stasi Commission (2003) reported, systematically contested courses in science and history, notably about the origin of the world and about the Holocaust. They moreover refused to participate in sports activities, and refused female institutional authority:

> Actually, the daily rhythm of the school is altered by systematic demands for absence once a week, as well as by interruptions of classes and exams because of prayer or fasting. Some students even contest entire parts of history and science. Some girls use medical certificates to skip physical activity and sports. Students and parents question the authority of female teachers and headmasters. (41)[32]

Within the public sector, the perceived defiance of communitarians, motivated by religious and/or gender demands, was equally present. The Commission proclaimed that even state functionaries and university students had demanded the right to wear symbols to display their religious identity (43). In hospitals, the Commission said, husbands and fathers, motivated by their religious conviction, prohibited their spouses and daughters being treated by, or giving birth with the aid of, male doctors (42). MPs such as Jacques Barrot (UMP) and André Gerin (SCR) made similar statements (see Barrot quoting Gerin in AN 2004a, 1296). Barrot went on to state that it was necessary not to fool oneself about "concrete threats" against secularism and the French ideal of peaceful coexistence—the much cherished "republican *vivre ensemble*."[33] It was up to the MPs to inform the public about the threat (AN 2004a, 1296).[34]

---

32 "En effet, le cours normal de la scolarité est aussi altéré par des demandes d'absences systématiques un jour de la semaine, ou d'interruption de cours et d'examens pour un motif de prière ou de jeûne. Des comportements contestant l'enseignement de pans entiers du programme d'histoire ou de sciences ... Certaines jeunes filles recourent à des certificats médicaux injustifiés pour être dispensées des cours d'éducation physique et sportive ... Des enseignants ou des chefs d'établissement, au seul motif que ce sont des femmes, voient leur autorité contestée par des élèves ou leurs parents."

33 "Nous devons nous rendre à l'évidence. Il existe aujourd'hui des menaces concrètes pesant sur le 'vivre ensemble' républicain et le principe de laïcité."

34 The French expression is *le vivre ensemble*, which here refers to the peaceful coexistance of different groups in a pluralistic society. See similar statements by MP Guy Tessier (UMP) (in AN 2004b, 1324) and MP Jean Lassalle (UDF) (in AN 2004b, 1321).

MPs from the benches of the left in the National Assembly made similar assessments. MP Marie-George Buffet (CR) saw a threat to the social and republican pact: "Let us first of all agree on the diagnostics: yes, secularism is threatened, and it is threatened in the most serious way by fractures that breaks the social and republican pact" (AN 2004a, 1294).[35] MP Jacques Brunhes (CR) agreed: "I have the impression that, today, secularism, this great French accomplishment, is threatened" (AN 2004b, 1327).[36] According to MP Danielle Bousquet (SRC): "This practice has no place in our Republic since wearing the veil goes against our constitutional principles" (AN 2004d, 1395).[37] As proof of what would happen were the veil left unregulated, MP Gabriel Biancheri (UMP) referred to an example of veiled women manipulating a good, willing employer in his electoral district in northern Drôme:

> We are also assisting a veritable offensive in public services and in businesses ... In my constituency, in Romans and in Bourg-de-Péage in northern Drôme, we are witnessing difficult situations in certain businesses. A young girl, indistinguishable from others, had a temporary contract [CDD], but as soon as she got a permanent contract, she appeared veiled. To her boss at the business she reclaimed her 'right to difference,' but what kind of difference? An owner of a business, confronted with a situation like this, is not encouraged to hire again. An attitude of this manner constitutes a set back for integration.[38] (AN 2004d, 1421)

MP Gilbert Le Bris (SOC), seemingly five years ahead of the debate, argued that if the veil was not prohibited today, tomorrow the problem would be burqas: "Islam has barely arrived in our country and already the religion represents a minority that refuses our values and traditions. We are witnessing the rise of a political and religious fanatism. The veil seeks to impose itself in the secular

---

35 "Accordons-nous, d'abord, sur le diagnostic: oui, la laïcité est menacée, et de la manière la plus grave par les fractures qui fissurent le pacte social et républicain."
36 "Cette laïcité, un grand acquis français, me semble aujourd'hui menace."
37 "Cette pratique n'a pas sa place dans notre République car le port du voile porte atteinte à nos principes constitutionnels"
38 "Dans ma circonscription, à Romans et à Bourg-de-Péage dans le nord de la Drôme, nous vivons des situations difficiles dans certaines entreprises. Une jeune fille, que rien ne distinguait des autres, travaillait en CDD, mais elle s'est présentée voilée deux jours après avoir obtenu un CDI. A son chef d'entreprise, elle a opposé son "droit à la différence", mais quelle différence? Un chef d'entreprise confronté à une telle situation n'est pas enclin à de nouvelles embauches. Une telle atitude constitue un frein à l'effort d'intégration."

space of the school. Why not the burqa tomorrow? We cannot accept this" (AN 2004f, 1463).[39]

• • •

In one sense, the first Veil Affair became a battleground for republican spokespeople to preach and confess their devotion to the Republic where every political representative sought to be the best defender of the republican model against communitarianism. "As if," to quote Geisser and Zemouri (2007), "an elected representative's or a candidate's capacity to exercise power was judged according to their aptitude to utter an alarmist diagnosis for French society, without for that matter really suggesting any concrete solutions" (6).

The situation described here was one where the other-subjects, Muslim women and fundamentalists in general, were responsible for their stigmatization. By living in the suburbs, they were responsible for their own exclusion from French society. Whether or not this was a correct depiction of the foundation of identity-based communities in the suburbs, republican spokespeople articulated religion, or more specifically Islam, Islamism, and fundamentalism, as the causes for the other's exclusion, discrimination, and economic segregation. In other words, republican spokespeople turned culture and religion into explicatory elements in the diagnosis of the Republic's socio-economic inequalities.

I refer to the logic underpinning these as *discursive displacement*. It is not only a question of creating a scapegoat to direct attention elsewhere (e.g., "it is them, not us, who are the true racists"), it is to neutralize and conceal one's own history through the other, by projecting one's own anti-Semitic past onto the other's imagined geographical origin. For example, the Dreyfus Affair and the Vichy Régime seemingly played no part in understanding anti-Semitism in France (see Noiriel 2007). Neither did France's exported anti-Semitism during colonial times, as when the *Union de races latines* organized several anti-Jewish leagues with the goal of driving the Jews out of French Algeria (see Ageron 1993, 109). Instead, an image was created of France as a universally benevolent and anti-racist nation (I discuss this in detail in Chapter Four).

While the statements presented here testify to a concern for the veiled women's bodies, freedom, and well-being, the deliberations equally articulated a concern for French men's right to access the other-woman's body. Republican

---

39 "A peine arrivée dans notre pays, voilà que la religion islamique présente le visage d'une minorité qui n'a que faire de nos valeurs et traditions. Voilà que l'on assiste à la montée d'un fanatisme politico-religieux. Voilà que le voile veut s'introduire dans l'espace laïque de l'école. Et pourquoi pas, demain, la burqa? Nous ne pouvons l'accepter."

spokespeople actually appear to have desired the Muslim woman and longed for her confirmation by projecting an excessive enjoyment onto the other (see Homer 2005, 62). Why? This is because her loyalty (manifested by letting French men see her hair and access her body) towards the Republic became an imagined closure of a republican *we*, as if the accessibility and conformity of the Muslim woman to Republican customs became a matter of national reproduction, symbolically (identity/we) and biologically (body) (Camiscioli 2009).

Since this desired other-woman in this secularist reasoning chose another path, the Islamic and communitarian one, Islam and communitarianism must have had something that the Republic did not, as if it had stolen something from the Republic (How could Muslim women choose fundamentalists over the Republic?). Žižek (2008) believes that "this results in a paradoxical relation; the subject is invested with a fundamental passivity, the object invested with agency and movement" (21). The failure of the Republic's closure is, in this logic, not a result of the Republic itself; it is displaced onto the object-other. The object-other thus not only becomes an antagonistic object, since it reminds the Republic of its own void, but also becomes an ever-present constitutive something for the Republic, meaning that "the epistemological change in the subject's gaze also changes the object's ontology—that is, the subject and the object are intrinsically mediatized" (22). In one sense, then, the subject as the Republic becomes passive, or rather perceives itself this way. Its self-realization is obstructed by the inevitable presence of the object-other (whatever form it might take), whereas the object-other is invested with an uncanny agency since it actively obstructs the successful realization of the true Republic, where the other, as the other, becomes an enemy of the political order and society; it becomes a post-political enemy. This is how the legislators legitimized their will to discipline the other through law. Think, for example, of when Interior Minister Nicolas Sarkozy filed a suit against a rapper for violating the principle and values of the Republic (see Chapter Two). The prevailing discursive logic exemplified here is one where the other can be disqualified from being French simply by critiquing French politics—the institutionalization of which can be seen in French laws of defamation, where the flag and the national anthem are proclaimed as sacred and it is illegal to insult them. Since figures like André Gerin and Nicolas Sarkozy appear to personally identify with the Republic, criticizing the Republic is to criticize and even discriminate against Gerin and Sarkozy.

Behind the Veil

In the eyes of the republican spokespeople, the Republic was thus threatened by fundamentalist communitarian Islam. Schools were prey to racist and discriminatory slander by veiled students. The veil appeared to be the visible sign of a perverted Islam—racist, anti-Semitic, and discriminatory—that was understood as representing new challenges to the Republic. If the veil was taken to be incompatible with the Republic, it is important to ask how this conclusion was drawn. Was the veil really *only* a religious symbol? Why did the veil pose a problem? How was the knowledge of the veil constructed? How were veiled female students construed? This search for knowledge was expressed in two questions: What does it represent? Why do these women choose to wear it?

What Does It Represent?

In one sense, a crucial issue regarding the veil was less of what it represented and more about its mere presence. The Debré Commission (2003a) explained that religious signs in themselves could provoke tensions that would divide schools and disrupt education (27). According to the Valade Commission (2004), the problem with the veil was its conspicuousness and its supposed religious nature (26). This immediate categorization was thought to exclude the veiled student and prevent her from integrating into school and society, as MP Valérie Pecresse (UMP) argued (AN 2004c, 1442).

A related issue was that of proselytism—the Stasi Commission (2003) even called veils in schools an "aggressive proselytism" (16).[40] MP Jacques Domergue (UMP) made a similar statement, arguing that the veil was "a symbol of a proselytizing Islam used by a minority" (AN 2004d, 1419).[41]

On the one hand, republican spokespeople articulated the veil as a religious symbol, but its simultaneous articulation as a symbol of communitarianism, fundamentalism, proselytism, ostentatiousness, and as a threat to the Republic, indicated that, as already noted, it had political connotations. The Debré Commission (2003a) accordingly reported that one should not reduce the veil to a simple religious symbol as it also brought with it a will to be different, a political affirmation, and a certain idea of women's place in society: "To the members of the commission the 'veil' cannot be reduced to a simple religious appearance. It often carries with it, even if this is not always the case, a political will to affirm difference and, perhaps even more so, a certain idea of the image

---

40   "[L]'affichage d'un prosélytisme agressif, particulièrement dans l'espace scolaire." See similar statements in the Clément Report (2004, 20).
41   "[L]e symbole d'un islam prosélyte brandi par une minorité de musulmans."

and the place of women in society" (8).[42] According to the Commission, the female student's will to wear the veil was even closer to ideology than to religion: "In school, these identity claims by certain young Muslims do not have anything to do with religious practice" (71).[43] The Valade Commission (2004) made similar statements; it put special emphasis on how the veil threatened "the principle of coeducation" and "equality between boys and girls" (25). There was, however, more to it: In their report, the Commission stated that the veil "was concealing hidden communitarian ideals" (19).[44] MP Jacques Myard (UMP) agreed with the Commission and argued that the veil was not only political, it was the first step in imposing Sharia law in France: "It is political and the veil hides the most crucial aspect—the creation of a society restructured in compliance to Sharia. In this society, certain women will be inferior to men, this is evident, but the objectives are more far-reaching than that. Let there be no mistake" (AN 2004e, 1458).[45]

MP Jean-Claude Guibal (UMP) saw the veil as a flag:

> The veil is a flag, a flag for radical Islamism's political and religious combat. This combat aims at exercising a social control over the 5 million Muslims that live in France, to enlist them, to make them into docile troops. Muslim women are the first victims, but the whole of the Muslim community will suffer from the consequences of the simplifying amalgamation wished for by some ... Nothing is more subversive to the republican order than communalism, for which the veil is the battle flag. (AN 2004e, 1433)[46]

---

42   "Pour les membres de la mission le "voile," qui est au centre de la polémique, ne peut être réduit à un simple signe d'appartenance religieuse. Il véhicule souvent, si ce n'est toujours, une volonté politique d'affirmation d'une différence et, peut-être plus encore, une certaine idée de l'image et de la place des femmes dans la société."

43   "[E]n milieu scolaire, les revendications identitaires de certains jeunes musulmans n'ont pas grand-chose à voir avec la pratique religieuse."

44   "Derrière le voile ... des dérives communautaires sous-jacentes."

45   "Il est politique et le port du voile cache l'essentiel: l'instauration d'une société formatée conformément à la charia, où certes la femme est enfermée dans un statut minoritaire, mais dont les objectifs vont beaucoup plus loin. Ne nous y trompons pas."

46   "Le voile est un drapeau, celui du combat politico-religieux de l'islamisme radical. Celui-ci vise à exercer un contrôle social sur les 5 millions de musulmans qui vivent en France, pour les enrégimenter ensuite dans une troupe docile ... Rien n'est plus subversif de l'ordre républicain que le communautarisme, dont le voile est l'étendard."

MP Dionis du Séjour (UDF) referred to an alleged majority of specialists on Islam and suggested that it was more pertinent to talk about an ideological veil:

> The majority of specialists on Islam agree on this point: the veil, in Saudi Arabia, in Iran or in European countries, is not the sign of a religious identity; it is exclusively a reference to fundamentalist tendencies ... We can therefore talk about an "ideological veil." The veil has become a sign of ideology and political propaganda; it is the consequence of proselytizing work carried out by Islamists in our neighborhoods, in a socially stigmatized context. (AN 2004b, 1337)[47]

MP Nicolas Perruchot (UDF) stated simply that the veil signifies the submission of women to men (AN 2004b, 1332) and, according to MP Martine David (SOC), certain religious symbols were worse than others. The veil was for "millions of human beings [the sign of] coercion, violence, and terror" (AN 2004c, 1390). MP Claude Darciaux (SOC) was worried that the veil might become "the uniform of the suburbs" and that to accept the veil was to "support political Islam and to legitimize an assault against women's dignity and her legal status" (AN 2004d, 1423; see also Dutoit in AN 2004b, 1346).[48]

Why Do They Wear It?

In the quest of seeking out why young women wore the veil, the republican spokespeople soon entered a problematic field. Even if the veil by itself was taken to be conspicuously religious, how could one actually know this without embarking on a theological reading of the religious meaning of the veil and the motivations for wearing it? Would it not appear as a contradiction in terms if a secular state engaged in theological debate? The Valade Commission (2004) stated that it was evidently not the MPs' task to conduct a theological debate (23). However, this was something that republican spokespeople could not avoid. This was the case with the Stasi Commission (2003), which, after

---

47 "La plupart des spécialistes de l'Islam sont d'accord sur ce point ... Ainsi peut-on parler d'un 'voile idéologique.' Le voile est devenu un signe idéologique et de propagande politique; il est la conséquence du travail de prosélytisme que mènent les islamistes dans nos quartiers, dans un contexte social très défavorisé."

48 "[L]'uniforme de nos cités ... Accepter le voile, c'est accepter une idée de la femme contraire à sa dignité et à son statut juridique, c'est encourager l'affichage des différences religieuses et, en quelque sorte, c'est soutenir l'islam politique."

its hearings argued that for the women wearing the veil, it could have different meanings: It could be a personal and religiously motivated choice, or the result of social and communal pressure (57). In the Clément Report (2004), MP Pascal Clément (UMP) discussed the problem of motivation in relation to the bandana (most often a triangular piece of cloth tied around the head) and a potential law prohibiting the veil: "Regarding symbols like the bandana, the term 'visible' does not facilitate the application of the law for the principals: in fact, since the law prohibits 'visible' or 'conspicuous' symbols, they [the principals] will always need to determine if the young girls wear the bandana by religious motivation or not" (21).[49]

Here Clément stated that it was crucial to understand whether students wore the bandana for religious or non-religious motives. A non-religious piece of cloth could thus be ascribed a religious meaning if the person wearing it did so for religious reasons. The veil thus seemed to pose questions of motivation in a double sense: Was it worn for non-religious reasons or religious ones? Was it worn for personal reasons or as the result of pressure? Even if the report brings up these alternatives, precedence was given to the understanding that it was worn for religious reasons *and* because of social pressure.

The Debré Commission (2003a) sought to gain a deeper understanding of social pressures pushing young women to wear the veil, and of those who supposedly choose it through free will; they did so by relying on a statement by Kaïna Benzaine. Benzaine, referring to "her own experience," explained that liberty is a problematic matter in relation to the veil. In Benzaine's case, she wore the veil out of free will, but it was in order to be left alone from the gaze of others and from a social tribunal judging good Muslims from bad—the ones who go to paradise and the ones who do not. Benzaine said that in reality she would not have worn the veil if she had a real choice. In the end, she concluded that wearing the veil was a result of coercion:

> "It is important to know what 'free' means when a young girl decides to wear the veil. I always refer to my case, which is not necessarily representative. Sometimes, I tell myself that if I wear the veil, I will be left alone and that I can dedicate myself to God ... In regard to the decision by these young girls to wear the veil several of indirect factors can be taken into

---

49 "Le terme "visible" ne rend pas l'application de la loi, pour des signes tels que le bandana, plus aisée pour les chefs d'établissement: en effet, que la loi interdise les signes "visibles" ou "ostentatoire," ceux-ci devront toujours déterminer si les jeunes filles portent ou non le bandeau pour des motifs religieux."

account. Even if no one directly obliges them to wear it, they have done it to be left alone, to avoid the gaze of this or that person. It's the logic of religion that dominates in the suburbs, because a young girl wearing the veil is extremely well viewed here, by the family as well as by the 'social tribunal.' Meanwhile, certain young girls, like me, do not want to wear it. Those who are veiled, although not all of them, taunt us and make us understand that, because they wear the veil, they are good Muslims, that they will go to paradise whilst the others are infidels. To me, that is an aggression. (28)[50]

Benzaine emphasized that she was talking of her own experiences and feelings. This did not stop the Commission from making her story into *the* true story about the veil, which also became a truth for the majority of the republican spokespeople analyzed here. The result of interpreting Benzaine's story as the true one led to the conclusion that even if free will guided students to wear the veil, it was interpreted as a false free will, a false desire, since it was a choice made under the influence of social pressure. In this sense, it became an even more problematic display.

The Debré Commission concluded that there were few who wore the veil without any social pressure: "Henceforth, we can question to what degree these young girls wear the veil by real free will. The hearings by the commission have clearly shown that their choice is not always free" (28).[51] The Valade Commission (2004) made clear that veiled students were "paradoxically seeking comfort in a symbol of women's alienation locking them into a spiral of

---

50 "Lors de son audition, Melle Kaïna Benziane a expliqué la contrainte très forte qui pèse sur les jeunes filles: 'Il faut savoir ce que l'on entend par "libre" quand une jeune fille décide de porter le voile. Je me réfère toujours à mon cas qui n'est certainement pas représentatif. A certains moments, je me dis que si je porte le voile, on me laissera tranquille et je pourrai me consacrer à Dieu (…) Plusieurs facteurs indirects peuvent entrer en ligne de compte dans la décision de ces jeunes filles. Même si personne ne les a obligé directement à le porter, elles l'ont fait pour être tranquilles, pour éviter les regards de telle ou telle personne, en raison de la religion qui domine dans la cité, car il est extrêmement bien vu pour une jeune fille de porter le voile dans les cités, tant par la famille que par le "tribunal social." Toutefois, certaines jeunes filles comme moi ne veulent pas porter le voile. Celles qui sont voilées, mais pas toutes, nous narguent et nous font comprendre que, parce qu'elles portent le voile, elles sont de bonnes musulmanes, qu'elles iront au paradis alors que les autres sont des mécréantes. Pour moi, c'est une agression.'"

51 "On peut, en effet, s'interroger sur la liberté réelle des jeunes filles de porter le voile. Les auditions menées par la mission ont clairement montré que leur choix n'est pas toujours libre."

exclusion" (24).⁵² For the Commission, the diagnosis of the situation was clear—fundamentalists and communitarians manipulated these young women for political ends (24).⁵³ These women, described as "lacking a voice," chose the veil to "protect themselves from the influence of Islamist networks, their parents, and their brothers" and "even other women who treat them as impure, as bad Muslims" (24).⁵⁴ Despite the almost unanimous condemnation of the veil as a symbol of religious fundamentalism, the Commission here concluded that the veil could protect women against what it symbolized. Hence, the majority of veiled women would prefer not to wear the veil and the reason why they put it on was the Republic's lack of protection against communitarian pressures. The Stasi Commission (2003) stated: "Paradoxically, the veil thus offers these young women the protection that should be guaranteed by the Republic. Those who do not wear the veil and perceive it as a sign of female inferiority that imprisons and isolates women are treated as 'impure,' as 'infidels'" (47).⁵⁵

Similar statements were made in Parliament. MP Jean-Pierre Grand (UMP) proclaimed that the most radical Islamists were manipulating religion and young girls for political ends (AN 2004c, 1444). MP Jacques Domergue (UMP) relied on personal experience to explain the gravity of the veiling of young women by juxtaposing them with older women. He said he Domergue had met veiled women and concluded that older women wore the veil out of religious conviction and nothing else, much as Catholic nuns do. These women wore their veils without the least provocation. However, when young women wear the veil to display their difference, the veil is no longer a religious sign. It then becomes a sign of communitarian resistance, a sign of a voluntary refusal to integrate:

> Some wear it conspicuously ... these women display the veil as a marker of their difference. The veil is no longer a religious sign, as for Muslim women from the old generation. It has become the symbol of communitarian

---

52   "Paradoxalement, elles expriment leur besoin de reconnaissance en adoptant un signe qui symbolise l'aliénation de la femme, et qui les enserre dans une spirale de l'exclusion."

53   "Leur déshérence identitaire et leur révolte morale et sociale les poussent finalement à se soumettre aux prédications de ceux qui, prenant appui sur la religion, les instrumentalisent à des fins politiques."

54   "Des sans voix, revêtent le voile pour se protéger des pressions, émanant des parents, des 'grands frères,' des réseaux islamistes, voire des autres filles voilées qui les traitent d' 'impures,' de mauvaises musulmanes."

55   "Le voile leur offre ainsi, paradoxalement, la protection que devrait garantir la République. Celles qui ne le portent pas et le perçoivent comme un signe d'infériorisation qui enferme et isole les femmes sont désignées comme 'impudiques' voire 'infidèles'."

resistance by a minority that does not feel integrated, and that does not want to integrate. To use a medical metaphor from the domain of organ transplantation I would say that this is a veritable "graft reacting against the host," which is to say the rejection of the welcoming country, the majority, by a transplanted minority that does not integrate.[56] (AN 2004d, 1419)

MP Dionis du Séjour (UDF) reiterated statements proposing that the veil signified the imprisonment of young women and that few young girls wore the veil out of a proper free will. Séjour thus concluded that to accept the wearing of the veil by minors in school would make the lawmakers accomplices to a fundamentalist reading of the Quran (AN 2004b, 1337).[57] MP Jean-Pierre Brard (CR) stated that, whatever was said about the veil, *we* know by experience that it is not worn through free will. The veil was the symbol of patriarchal control and the submission of women:

> What are the motivations for wearing the veil and what is its signification? Is it really a free and emancipatory act that certain women claim? We know by experience that this is sadly not the case. Those to which we in particular should aim our thoughts are the silenced young girls, reduced to mutism, kept under permanent submission by an authority and under masculine social control, in the family, in the apartment building, and in the neighborhood. The veil is indeed the symbol of inferiority and the submission of women. (AN 2004b, 1323)[58]

MP Jacques Barrot (UMP) was one of the few who argued that even young women could wear the veil with an honest religious conviction. Barrot, however,

---

56 "Certaines le portent ostensiblement ... ces femmes arborent le voile comme la marque de leur différence. Le voile n'est plus le signe religieux des musulmanes de la vieille génération. Il est devenu le symbole de la résistance communautariste d'une minorité qui ne se sent pas intégrée ou qui ne veut pas s'intégrer. Pour user d'une métaphore médicale empruntée au domaine de la transplantation d'organe, je dirai que c'est une véritable "réaction greffon contre hôte," c'est-à-dire le rejet du pays d'accueil, majoritaire, par une minorité transplantée qui ne s'est pas intégrée."

57 See similar statement by MP Martine David (SOC) (AN 2004c, 1390).

58 "Quelles sont les motivations et la signification du port du voile? Est-il vraiment un acte volontaire d'émancipation que revendiquent certaines femmes? Nous savons d'expérience que ce n'est malheureusement pas le cas. Celles auxquelles nous devons penser particulièrement, ce sont les jeunes filles silencieuses, réduites au mutisme, soumises en permanence à une autorité et à un contrôle social masculin, dans la famille, dans l'immeuble, dans le quartier. Le voile est bien le symbole de l'infériorité et de la sujétion des femmes."

concluded that when this was not the case, when it was worn as a result of social pressures, it was, as stated by other MPS, "a battle flag for the refusal to integrate" (AN 2004b, 1296). MP Danièle Bousquet (MP) referred to the young women as "manipulated banner-bearers" of a fundamentalist movement (AN 2004d, p. 1396). According to MP Jacques Rivière, the nature of the manipulation was a form of "seduction" that was gravely hurting French tradition and society (AN 2004e, 1452).

If young women were manipulated or even seduced into wearing the veil, into carrying battle flags against the republic, how were the actions of these women rationalized? Were they mere empty vessels in the hands of the fundamentalists? According to the Debré Commission (2003b), they were voluntarily submitting to the fundamentalists and communitarians, which was the even case for fourteen-year-old adolescents. The Commission referred to the famous psychoanalyst Élisabeth Roudinesco when reaching this conclusion, thus giving the conclusion scientific credibility (28).[59]

This sort of voluntary servitude suggested that the young women played an active part in the fundamentalist and communitarian threat since they willingly let themselves be manipulated, and that these young women actually took an active part in the defense of their right to wear the veil should thus be interpreted as a successful manipulation of them by the fundamentalists (23). Young girls wearing the veil knew more and more about French legislation according to the ambiguous decree by the *Conseil d'Etat* from 1989 (see Chapter Two). The Commission quoted Philippe Guittet, the Secretary General of the teacher's union, *Syndicat national des personnels de direction de l'éducation nationale* (SNPDEN), confirming the above conclusion. The more these young women learned about the law, the more they became determined in keeping their veils on: "They know about the verdicts from the *Conseil d'État* and have a much more determined approach to the problem" (23).[60] That the students informed themselves about the present legislation, taking an active part as republican citizens, was in other words not welcome.

One of the few critical voices amongst the virtually unanimous condemnation of the veil, MP Jean-Claude Lefort (CR), accused his colleagues in Parliament of losing focus. Lefort argued that the debate had become politicized, that it had come to stigmatize the French Muslim youth by treating them as if they were not fellow citizens, and that it had lost proportionality: "A veil, a

---

59   "Mme Roudinesco, psychanalyste, a parlé de 'servitude volontaire'... même chez des adolescentes de 14 ans'."

60   "Elles connaissent les arrêts du Conseil d'Etat et ont une attitude beaucoup plus déterminée face au problème."

simple veil, worn by young schoolgirls, and all of a sudden the foundations of secularism are threatened!? These young girls, who are targeted by unworthy and sickening statements, are French. They are French just as much as you and I! In addition, this is their home as much as it is for you and I! Are we also going to reconsider their nationality?" (AN 2004c,1377–1378).[61] Lefort's statements did not resonate in Parliament, although many anti-racist and human rights organizations, academics, journalists, religious spokespeople, and intellectuals made similar statements (see Chapter Two).

•••

Considering the veil's constructed meaning, Asad (2005) pointed out that what "is signified by the veil is not some historical reality but another sign— the externally fixed Islamic religion, which is used to give the veil a stable meaning" (502). Indeed, the veil was embodied as the Republic's antithesis since it did what the Republic ought to have done: provide protection. It appears as if the republican spokespeople could have direct access to this externally fixed Islamic religion without speaking to those who were supposedly its subjects. The reports undertook virtually no interviews with veiled students and they ignored scholarly accounts on the matter.[62] Instead, the reports relied on secondhand information and state officials recounting anecdotical stories and self-referential truths ("to others the veil signifies," "specialists are in agreement," "we all know," etc.). One exception was the few women who had been brought up in the suburbs (Amara and Benzaine). When the Commissions or the debate in general took interest in a Muslim woman's story, it was in the form of the formerly veiled woman (see Geisser 2003; Rigouste, 2005), the internal informant, the successfully integrated (ex-)Muslim. That is, since the veiled students were not to be trusted, the only one who could bear witness about the veil's true essence was someone from "over there" (see Chapter Two).

One can relate the absence of voices from veiled young women to at least two reasons. First, that they were so few and hard to find or, second, that they were not credible as informants—when the students' legal reasoning to justify the wearing of the veil was understood not as a young citizen's manifested interest in republican law but as a problem, as a manifestation of her submission

---

61   "un voile, un simple voile, porté par des jeunes filles à l'école, et voilà que la laïcité serait menacée dans son principe! [L]es jeunes visés par ces propos indignes et écœurants sont Français. Ce sont des Français comme vous et moi! Et leur 'ailleurs,' comme pour vous et pour moi, c'est ici. Va-t-on aussi les déchoir de leur nationalité?"

62   Compare to the seminal study by Gaspard and Khosrokhavar (1995).

to the communitarians and fundamentalists. Hence, republican spokespeople deemed the students incapable of coming up with a strategy of resistance against family or social pressure. They were the imagined silent majority in need of republican salvation. When they showed agency, they were no longer exclusively perceived as victims of authoritarian fathers and/or brothers. They were described as having a paradoxical voluntary servitude: They chose their own submission, which made them even more dangerous and devious.

As Asad has pointed out, the veil was detached from desire because it simply could not be a proper object of it. To the commissions and the politicians, the idea that a student wanted to wear the veil but did not have the courage to do so, fearing the gaze of the Republic, did not appear as a possibility. Female desire thus had one endgoal—to unveil. In this logic, you either had the wrong desire or the right one (Asad 2005, 503; see also Chouder, Latrèche, and Tévanian 2008; Wafika Ouhhabi in Bronner 2011; Yankelevich 2004). Žižek (1999) has suggested that the only officially recognized alternative for the other to break through this sort of silenced subject-position, to achieve a semi-political recognition, to become a subject with agency, is to go through the situation of forced choice "by means of which the subject emerges out of the act of freely choosing the inevitable" (18). To emerge as a citizen in the first place, to be invited to dance with the republican state apparatus, the subject not only needed to want to do it—to have the desire to do it—but the will and desire needed to conform with the hegemonic discourses' *pre-established* articulations of desire and will. In addition, even when these qualifications were attained, the other remained an ex-other, a former Muslim.

Conclusion

In this chapter, I have sought to answer the following questions: What was the rationale for the reasoning underlying the deliberations for the Law of 2004? In what ways were Islamic female students and their veils understood to undermine the foundation of the French Republic? What kind of identity was ascribed to them? What kind of politics (identity and technique of governance) did they legitimize?

As my analysis suggests, the Muslim-other, and the veiled young Muslim woman in particular, was a subject-object that created a strong will to know their innermost desires and motivations. It was as if the veiled woman forced the republican state apparatus and its spokespeople (as well as the national media) into an unwanted but indeed necessary debate to come to terms with the challenges posed by the veil. However, given the orientalist reasoning underlying the will to know her, the veiled young Muslim woman was perceived as both a symptom of contemporary political, social and economic inequalities in the Republic and the reasons for them. She was an imagined extension of fundamentalist Islamism threatening to tear the republican unity to shreds. To get to know her, a number of republican spokespeople set out to reason objectively about the veil's true meaning. As enlightened, goodwilled, and civilizing secular republicans, they sought to prescribe the sartorial, moral, and spatial limits of the Republic through a negative identification with the veil. For the spokespeople, it was a matter of winning back the veiled woman to the Republic—to direct her desires to the warming embrace of the French Republic instead of Islam and, by so doing, affirm the Republic's universal benevolence. The women themselves were given two options. They could either accept their place as other-subjects, as veiled Muslim women, or as formerly other-subjects and formerly veiled Muslim woman. In either case, their otherness could not be disassociated from their bodies; they became civilizational-biological threats creating a state of emergency calling for exceptional political measures.

The Muslim-other was here articulated as a post-political other and, partly, as a post-political enemy—an external intruder in the midst of the French society. It was the other's culture, religion, and ethnicity that mainly defined the characteristic moments in the identity ascribed to the other in republican discourse on secularism. As I will show in the following chapter, this is a key aspect in understanding how secularism as governmentality came to function during 2003 and 2004.

CHAPTER 4

Inventing Secularism

In the previous chapter, I showed how veiled female students were articulated as embodiments of a post-political threat (communitarianism and Islamism) during the deliberations preceding the Law of 2004 prohibiting conspicuous religious symbols in public schools. To the republican spokespeople, the veiled other-woman's disobedient presence called into question French secularism and was understood as opening a gateway for devastating forces threatening national cohesion. To quote the Minister of Education, Luc Ferry (2003), who proclaimed that, "thanks to secularism, the republican school had been a safe haven until the intrusion of the veil, protected from racism, anti-Semitism, and communitarianism."[1] National unity was in peril, at least so the story went.

In this chapter, I will analyze how republican spokespeople sought an answer and solution to the imagined challenges and threats posed by the veil during the first Veil Affair. I aim to understand how republican discourse on secularism found its *modus vivendi* in the discourse of the Muslim-other. In other words, I analyze how republican discourse on secularism as post-political governmentality (as a mode of governance and as a mode of identity) was articulated and practiced, and the kinds of subjects that needed to be fashioned for secularism to function. The main argument of the chapter is that the state of emergency articulated by the discourse about the Muslim-other legitimized a state of exception—an exceptional and illiberal political solution to the imagined enemy-other.

The chapter is structured around the following questions: What was secularism's articulated history? What were the conclusions drawn from this history? What was the content of secularism? What was its purpose, if there even was one? Moreover, if there was a purpose, how was it to be implemented? I end this chapter by discussing secularism in relation to the Muslim-other (Chapter Three), post-politics, universalism, and nation.

---

1 "C'est au nom de cette conviction [laïcité] que la République française a su jusqu'à présent préserver son école des intrusions inacceptables du racisme, de l'antisémitisme et du communautarisme."

An Unruly March Towards Unity

To the President, the Prime Minister, and a large number of MPS, the development of secularism was an integral part of what it meant to be French where freedom and tolerance are its most important markers. Even though the history of secularism was confrontational and violent, it had led to a peaceful unity, to atonement. It was this atonement that the Muslim-other was thought to disrupt (as discussed in Chapter Three). However, as will become clear, there was more than just an atonement to disrupt. Secularism was understood as something more: it was exceptional and the embodiment of universal spirit embodied in the French Republic. As such, it was understood to have certain uncompromisable principles dating as far back as Jesus Christ and Ancient Greece. Although the history of secularism was a contested one, the spokespeople united around three crucial moments in its history and development: the French Revolution of 1789, the Law of 1905 separating Church from State, and the 1946 Constitution declaring that the Republic is secular (*laïque*).

From Clash to Atonement

Talking in general terms, President Chirac (2003b) stated that secularism was a central part of French identity: "Secularism is inscribed in our traditions. Secularism is close to the heart of our Republican identity."[2] The development of secularism had been a "long march towards unity" which carried with it the marks of "religious wars and persecutions." In Chirac's view, secularism harbored an "emancipatory exceptionality." It had succeeded in uniting France around a "consensus" founded upon "freedom of religion" and "tolerance" which, most importantly, had led to the emancipation of women.[3] The Debré Commission (2003a) talked about "the long march towards unity," but also as a quarrel of the "Two Frances." It was a quarrel that played out between the Catholic-clerical France (*ultra-montaine*) and the republican, anti-clerical France.

When did this journey towards emancipation of women begin? While none of the republican spokespeople disputed the claim that the revolution of 1789 brought about the first proper emergence of secularism, a number of statements sought to trace its roots even further back in time. Both the Stasi and Valade Commissions traced it back to Ancient Greece. The former explained that the historical thresholds of secularism were Ancient Greece, the Renaissance, the Reformation, the Edict of Nantes, and the Enlightenment. Each step

---

2   "La laïcité est inscrite dans nos traditions. Elle est au coeur de notre identité républicaine."
3   For similar statements see PM Jean-Pierre Raffarin (UMP) (AN 2004a, 1286), MP Daniel Paul (GDR) (AN 2004b, 1333), and MP Jean Glavany (S) (AN 2004c, 1375).

had contributed in bringing about personal autonomy and freedom of thought (Stasi 2003, 10). The Valade Commission (2004) stated that "the French term (laïcité) has its roots in the Greek concept *laos*, designating a people united around a common social project where everyone was regarded as equals" (6).[4] It was as if a self-evident democratic kernel inhabited French secularism.

Another prevailing and interrelated statement by the PM and certain MPS was that secularism had Christian roots. For example, PM Raffarin referred to France as an "old Christian country" (AN 2004a, 1286). MP Jacques Domergue sought to remind his listeners that France's Judaeo-Christian origins had shaped the Republic's secular foundations (AN 2004c, 1419). MP Pierre Bourguignon (S) found secular ideals in the words of Jesus Christ from Matthew 22:21: "Give to Caesar what belongs to Caesar, and give to God what belongs to God" (AN 2004e, 1455). MP Bernard Carayon (UMP) similarly stated that *our* Judaeo-Christian identity defined the exceptionality of French secularism. French secularism's supposed strict line of demarcation between the religious sphere and the political sphere went back to early Christian times where the seed of democracy was planted (AN 2004d, 1410). Carayon even stated that "equality between men and women had always been a fundamental aspect in *our* Greco-Latin civilization and in the Judaeo-Christian civilization" (AN 2004d, 1410).[5]

Yet another take on secularism's roots was provided by MP Xavier Bertrand (UMP), who retraced secularism to when Philip IV contested the Papacy's power over the French church at the end of the thirteenth century (AN 2004f, 1434). Philip's influence on secularism was, according to Bertrand, thought to have inaugurated the Gallican or tutelage model of the State-Church relationship.

However, according to the President, the French Revolution of 1789 was the first time in history when the Republic institutionalized secularism (Chirac 2003a; also see Ferry 2004a; Buffet in AN 2004a, 1294). It was in article ten of the Declaration of the Rights of Man and of the Citizen (1789) that one could find the core foundation of secularism. The article states: "No one shall be disquieted on account of his opinions, including his religious views, provided their manifestation does not disturb the public order established by law."

---

4 "Le terme laïcité tire en effet ses racines du grec laos, qui désigne le peuple rassemblé dans un projet de société, autour d'un engagement commun, où chacun est à égalité." That the Greek laos was the marker for a democratic and equal society can of course be qualified since it only referred to citizens, not women, slaves, blacks, etc. See Bernal (1991).

5 "dans l'histoire de notre civilisation gréco-latine puis judéo-chrétienne, l'égalité de l'homme et de la femme a constitué une référence obligée."

Here, it is important to note that legislation could clearly limit the manifestation of religious views; that is, a personal manifestation of a religious conviction must not disturb public order. MP Jean Glavany (S) gave an account of the revolutionary roots of secularism by suggesting that the only true secular constitution was the one adopted by the National Convention [*conventionelles*] in 1793. Glavany paid special homage to the Convention's famous republican calendar, a calendar that still today makes secularists "dream" (AN 2004c, 1374).[6]

The second major institutionalization of secularism was the Law of 1905. Chirac (2003b) described the 1905 Law as *the* embodiment of secularism. Here secularism finally became one of "the great accomplishments" of the Republic. It was moreover a "great law" that adapted itself to the "evolutions" of French society while at the same time respecting "the particularities of every religion" (Chirac 2003a). He also understood the law to safeguard the primacy of national law over particular interests (Chirac 2003b). In the words of MP René Dosière (S), with this law secularism "took root" in the Republic (AN 2004c, 1382).[7] The Stasi Commission (2003) declared that secularism was constitutive of our collective history and that it was with the Law of 1905 that France became a secular republic (2). The essence of the law was explained in articles one and two.

> 1st article: The Republic assures liberty of conscience. It guarantees the free exercise of religion under the sole restrictions of public interest prescribed hereafter.
> 2nd article: The Republic does not recognize, remunerate, or subsidize any religion.[8] (Stasi 2003, 14)

Similar to the Declaration of 1789, these two articles make clear that freedom of conscience is guaranteed within the restrictions of public order and that the

---

6 The National Convention was the elected legislative body inaugurated 20 September 1792. It lasted until 26 October 1795. In the reigning consensus over secularism's founding period a dividing fissure prevailed regarding the role attributed to the Jacobins. In the 1789 post-revolutionary era the left-block saw the birth of the "revolutionary," "combative," and "republican" features of secularism whilst the Debré Commission and, as we will see, parts of the right-block in general, referred to this period as the "terror." Secularism here was articulated as anti-religious and non-tolerant (Debré 2003a, 14).

7 For a similar statement see Pierre Bourgignon (S) (AN 2004e, 1455).

8 "La République assure la liberté de conscience. Elle garantit le libre exercice des cultes, sous les seules restrictions édictées ci-après dans l'intérêt de l'ordre public." "La République ne reconnaît, ne salarie ni ne subventionne aucun culte."

Republic does not acknowledge or subsidize any religion (see Chapter One for a discussion about these statements).

According to Chirac (2003b), the last institutionalization of secularism was the asserted inscription of secularism into the Fourth Republic's constitution in 1946, where it was stated that France is a secular Republic: "The human rights and those of citizens have been progressively conquered, consolidated, and deepened, from the declaration of 1789 to the preamble of 1946."[9] According to the Stasi Commission (2003), it was through the Constitution that the principle of secularism acquired a constitutional value (19). The Debré Commission (2003) similarly confirmed that it was in 1946 that the Republic was permanently established in France (22). MP Jacques Brunhes (DCR) stated that the Constitution was the marker of secularism's quasi-total support by the French population (AN 2004b, 1327).[10]

With the exception of the 1789 Declaration, the 1905 Law, and the 1946 Constitution, a number of laws, concords, circulars, decrees, bills, agreements, and declarations were mentioned in the reports and during the deliberations.[11] So were a number of founding fathers: Jean Jaurés, Léon Gambetta, Emile Combes, Voltaire, Jean Bodin, Thomas Hobbes, John Locke, Jean-Jacques Rousseau (Debré 2003, 12ff), and Ernest Renan (Valade 2004, 5). Jules Ferry and the school reforms of the late nineteenth century in particular were attributed unique status. Jean Glavany (S) talked about Ferry as "the real one," "the grand one!" (AN 2004a, 1302). Jean-Pierre Brard (GDR) asserted that secularism was "the fruit of a courageous battle" by Ferry (AN 2004b, 1322).[12] MP Martine Aurillac (UMP) referred to the Ferry Bill of 1883 as a "beautiful maxim" (*une belle maxime*) (AN 2004c, 1383). Régis Debray (UMP) (2002), appointed

---

9   "Les droits de l'Homme et ceux du citoyen ont été progressivement conquis, consolidés, approfondis, depuis la Déclaration de 1789 jusqu'au Préambule de 1946."

10 For a similar statement, see MP Yves Bur (UMP) (AN 2004b, 1312). Secularism's history as presented here, however, is not the whole story. For example the Debré Commission, the Stasi Commission, and a few MPs, argued that unity was accomplished first in the wake of the the Great War, in 1924, when the French government re-established its friendship with the Holy See. According to them, it thus took the 1905 law some 20 years to take hold in France and to completely unify the "Two Frances" into one. This does not however change the narrative presented in the text.

11 In the Debré Report 2003 and the Stasi Report 2003: the Napoleon Concordat 1802, the Guizot Law 1833 vis-à-vis the Falloux Law 1850, the Ferry law 1882, the Goblet Law 1886, the Algiers Toast 1890, the Debré Law 1959, and the International Covenant on Civil and Political Rights 1966.

12 "[L]a laïcité est le fruit d'une lutte âpre et courageuse menée par des républicains contre des forces hostiles très puissantes, que Jules Ferry dénonçait en 1882."

commissioner by the Minister of Education, alluded to this period as the "high époque of the secular and republican laws" (21).

Another important figure was Ferdinand Buisson (the appointed reporting councilor of the 1905 Law). MP Frédéric Reiss (UMP) referred explicitly to Buisson and said that Buisson had "nurtured secular education as a parent nurtures a child" by "feeding and raising it, to finally give it an identity" (AN 2004f, 1481).[13] A number of MPs saw Buisson, from the then Republican radical and radical-socialist group in Parliament, as the founder of secularism.[14] No women were mentioned, nor was the attempted separation of church and state during the Paris Commune in 1871.

Exceptionality

Regardless of the rather diverse nature of the statements presented here, and even though the Stasi Commission (2003) stated that two models of secularism opposed each other—one combative and anti-clerical, the other liberal and tolerant (11)—a consensus reigned among the republican spokespeople suggesting that the long history of secularism, whatever its specific history, had led to a profoundly rooted societal consensus and an exceptional form of secularism.[15] Secularism had been born out of a historical compromise between left wing and right wing republicans, to paraphrase MP Jean-Pierre Balligand (S) (AN 2004b, 1320).[16] According to MP Jean Glavany (S) and several other MPs, "secularism was a historical battle of reason, rationality, and free will against all sorts of fundamentalism" (AN 2004b, 1375).[17] Glavany, moreover, saw secularism as a universal value that constitutes the foundation for freedom of conscience and, to Glavany, secularism as a value was a direct outcome of progress and reason. This was something society was in need of: "I believe that what society needs is reason, rationality, a critical spirit ... Secularism is all that" (AN 2004b, 1375).[18] All this, in the words of the Debré Commission (2003a), defined the exceptionality of French secularism (28).

---

13   "L'enseignement laïque, Ferdinand Buisson l'a porté comme on porte un enfant; il l'a nourri et élevé pour lui forger une identité."
14   Some scholars have elevated Buisson to the status of the founding father (Baubérot 2004).
15   See for example Christian Vanneste (UMP) (AN 2004d, 1406).
16   For similar statements see for example MP Christian Bataille (S) (AN 2004b, 1325) and Aurillac (AN 2004b, 1384).
17   "[L]a laïcité est un combat historique de la raison, de la rationalité et du libre arbitre, contre l'obscurantisme." See also Jean-Claude Perez (S) (AN 2004b, 1331).
18   "Je pense que la société a surtout besoin de raison, de rationalité, d'esprit critique ... La laïcité, c'est tout cela."

Another related issue in the recounting of secularism's history is the silence on French colonial history; indeed, colonialism was a next-to-absent topic. The Stasi Commission (2003), however, mentioned it in passing by commenting on the unequal implementation of the Law of 1905 in Algeria.[19] The Commission thus pointed to a disturbing moment in secularism's history: "The declaration of the republican secular principles and their derogatory application in Algeria reveals a genuine contradiction in the French colonial state" (12).[20] The conclusion drawn from this excursus was that the non-application of secularism had had a direct negative impact on Islamic theology, namely "its possibility to develop in a secular society" (12).[21] While this insight could have served to problematize French history and secularism as a road to equality, tolerance, and freedom, the opposite conclusion was drawn. If anything, the problem in France today was that there was too little of France itself, especially its secularism. MP Jacques Ayrault (S), whose statement was followed by applause in the Assembly, suggested this: "Anti-Semitism, racism, hate of Islam is not the venomous fruit of too much secularism, but of too little" (AN 2004b, 1299).[22]

• • •

These statements inscribed secularism in a long republican history, where it was articulated to emanate from various historical moments from Jesus to the French Revolution. Even though one might see these historical moments as contradictory, secularism here appears to harbor a benevolent and emancipatory kernel. Secularism was both transcendental-teleological, in that it was what has always been and, as such, it served a certain purpose, and immanent, since it was the purpose itself, embodied in the Republic, in the nation, in law. It was thus articulated as a dual emancipation-separation—emancipation for the citizen from religious or ideological indoctrination (i.e., freedom from religion ensured by the state) and separation between church and state or religion and politics. Secularism was here given the status of a telos-spirit invested with agency. As such, by separating religion from the Republic it had

---

19   See Stasi 2003, 11.
20   "L'énonciation de principes républicains laïques et leur application dérogatoire sur un territoire donné sont révélateurs d'une contradiction propre à l'Etat colonial français."
21   "Ce processus interdit tout épanouissement de la théologie musulmane dans un environnement laïque."
22   "L'antisémitisme, le racisme, la haine de l'islam ne sont pas les fruits vénéneux de trop de laïcité, mais de trop peu de laïcité. (Applaudissements sur plusieurs bancs du groupe socialiste)."

offered protection and guaranteed the Republic's democratic foundation. However, in this view, secularism similarly arose organically over time and was by now embodied in the republican spirit.[23] It was both universal-civilizational (Greek-Latin/Judaeo-Christian) and particularly French (national-republican), and thus, eternally, not Islamic. As such, French republican secularism was elevated to the universal. That is, secularism's history was as much universal history as French history. The historical unfolding was made possible by the 1789 revolution, its embodiments, and its founding fathers—as if France made possible the full blooming of secularism, planted by and prepared for by the Greeks and Jesus. In addition, if French history was conflated with secularism's history, and secularism's history in its turn with universal history, not only was the demarcation between religion and politics built into French-Christian history and manifested in secularism, it was the prerequisite for democracy and women's emancipation. The secular Republic was portrayed as a yet-to-be-accomplished universal, whose prime task was to fulfill itself.

Here, the opposition to Islam, described in the previous chapter, ignored conspicuous contradictions in the articulation of French history and the history of secularism. Through discursive displacement, the other became a legitimizing moment in the implementation of secularism based on the logic of the state of emergency (see discussion about Schmitt, Chapter Two). In this regard, the unequal implementation of the Law of 1905 in Algeria that made Muslims second-class citizens was understood as a missed opportunity for Islamic theology, since it did not have the chance to modernize through secularism. The horrific Vichy regime was seen as a fluke in the otherwise progressive and emancipatory history of the Republic. The Dreyfus Affair was taken as evidence of the benevolent and anti-racist spirit of the French, and the Third Republic's imperialist and colonialist politics were simply omitted. Finally, the Revolution was not understood as the birth of the racial- and gender-divided nation-state, but as the installment of an emancipatory universal republic.

It was this kind of ideological displacement that led to Chirac's (2003b) juxtaposition of secularism with other republican accomplishments, such as universal suffrage, female suffrage, liberty of the press, liberty of association, and, thus, made even the acknowledgment of Captain Dreyfus's innocence logical. The next challenge for secularism was to further enhance equality and to liberate women. According to him: "A society's level of civilization is measured

---

23   Bowen (2007) has similarly pointed out that narratives "about laïcité give to these elements both a temporal continuity and a historical telos or purpose" (20). Bowen however has not analyzed in what ways these narratives feed into the republican-secular imaginary in terms of it as a contemporary ideological sign.

by women's status in that society" (Chirac 2003b).²⁴ It was a secular, Christian, and French understanding of what civilization entailed.

The Cornerstone of the Republic

During the parliamentary debates the imagined secularist historical kernel was thought of as embodied or waiting to be embodied in and through the French republic's cardinal values: liberty, equality, and fraternity. Chirac (2003a) explained that secularism was "both the liberty to believe and the liberty to abstain from believing"; it was both positive and negative. It was, furthermore, "signified by equality between citizens as it did not distinguish between citizens' religious belonging." Finally, secularism was "brotherly" in that "it united the French around common values, transcending any communitarianism."²⁵

PM Raffarin tuned in by arguing that these three values (liberty, equality, and brotherhood) were integral parts of secularism (AN 2004a, 1286), while MP Philippe Folliot (UDF) claimed that the words "liberty, equality, fraternity" inscribed above the entrance to the National Assembly "would not be what they were without secularism" (AN 2004b, 1315).²⁶ MP Jean-Pierre Brard (DCR) saw secularism as "the cornerstone of the republican values" (AN 2004b, 1321).²⁷

(Forced) Liberty

Chirac thus saw secularism as a total freedom of religion and expression. But if, under the heading of *total freedom of religion and expression*, a ban against religious insignia could be legitimized, what was this freedom taken to mean and where was the line between the freedom of an individual to express their religious convictions (the freedom to) and another individual's freedom to not be imposed upon by religion (freedom from)?

MP Jean-Pierre Grand (UMP) argued that the debate on the veil and secularism revealed a conflict between these two freedoms. On the one hand, Grand stated,

---

24   "Le degré de civilisation d'une société se mesure d'abord à la place qu'y occupent les femmes."
25   "Car la laïcité est la traduction la plus directe de l'exigence de liberté, d'égalité et de fraternité inscrite dans notre devise républicaine. La laïcité, c'est d'abord une totale liberté de religion et d'expression, conçue à la fois comme liberté de croire ou de ne pas croire. C'est l'égalité entre les citoyens, sans distinction de religion. C'est enfin la fraternité, la volonté de réunir les Français dans une seule collectivité, dépassant tous les communautarismes."
26   "'Liberté, Egalité, Fraternité'... ne peuvent être ce qu'elles sont sans la laïcité."
27   "Pierre angulaire des valeurs républicaines."

the state apparatus was dealing with an individual freedom—the absolute freedom of expression. On the other hand, it was a matter of a collective freedom that guaranteed social cohesion by transcending ethnic and religious conflicts. Grand concluded that when the individual freedom of expression became a collective demand or manifestation, conflict was born. This was the current state of affairs in France (AN 2004e, 1444).

For freedom, and thus secularism, to function, a certain type of sensibility was demanded. In the words of the Minister of Education Luc Ferry (UMP) (2004a), secularism implied "human dignity that could render an individual's communitarian roots abstract." This was, according to Ferry, "an abstract humanism"[28] that demanded, however, an abstracted subject that could raise her- or himself above any linguistic, cultural, religious, or ethnic origin. While Ferry stated that secularism belongs to a long republican tradition of human rights, he also suggested that secularism as a republican human right could only function insofar as the subject targeted by secularism actually was abstracted: "Secularism belongs to the republican tradition of human rights. These rights, let us repeat it, mean that each human being must be respected in his own right, in abstraction from the linguistic, cultural, ethnic, and religious community to which he belongs" (Ferry 2003).[29] Secularism was thus not only portrayed as a fundamental value of the French republic but also, in the words of PM Raffarin, "a fundamental value of French humanism" (AN 2004a, 1286).

The sort of human being described here and the human being subjected to human rights distributed by the Republic bore significant marks of Enlightenment ideals, where the common human nature was said to reside in the universal. We thus confront a freedom guaranteeing the individual citizen free conduct, insofar as this conduct is restricted to the mind of the individual and does not transgress the linguistic, cultural, ethnic or religious identities (e.g., Stasi 2003, 9). As I have argued in the preceding chapter, republican spokespeople did not see the Muslim other as an abstracted subject, making the scope for secularism's liberating potential highly restricted.

---

28 "La dignité des êtres humains dépasse toutes les appartenances communautaires: c'est cela que l'on a appelé, à juste titre, 'l'humanisme abstrait,' dans la mesure où il fait abstraction des enracinements communautaires."

29 "[L]a laïcité à la tradition républicaine des droits de l'Homme. Ces derniers, redisons le simplement, signifient que tout être humain doit être respecté en lui-même, abstraction faite de la communauté linguistique, culturelle, ethnique ou religieuse à laquelle il se sent appartenir."

Equality and Neutrality

Equality was articulated in relation to tolerance and neutrality. As the argument was laid down, for equality to prosper, for everybody to be free to choose their own religion with all the predicaments involved, the state needed to retract itself; it could not favor any one religion over the other. In their report, the Valade Commission (2004) sketched a historical lineage of neutrality. The Commission stated that neutrality derives from the Latin *neuter,* meaning neither one nor the other, and that, on a religious level, neutrality aspired to guarantee liberty through equal respect of all beliefs and to permit the harmonious coexistence of different religions (5). PM Raffarin explained that secularism implies neutrality and especially neutrality from the state officials (AN 2004a, 1286), which does not mean hostility towards religion. He claimed that neutrality is not the negation of religion (AN 2004a, 1287).

MP Guy Teissier (UMP) (2004b) suggested in a similar fashion that the respect for the neutrality of the public space made possible "a harmonious coexistence of different religions." Religious freedom thus *implied* neutrality. Teissier, moreover, made clear that secularism is not only a question of prohibitions; citizens still had the "right to choose among spiritual and philosophical options" (AN 2004b, 1324). Here the MP seems to argue that although every citizen is free to hold whatever belief they want, the respect for neutrality in the public space implied that religious symbols should be prohibited (as discussed in the previous section). In the words of MP François Bayrou (UMP), "secularism takes humanity and all humans into account" (AN 2004a, 1304).[30]

According to MP Pierre Bourguignon (S), secularism, "one of the Republic's great conquests," had no other "objective than to assure the equality of every citizen" (AN 2004e, 1455).[31] MP Yves Durand (S) stated that secularism assures equal opportunities for all the children of the Republic: "Secularism is above all the possibility given to everyone to freely dispose over his or her life and to construct his or her own destinies. Secularism is the will to give every little French girl and boy the same chance for success without distinction of their origin or religion" (AN 2004c, 1389; also see Aurillac in AN 2004c, 1384).[32]

Neutrality here appears to mean that, on the one hand, organized religion (*cultes*) under the tutelage of the state was not only not tolerated by the state

---

30   "La laïcité, c'est la prise en compte de tout l'Homme et de tous les homes."
31   "[La laïcité] n'a pas d'autre objectif que d'assurer l'égalité de tous les citoyens."
32   "La laïcité, c'est avant tout la possibilité offerte à chacun de disposer librement de sa vie et de construire son propre destin comme il le veut. La laïcité, c'est la volonté de donner à chaque petite Française, à chaque petit Français, la même chance de réussite, quelle que soit son origine ou sa religion."

but that it also positively provided for a harmonious societal foundation based on equal respect towards all religions. In this sense, secularism was thought to open up for an inclusive neutral public space, a common ground for all French people, where origin, belief, and skin color were of no importance. On the other hand, neutrality seems to have meant the removal of religious signs in public space. It was not only a question of creating a neutral and thus equal public space, the Muslim-other had to be neutral in the eyes of the Republic before entering public spaces (see Chapter Two). Here, the abstracted subject and neutrality as pillars in secularism and as a technique of government worked in tandem to demand of the Muslim-other that they reduce their religiosity to a question of "religious and philosophical options" but not visible manifestation, while it coded the neutral and equal public space with a certain conception of religiosity (Liogier 2012). In other words, the question of neutrality was displaced and transferred onto the other-citizen instead of the Republic and its official representatives (see Hennette-Vauchez and Valentin 2014; Hennette-Vauchez, Pichard, and Roman 2014).

Brotherhood, Integration and French Communitarianism

Chirac (2003a) said that *brotherhood* referred to "the will to unite all citizens into one single collectivity that overreached all sorts of communitarianism."[33] In the will to unite, brotherhood was closely linked to integration, and, in the words of the National Assembly's president, Pascal Clément (UMP), secularism was a formidable instrument that served the French model of integration (AN 2004a, 1290). According to PM Jean-Pierre Raffarin (UMP), secularism as integration was inscribed in a long French tradition. Being originally Christian, France had been enriched by the influx of different cultures: "The French tradition is an open tradition. Our country, ancient Christian soil, has been enriched, and still is, by contacts with diverse cultures, especially with women and men coming from all horizons and that, in the logic of national integration, today has become French" (AN 2004a, 1286).[34] According to MP Jean-Claude Leroy (S), the French secular brotherhood was one that integrated all citizens into a single community without distinguishing between race, origin, or belief: "Secularism, a constitutional principle and foundation of our Republic,

---

33 "C'est enfin la fraternité, la volonté de réunir les Français dans une seule collectivité, dépassant tous les communautarismes."

34 "La tradition de la France est une tradition d'ouverture. Vieille terre de chrétienté, notre pays s'est enrichi au contact de diverses cultures et continuera à le faire, notamment par l'intermédiaire de femmes et d'hommes venus de tous horizons, qui y ont aujourd'hui fait souche, dans une logique d'intégration à la nation."

is a principle of tolerance, respect, and neutrality that guarantees each and everyone's integration regardless of race, origin, of belief" (AN 2004b, 1326).³⁵

In adding integration as a foundational principle of secularism, it became an activity. It was something that could and should act. In the words of MP Daniel Vaillant (S), secularism "was an active principle of liberation and integration," it is "the heart of the republican pact" (AN 2004b, 1313).³⁶ The Valade Commission (2004) quoted the philosopher Henri Pena-Ruiz and assessed that secularism unites everyone, and followed with a quotation from the historian Jean Baubérot by which the Commission concluded that secularism was "the art of living together in a diverse society" (6). The commission, furthermore, stated that secularism's uniqueness resided in how its universal reach was coupled with the particularity of the French national community. This specificity guaranteed national cohesion, mutual respect among the French citizens, and civil peace: "In France secularism is one of the most precious principles of the Republic, guarantor of our national cohesion, of our mutual respect, and of civil peace. Through its universal reach, secularism incarnates our republican model of integration, based on an identification with the national community" (6).³⁷

Secularism was not only about rights; it was also an obligation. President Chirac (2003a) explained that it implied a sort of "reworking of the self." This meant that citizens needed to "limit public expressions of their particularities," as previously mentioned. It furthermore implied "a will to educate and for empathy—to put oneself in the place of the other."³⁸ To Chirac, that secularism implied obligations was crucial since, without this emphasis, one was easily led to believe that secularism could mean that anything goes. "To present secularism as a simple right and not as an ensemble of demands imposing themselves on everybody" was thus, according to Chirac (2003a), "to lose the sight of its importance—to open up the door for all sorts of demands."³⁹ According to PM

---

35 "La laïcité, principe constitutionnel et fondement de notre République, est un principe de tolérance, de respect et de neutralité, qui garantit l'intégration de chacun de nos concitoyens sans distinction de race, d'origine et de croyance."

36 "La laïcité n'est donc en rien une simple garantie passive. Bien au contraire, c'est un principe actif de libération et d'intégration. C'est le cœur du pacte républicain."

37 La laïcité est en France l'un des principes les plus précieux de la République, garant de notre cohésion nationale, du respect mutuel et de la paix civile. Elle incarne, par sa portée universelle, notre modèle républicain d'intégration, fondé sur l'identification à la communauté nationale.

38 "[Secularism implies] un effort sur soi: elle nécessite de mettre des limites à l'expression publique de ses propres particularités, elle nécessite de comprendre l'autre, de se mettre à sa place."

Raffarin, the Law of 2004 was a means "to mark the frontier between what was acceptable and what was not; a clear answer to those who would like impose their communitarian identity on the laws of the Republic" (AN 2004a, 1287).[40]

As a foundational value and a tool for integration, MP Hervé Mariton (UMP) claimed that secularism "was a vertical unity, a moral and spiritual foundation for society" (AN 2004d, 1402).[41] Some republican spokespeople went further: "Secularism is a sacred value of our Republic", opined André Gerin (GDR) (AN 2004b, 1217).[42] He continued by declaring that there was something sacred about the Republic and that the school ought to be "a sanctuary where the motherland, reason, and humanity melded" (AN 2004b, 1218).[43] Chirac (2003b) made similar statements. According to the President, the school was the institution per se in "molding future republican citizens in critical thinking, dialogue, and liberty ... where the key to the future is given to the young"; "it was a republican sanctuary."[44]

The *sacred* and *sanctuary* as articulated here do not necessarily have to be understood as a secularist paradox—that only religious declarations might articulate something sacred. Rather, one might understand secularism as a way to articulate, emphasize, and hegemonize a particular understanding of the Republic, to neutralize it and render any critique of secularism into a critique of France, the Republic, Human Rights, and universalism as such.

⋯

---

39   "Présenter la laïcité comme un simple droit, et non comme un ensemble d'exigences s'imposant à tous, ce serait, en effet, perdre de vue sa signification ... [c]e serait ... d'ouvrir la porte à toutes les recuperations."

40   "[L]e moyen de marquer la frontière entre ce qui est acceptable et ce qui ne l'est pas ... de répondre à ceux qui voudraient mettre leur appartenance communautaire au-dessus des lois de la République." MP Jean Dionis du Séjour (UDF) opted for the construction of an open and tolerant, but also a strong and firm secularism (AN 2004b, 1338). The Stasi Commission (2003) opted for "reasonable accommodations" allowing everyone to exercise their religious liberty (12).

41   "[U]ne unité d'une autre sorte—verticale—morale et spirituelle: c'est la laïcité."

42   "La laïcité est une valeur 'sacrée'—j'emploie le mot à dessein—de notre République."

43   "Nous devons sans crainte sanctuariser l'école, admettre qu'il y a quelque chose de 'sacré' dans la République, où se mêlent la patrie, la raison et l'humanité."

44   "[U]n sanctuaire républicain ... L'école est au premier chef le lieu d'acquisition et de transmission des valeurs que nous avons en partage. L'instrument par excellence d'enracinement de l'idée républicaine. L'espace où l'on forme les citoyens de demain à la critique, au dialogue, à la liberté. Où on leur donne les clés pour s'épanouir et maîtriser leur destin."

In this section, I have sought to highlight how secularism as a mode of governance, as a political doctrine, and as a mode of identity was articulated around liberty, equality, and brotherhood. As my analysis suggests, for secularism to function, it needed to refashion the ungovernable-other into an abstracted human being. It was only the abstracted human being that could be a proper subject benefiting from neutrality, and thus become a full member of the French community. However, it is apparent that abstraction, neutrality, and community could be thought of as universal while coded with a French particularity. The links between secularism's history, secularism as a political doctrine, and secularism as a republican universal-particular social order, created the already-accomplished secularism. One example of this is the attempt to write the official history of secularism manifested in the *Guide Républican* (SCEREN 2004). In the Guide, François Fillon, the Minister of Education, proclaimed that "the republican ideal was always modern" but constantly "needed to be enriched and actualized while conserving its cultural essence." Fillon saluted President Chirac's definition of secularism as pragmatic and firm while praising the President for having invited the republican spokespeople to ground the Republic in modernity (SCEREN 2004).

It is as if the Republic always *already-was*, and always *is-becoming* itself simultaneously. However, the Republic was not free from conflict. Ideology, communitarianism, fundamentalism, and criminality all had a hold on the Republic. The reason for the already-established order's failure to be realized was because of the imagined enemy of this very order: the Muslim-other. The French people's continued existence thus depended on the eradication of the universal order's enemy. In this sense, the Muslim-other was not only articulated to be a religious- and civilizational-other, but also a moral-other. The Muslim-other was thus seen as a post-political enemy of the historically- and naturally-established universal order manifested in the French Republic. This negative identification with the other reveals the parasitic and paradoxical base of contemporary French secularism. Secularism here needed to produce a difference and alterity that could never be overcome. While integration provided a path for the excluded-other to be included, it simultaneously produced the very markers that excluded the other from the imagined French community. Secularism as governmentality became the impetus, the stimulus of a colonial judicial regime dividing its population into two types of citizens: the *souches* and the *sujets*, the pure French and the colonial subjects (see Rouland 1994, 387).

A reading of Jean-Jacques Rousseau's *general will* clarifies the sort of reasoning in play here. The general will, Rousseau's solution for all to be free (Rousseau 1987, 141), resides in the social contract whereby individuals entering into society, by virtue of their delegated citizenship, substitute primal instincts for moral virtue (150). It is this aggregated body of citizens that amounts to the general will, meaning that this body is what constitutes the sovereign ruler, the lawgiver. Since the sovereign ipso facto is its own subject, Rousseau conceded, "the general will is always right" (160) and, subsequently, "the sovereign, by the mere fact that it exists, is always all that it should be" (150). In the case described here, the general will was coded as that of the white French and non-Muslim majority, where the Muslim-other conspicuously went against the general will. However, since the general aggregated will was the true will, the individual and potentially selfish will must be understood as a negation of the individual's true, proper will. This is why, in Rousseau's logic, "whoever refuses to obey the general will, will be forced to do so by the entire body," which "means merely that he will be forced to be free" (150). This entailed that the gaze "of his compatriots rests upon him every moment of the day" (as cited in Hulliung 2001, 3). Here a complement to the Muslim-other's forced free choice is revealed (see Chapter Three). If the other did not choose the right option, the Republic needed to force them to do so. In other words, the other-subject needed to be refashioned into abstraction.

Legislation, Education

How, then, was secularism as governance and identity to be implemented? At this stage in the analysis it should come as no surprise that its implementation was the Law of 2004. To the elected legislators, a problem going back to Rousseau's writings was posed:

> It is not enough to say to the citizens: be good. They must be taught to be so; and example itself, which is in this respect the first lesson, is not the only means to be used. Love of country is the most effective, for as I have already said, every man is virtuous when his private will is in conformity with the general will in all things, and we willingly want what is wanted by the people we love. (Rousseau 1987, 120)

By translating Rousseau's words to this specific context, the question asked was how to teach the Muslim-other to be a good and loving citizen, if it ever could. As my analysis, and those of other scholars, suggests (see Chapter 2), the Law of 2004 was explicitly aimed at educating the other of the benefits of secularism as a means to protect the other-woman from communitarian temptations. However, since secularism was not hostile towards religion, according to the republican spokespeople, the deliberations of the implementation of the Law also sought to provide a place for Islam in the Republic. These discussions were marked by a strong sense of consensus regarding the need to legislate, an urgency to legislate now, and the need to discipline Islam and Muslims through legislative pedagogy.

Consensus

Were all the republican spokespeople in agreement of what secularism really meant? When the Stasi Commission had finished its work, the Commission's president, Bernard Stasi, was content that it had reached consensus. It was a "miracle" as he put it (quoted in France 5 2003b). Baubérot, who was a member of the commission, was the only one who abstained from voting for or against the Law of 2004. He criticized the Commission's work for being too hasty, and for not allowing the different members' differing opinions to be discussed thoroughly. Baubérot wanted the law to make a distinction between a "discreet" veil and a "conspicuous" veil; then, he said, "I would have voted" (France 2 2004).

In one sense, even with only one member abstaining from voting, the word miracle seems to be a rather exaggerated or misplaced description. However, one might also understand the miracle as an expression of the fact that they managed to produce a report about secularism in the first place. For example, the Debré Commission argued that secularism evokes all kinds of "phantasms" (Debré 2003a, 11). MP Armand Jung (S) suggested that everybody was defining secularism in the light of their personal experience and their philosophical or religious opinions (AN 2004e, 1438). MP Jean Glavany (S) conceded that "if one asked the 577 deputies in the National Assembly to give a definition, one would be surprised by the diversity of answers" (AN 2004c, 1375).[45]

It appears, nonetheless, that given the overdetermined and contradictory meaning ascribed to secularism by republican spokespeople, there were few who denied its importance in what it meant to be French and what the Republic stood for. Indeed, regardless of whether republican spokespeople had a hard time grasping what exactly they were legislating about, except for legitimating a ban on wearing the veil, their seeming confusion on the matter was never discussed in detail, either by the commissions or the President. In general terms, the problem was not that *we* did not know what it was; it was that the *other* did not.

---

45   "[S]i l'on demandait aux 577 députés d'en donner une définition, on serait surpris de la diversité des réponses."

The Stasi Commission (2003) declared that French citizens in general were attached to secularism, which is why it was important that secularism was "respected and defended" every time it was "threatened" (6). The Commission, however, added that "for a number French citizens secularism was not such a familiar concept" (50).[46] Chirac (2003a) also explained that certain French citizens did not always understand what secularism stood for. Minister of Education Luc Ferry (2004a) (UMP) suggested that the meaning of secularism was ambiguous, at least outside of France, but that there was nothing wrong with it: "I know that is sometimes difficult to explain our position abroad. Secularism is often contested and appears as an exception. But we have no guilt, no shame. On the contrary, we should be proud of this French exception."[47]

MP Alain Juppé (UMP) blamed himself and his colleagues for not being sufficiently clear in what secularism meant and what values in entailed (AN 2004c, 1366). This was especially true for middle- and high-school students. MP Philippe Vuilque (S) suggested that the word *secularism*, "sadly enough, did not mean much to them at all" (AN 2004d, 1418).

A problem facing the apologists of secularism was, then, how to convince the non-believers and those who simply did not understand the merits of secularism and the universal and emancipatory bliss of the Republic. MP Yves Durand (S) asked how the MPS could explain that secularism meant both emancipation and prohibition or, rather, emancipation through prohibition: "How can we explain to the students that a secularism that sometimes forbids is also, for them, a secularism that emancipates?" (AN 2004c, 1389).[48] The solution, in the words of MP Jean-Pierre Blazy (S), was simply to be persistent and to "explain that the supreme aim of the republican ideal is human emancipation"; a path to "break free from oppression" (AN 2004a, 1447).[49]

---

46 "La laïcité n'est pas une notion familière pour nombre de nos concitoyens."

47 "Je sais que notre position est parfois difficile à faire comprendre à l'étranger. Très souvent contestée, elle apparaît comme une exception. Mais nous n'avons aucune culpabilité, aucune honte à ressentir; au contraire, nous devons tirer fierté de cette exception française."

48 "Comment leur faire comprendre que la laïcité, si elle doit quelquefois interdire, est aussi, pour eux, la laïcité qui émancipe?"

49 "Nous devons expliquer à nos concitoyens, et particulièrement à ceux qui doutent aujourd'hui, que la fin suprême visée par l'idéal républicain est l'émancipation humaine ... en même temps qu'elle [the school] lui donne les moyens de s'émanciper des tutelles et des oppressions."

Urgency

If republican discourse on secularism articulated a strong sense of consensus, an expressed urgency to act upon that consensus followed. In warlike rhetoric, President Chirac (2003b) explained this sense of urgency. For France to remain the same, the Republic needed to answer the challenges posed by "the new situation" and "diffuse tensions" in society. The response, the antidote, to the challenges of communitarianism and political religion resided in the re-establishment of the Republic's values. PM Raffarin stated that it was time for republican secularism to reaffirm its grand principles and to establish clear limits against *them*: the communitarians—the ones who seek to make politics out of religion. According to Raffarin, "if the Republic had withdrawn from action, from legislating against the veil, it would have been a grave mistake." Since the state was seen as the protector of freedom of conscience "it was even *obliged* to act," especially since gender equality was threatened—an equality that, according to the PM, "resided at the heart of the republican pact" (AN 2004b, 1287).[50] The UMP group applauded Raffarin's statement.

By recalling secularism's history, the issue of women's rights was not only the Republic's top priority; according to Chirac (2003b), it was how a society's degree of civilization was measured. He thusly reassured, "I will personally engage in this question." If the Republic did not act, Chirac claimed, "it would sacrifice its heritage, it would compromise its future, and it would lose its soul."[51] In a similar fashion, MP Yves Bur (UMP) stressed the urgency "to not give in to the staggering blows of the fundamentalists" (AN 2004b, 1312: see also Goasguen in AN, 2004d, p. 1399).[52]

The answer from the parliamentarian Left to the threats against "individual liberty and especially women's liberty was," according to MP Jean-Claude Perez (S), "to slam the door in the face of religious extremists" (AN 2004b, 1331).[53] MP Alain Néri (S) stated that the task, and even the responsibility, of

---

50 "Il faut aujourd'hui réaffirmer pour eux cette force de nos valeurs, cette force de la laïcité républicaine. Parce que l'Etat est le protecteur de la liberté de conscience, il se doit d'intervenir quand le prosélytisme, le repli communautaire, le refus d'égalité entre les sexes menacent cette liberté fondamentale qui est inscrite au cœur de notre pacte républicain ... dans la République française la religion ne peut pas et ne doit pas être un projet politique (Applaudissements sur les bancs du groupe de l'Union pour un mouvement populaire)."

51 "Elle [the Republic] y sacrifierait son héritage. Elle y compromettrait son avenir. Elle y perdrait son âme."

52 "La République n'a pas à plier sous les coups de boutoir de quelque fondamentalisme que ce soit."

53 "[L]a volonté pour claquer la porte aux extrémistes religieux, coupables de s'attaquer à nos valeurs de liberté individuelle et notamment à la liberté de la femme."

the elected MPS was "to defend secularism and liberty against" what he called "the deadly poison—fundamentalism" (AN 2004e, 1436).[54] MP Conchita Lacuey (S) agreed by saying that it was time "to fulfill the Republic's long tradition of fighting for equality, justice, and against racism by giving a final blow against fundamentalist Islam"; "the stability of the country" depended on this (AN 2004b, 1349).[55] To maintain the stability of the country, the republican sanctuary needed protection. MP André Gerin (GDR) stated that the new law would help national education to get out of its "autism," to stand up for abandoned teachers, and "to help young girls to escape from the rule of criminals and Islamists in the suburbs" (AN 2004b, 1318).[56] MP Nathalie Gautier (S) expressed a similar concern, stating that she "refused" the entry of religion into secular schools. Religious convictions were a "personal matter." Gautier moreover refused the veil because it was "a discrimination against women," especially since, according to her, "the Republic had made gender equality a constitutional principle" (AN 2004e, 1443).[57]

Legislative Pedagogy
The reaffirmation of secularism, the slamming of the door in the face of fundamentalists, the respectful announcement of French fundamental universal values was articulated into the need for action, for a law protecting the school, and the establishment of a secular-republican pedagogy explaining the necessity of the former. For example, according to MP Guy Teissier (UMP), the debate preceding the Law of 2004 was an occasion for the French to unite around the essential and to act (AN 2004b, 1324).

President Chirac (2003b) called for the respectful announcement of a clear and firm republican rule. Reform of secularism was not necessary; it was a

---

54 "Aujourd'hui, notre devoir—et notre responsabilité—est de défendre la laïcité et la liberté contre le venin mortel de l'intégrisme."
55 "[N]otre pays, qui a une longue tradition de lutte pour l'égalité, pour la justice et contre le racisme ... Pour engager ce vaste débat sur la laïcité, il fallait donner un coup d'arrêt à l'islam intégriste." For a similar statement see MP Pierre Bourgignon (S) (AN 2004e, 1456), MP Jean-Marc Ayrault (S) (AN 2004a, 1305) and Chirac (2003b).
56 "d'aider les jeunes filles à refuser de voir leur vie brimée, leur statut de femmes bridé, d'être les victimes de représailles de la part de caïds et d'islamistes."
57 "je refuse l'entrée du religieux dans l'école laïque. La conviction religieuse est une affaire privée. Or, l'école appartient à la sphère publique et ne peut être assujettie à quelque croyance que ce soit. Je refuse également la discrimination à l'égard des femmes qu'exprime le port du voile islamique, lequel fait de la femme une citoyenne de seconde zone, exclue de l'espace public, alors même que la République fait de l'égalité entre la femme et l'homme un principe constitutionnel."

matter of implementing what already was: "It is not a matter of inventing new rules or to push the boundaries of secularism. It is however a matter of respectfully announcing a rule, clear and firm, that has been a fundamental part of our customs for a very long time" (Chirac 2003b).[58] According to PM Raffarin, it was "natural" that the parliament pronounced itself through legislation on such a fundamental value as secularism. Once again accompanied by applause from the UMP benches, Raffarin stated that this soon-to-be-passed law was about to answer French expectations, "especially those of teachers and principles" (AN 2004a, 1287).

Pascal Clement (UMP), president of the National Assembly, explained that, from now on, teachers and principles could lean on clear legislation with the purpose of protecting school neutrality (AN 2004a, 1291). Besides supporting the headmasters and their personnel, Clement added that a law would permit the students in school to unite around common values instead of being separated by religious signs (AN 2004a, 1291).

In the words of MP Gabriel Biancheri (UMP), the law should not only reaffirm but "hammer home" the equality of rights between women and men (AN 2004d, 1421).[59] Following Biancheri, MP Jean Dionis du Séjour (UDF) argued that by prohibiting the veil, the legislators were clearly manifesting a refusal of communitarianism and fundamentalism and were, moreover, making possible the emancipation of Muslim women in France. As such, a prohibition of the veil would inscribe "itself in the tradition of banning circumcision and polygamy" (AN 2004b, 1337).[60] Jean-Pierre Brard (DCR) saw the ratification of the law as an occasion to put into practice "the courageous republican ancestor's convictions [in order to] ensure the continued existence of an essential republican principle, secularism" (AN 2004b, 1323).[61]

In the end, the deliberations boiled down to legislating on the Stasi Commission's (2003) proposal, in respect to freedom of conscience, "to prohibit clothes and symbols [big crosses, veils, and Kippahs] that manifest a religious

---

58   "Il ne s'agit pas d'inventer de nouvelles règles ni de déplacer les frontières de la laïcité. Il s'agit d'énoncer avec respect mais clairement et fermement une règle qui est dans nos usages et dans nos pratiques depuis très longtemps."
59   "marteler."
60   See also MP Jean Leonetti (UMP) (AN 2004b, 1319) and MP Pierre-André Périssol (UMP) (AN 2004d, 1396).
61   "nous nous placerons dans la lignée des positions courageuses de nos lointains prédécesseurs, qui ont mis en pratique … leurs convictions républicaines. Nous ferons vivre un principe républicain essentiel, la laïcité."

or political belonging" (58–59).[62] The final law, ratified in March 2004, stated that "signs or clothes by which a student conspicuously manifests a religious belonging are forbidden" (Loi n°2004-228 du 15 mars 2004).[63] The law postulated that before a student was subjected to disciplinary measurements, the student should go through a period of dialogue with the school's board of education.

To a number of republican spokespeople a simple law was not sufficient. It needed to be accompanied by other pedagogical measurements that could fight against racism, anti-Semitism, and communitarianism. Minister of Education Luc Ferry (UMP) (2004b) explained that a republican guide, *Le guide républicain*, would clarify, as he put it, "the origin, the force, and the modernity" of the principles on which the republican school rests. Ferry urged the necessity to enlarge civic education in schools to incorporate the foundational principles of secularism. Echoing Rousseau, MP Yves Durand (S) explained that the socialist MPS wanted to enforce secularism in school by making it "lovable" (AN 2004c, 1389).[64] Some MPS even expressed the belief that citizens ought to be "faithful" to secularism.[65]

When discussing the school curriculum, MP André Gerin (DCR) stated that it was "vital and urgent" to reinforce education by strengthening the bond between secularism and the Republic. The goal was to form citizens capable of "resisting economic, social, moral, and cultural pressures" (AN 2004b, 1317).[66] In addition to the new law and the secular pedagogy, MP Martine David (S) saw the need for a "formal charter of secularism and citizenship" (AN 2004c, 1390). Jean-Pierre Balligand (S) stated that the law would decide and the charter of secularism and citizenship would unite the Republic, and, as such, act as "the fourth pillar of the Republic" and undercut the communitarians

---

62 "Dans le respect de la liberté de conscience … sont interdits dans les écoles, collèges et lycées, les tenues et signes manifestant une appartenance religieuse ou politique … cette disposition serait inséparable de l'exposé des motifs suivant: Les tenues et signes religieux interdits sont les signes ostentatoires, tels que grande croix, voile ou kippa…"

63 "Dans les écoles, les collèges et les lycées publics, le port de signes ou tenues par lesquels les élèves manifestent ostensiblement une appartenance religieuse est interdit."

64 "Nous voulons aujourd'hui … renforcer la laïcité à l'écol …. si nous savons aussi la faire aimer."

65 See Teissier (AN 2004b, 1324), Bur (AN 2004b, 1312), and Brard (AN 2004b, 1322).

66 "Il est vital et urgent de redonner corps à une éducation où laïcité se conjugue avec République, pour former des citoyens, des républicains capables de résistance face à la paupérisation économique, sociale, morale et culturelle." For a similar statement see MP Martine David (S) (AN 2004c, 1390).

(AN 2004b, 1320). MP Jean Glavany (S) explained that the socialists in Parliament wanted to "organize ceremonies" around the teaching of the charter's principles. According to Glavany, these ceremonies could function as a rite of passage to celebrate the young citizen's coming of age or on gaining citizenship. It could even be a "new foundation for republican citizenship all together" (AN 2004c, 1376).[67]

An Anti-Islamic Law?

Given the conspicuous link between the law and the veil, Parliament expressed some anxiety about the law's reception in the French Muslim community. Even if the laws promoting secularism aimed at educating, integrating, and disciplining the Muslim-other into the republican unity, questions were raised about whether the law was anti-Islamic. According to the large majority of the republican spokespeople, the answer was clearly "no." Integrating Islam into the Republic in no way meant its effacement. In the words of Minister of Education Luc Ferry (UMP) (2004b), the core of the problem was that the law was aiming simultaneously at both prohibition and liberation. According to MP Jean-Pierre Brard (DCR), the law only revoked what Jules Ferry did in 1882 when he was defending the state from political Catholicism while also urging for the respect of religious Catholicism: "In 1882, Jules Ferry declared: 'We have been chosen to defend the laws of the State against a certain Catholicism that I call Political Catholicism. Religious Catholicism, however, deserves our respect and protection'" (AN 2004b, 1322).[68]

To reassure Muslims who were living under the impression that the law was stigmatizing them, MP Éric Raoult (UMP) explained the importance of telling Muslim citizens that it did not aim to exclude them but, instead, to acknowledge them (AN 2004c, 1381). MP Alain Juppé (UMP) assured every Muslim in France that the law was not against Islam (AN 2004c, 1366). Following this logic, MP Jacques Domergue (UMP) claimed that because "he respected French

---

67 "C'est pourquoi les socialistes ont proposé l'élaboration d'une charte de la laïcité, une charte que nous pourrions élaborer consensuellement ici, à partir de nos grandes lois laïques, une charte qui pourrait être enseignée, autour de laquelle on pourrait organiser des cérémonies républicaines dans nos mairies, prestation de serment à l'appui quand on accède à la majorité ou à la nationalité, donc à la citoyenneté, bref une charte de la laïcité comme instrument de base de la reconstruction de la citoyenneté."

68 "Jules Ferry dénonçait en 1882 en affirmant: 'Nous sommes institués pour défendre les droits de l'Etat contre un certain catholicisme que j'appellerai le catholicisme politique. Quant au catholicisme religieux, il a droit à notre respect et à notre protection dans la limite du contrat qui lie les cultes avec l'Etat'."

Islam and his Muslim compatriots," he would vote for the law (AN 2004d, 1420).

On the left wing of the Assembly, MP Marc Dolez (S) said that the law was "necessary" but added that its purpose was "not to judge the worth of any religion or any religious practice" (AN 2004d, 1416).[69] The prohibition of the veil in schools was thus not "to point fingers at the Muslim religion" (AN 2004d, 1416). MP André Gerin (CR) expressed a wish to create an open and modern Islam with "minarets worthy of the twenty-first century," as he put it. The short-term aim was to put an end to prayers in cellars but the long-term aim was to reach out to Muslims and to encourage them to mobilize against radical and political Islam. Gerin wanted to open up Islam to universalism, to make it tolerant and compatible with Republican ideals: "With this law we should reach out to Muslims, to work with them in a Republican reconquest, to encourage them to engage and to express themselves, to mobilize in favor of a tolerant and popular Islam that adapts to the republican ideals, to everything that is universal. Let us call upon the Muslim majority to fight against a radical and political Islam" (AN 2004b, 1317).[70]

MP Gérard Bapt (S) similarly talked about secularism as a chance for French Muslims to live a life without stigmatization (AN 2004b, 1336). According to the Stasi Commission (2003), secularism could even "spur a full intellectual blooming of Islamic thought and protect it from the constraints of power" (16).[71] In this regard, President Chirac (2003b) declared that he saw the creation of the *Conseil Francais du Culte Musulman* (CFCM) in 2003 as an important step towards the integration of Islam, but acknowledged that much remained to be done in the domain. For example, the creation of new, dignified places of worship and an imam education programme would create an "Islam rooted in French culture." MP Jean Dionis du Séjour (UDF), however, cautioned that the law was the start of a very long journey to solve the tensions between the Republic and Islam. The length of the journey was not clear, at least not to the MP, but he assured his listeners that in the end the Muslim community would adapt to the Republic, just as the Catholic community had:

---

69 "Oui, une loi est aujourd'hui nécessaire, mais évidemment pas pour juger une religion ou une pratique religieuse."

70 "Avec cette loi, nous devons tendre la main aux musulmans, pour travailler avec eux à une reconquête républicaine, pour les appeler à s'engager, à s'exprimer, à se mobiliser en faveur d'un islam tolérant et populaire, un islam qui s'adapte aux idéaux de la République, à tout ce qui portent les valeurs universelles."

71 "la laïcité peut permettre le plein épanouissement intellectuel de la pensée islamique à l'abri des contraintes du pouvoir."

"How long will the journey last? Twenty years? Fifty years? History will tell. My friends, ratifying this law is no reason to lie to ourselves. Yes, today there are tensions and difficulties between Islam and the French Republic. To deny it is to deny ... reality. Yes, the Muslim community will adapt to the Republic" (AN 2004b, 1338).[72]

• • •

The statements in these sections refer to an imagined emancipation where this secularist legislation has become a post-political moment articulated around Republic, Christianity, and nation. It was a matter of having faith in the Republic, of being truthful to it and, first and foremost, to have and to manifest a desire of belonging to it. Thus, a focus on common values and a shared destiny can be understood as an articulation of a post-political consensus performed by republican spokespeople asking for, and at the same time demanding, loyalty of the people. It was a loyalty expressed in love for and fidelity to the nation, where the legislators appear as simple technocrats implementing the imagined universal and Republican order. And for those who had lost their love and fidelity, the elected in Parliament set out, through a modern *mission civilisatrice* effectuated by law, to set them on the straight path and/or, in an Enlightened and chivalric manner, to defend the nation with legislation against threats to the love for and the fidelity to the nation.

One point to highlight here is that any pure post-politics, as Žižek has it, any "regime whose self-legitimization would have been thoroughly 'technocratic,' presenting itself as competent administration" would be utterly impossible since "any political regime needs a supplementary 'populist' level of self-legitimization" (2006). Not only is this populist or ostensibly ideological level visible in any particular articulation of the French-universal, a republican-liberal credo such as tolerance works side by side with different mechanisms and techniques that have been set in motion to establish *our* true identity, value base, or essence. And once the universal got attached to an ethnic marker, its inherent potential inequality appeared. Thus, since the Muslim-other was articulated as a civilizational and moral enemy, a national majority could rationally be articulated as the oppressed minority, or even as a potentially

---

72 "nous commençons aujourd'hui un vaste chantier ... Quelle en sera la durée? Vingt ans? Cinquante ans? L'histoire nous le dira. Mes amis, aujourd'hui, en votant cette loi, nous n'avons pas le droit de nous mentir. Oui, aujourd'hui, il y a tension et difficulté entre l'islam et la République française. Le nier, c'est nier ... la réalité française ... Oui, la communauté musulmane s'adaptera à la République française."

future minority, if the repressive minority was not tamed. Disciplining Muslims and Islam was thus not a matter of simply purifying the nation from a foreign element through a logic built on an impossible integration; it was a matter of saving and preserving humanity as such. One can thus understand the will to discipline the Muslim-other and the desire to win over the Muslim woman to the Republic as a symbolical-nationalist technique of governmentality and as a bio-political technique of governmentality to ensure the future of the French race. This relates to the concept used by Foucault to analyze how power, politics, and governance in modernity have targeted human life as a subject-object: bio-power. Bio-power seeks to capture how the state apparatus has come to treat the population based on statistics of birth and death, age curves, and health (Foucault 2001c, 1012ff). In this focus on human life and the human body resides the possibility of a radical inequality, polarity, and discrepancy (see Schmitt 2007, xxii). That is, the signifier *humanity* has the potentiality of becoming an asymmetrical sign where the one speaking in defense of universal humanity can remove the human qualities from the articulated enemy, which then renders the imagined enemy into a non-human object—into an object of bare and useless life (see Agamben 1998, 71ff). This transformation has been carried out through racial markers distinguishing the pure from the impure, but as I argue, culture and religion carry the same function in the Islamic Veil Affair (see Balibar 1991).

During the 19th and 20th centuries, the state apparatus sought to preserve the French nation's virility and racial purity from ignorant races and degenerate social classes, who were thought to procreate on a level with which the educated and civilized French could not compete. Today the imagined massive growth of the Muslim population in France would appear to reiterate this discourse of national purity and prosperity. The continuation of the Republic and civilization as such becomes a matter of containing and managing life transformed into, on the one hand, numbers and statistics, and, on the other, numbers that seemingly pose a threat to *our* survival if they are not contained. Two potential paths thus seem to have opened up. The first one promotes *le bon métissage*, a proper racial mix, by infusing the Muslim-other with republican secularism, the republican soul, so that they might become French Muslims. However, this is a path where their Muslim identity signals that they are still not fully secular French citizens. The second was to exclude the Muslim-other from the universal interiority (the school and the Republic), to strip the other of its humanity. The veiled woman had chosen not to contribute to the prosperity and continuation of the nation thus her life became useless for it. As Foucault put it: "What follows is a kind of bestialization of man achieved through the most sophisticated political techniques. For the first time in history, the possibilities of social sciences are made known, and at once it becomes possible both to protect life and to authorize a holocaust" (quoted in Agamben 1998, 3).

The imagined purification of the other through the republican ethos thus becomes a manner for the republican spokespeople to complacently rejoice in the other's desire to become like *us*. The other is thus only accepted as the image of us, but never as us. One of the results of the imaginary frontiers created through culture and religion, to paraphrase Brown (2008), is that the enlightened and universal *we* choose culture. *We* choose the particular as a personal addition to our universal identity, whilst *they*, due to their primordial culture, cannot cast culture off; they *are* culture (21). This relates closely to a point made by Camiscioli (2009), who argues that the other as an "embodied person cannot function as the abstract individual of Republican universalism" since that other's particularist identities will always potentially reappear and therefore be taken to dictate any actions or experiences of the other (10).[73] In this sense, disciplining the eternal-other opens up for a potentially endless expansion of state sovereignty.

Conclusion

In this chapter, I have analyzed republican discourse on secularism as governmentality (governance and identity). I have structured the chapter around the questions: What was secularism's articulated history? What were the conclusions drawn from this history? What was the content of secularism? What was its purpose, if there was one? If there was a purpose, how was it to be implemented?

I have tried to show the articulation of a secular-national identity channeled through the Muslim-other, making possible a self-righteous and self-legitimizing republican discourse on secularism, and leading to a legitimization of state power. The Muslim woman appears as a seemingly permanent object of desire for an expansive national judicial and identity apparatus expressed in the always accomplished but never fulfilled national ethos. The discourse of the Muslim-other thus worked to legitimize an imagined closure of a national *we*. The republican spokespeople's way to suture and maintain this imagined closure, the creation of a national ethos, was to create a secularist imaginary in which the French republican ego was fueled by a narcissistic

---

73 This point is also made by Scott (2005), who discusses the problem of abstract individualism in relation the idea of "difference of sex" during the the Parité-debates in the 1990s (4–5;11ff).

self-celebration of its own grandiosity—as if the Islamic Veil Affair was the expression of a republican neurosis, deeply protecting a traumatized subject. As such, the debate might be read as a self-therapeutical session of a subject in despair. Thus, in the words of Lionel Bailly (2009), "in the absence of a true demand, the Subject [sic], in talking, develops more and more sophisticated methods of skirting around the core issues, building upon the neurotic structures of repression and ego already in place" (169). This was expressed in the republican state apparatus' neurotic compulsion to appropriate French history and contemporary social reality, which can be read as an attempt to bring closure to the overdetermined character of discourse manifested in the republican officials' desire to neutralize a traumatic anti-Semitic, racist, imperialist, colonial, and immigration history through ideological displacement.

PART III

The Second Islamic Veil Affair

∵

CHAPTER 5

The Tip of the Iceberg

In this chapter, I analyze how the Muslim-other was articulated in neo-republican discourse on secularism during the deliberations preceding the ratification of the Law of 2010 prohibiting the Islamic full-face veil in public space. I also incorporate speeches by President Sarkozy and certain ministers preceding the deliberations in my analysis. The analysis follows the same structure as in Chapter Three. This means that I set out to reveal and understand the different discursive techniques in play when producing alterity, and how these techniques of othering worked to produce a subject to govern.

Similar to the deliberations in 2003 and 2004, the Muslim-other was construed as a post-political enemy—as a temporal, geographical, religious, national, and civilizational but still uncivilized other. Just as in the previous debate, this created a sense of exceptionality and urgency justifying a state of emergency aimed at neutralizing the other-enemy. However, while the 2003 and 2004 debates were mainly restricted to the schooling milieu, to the "sanctuary of the Republic," the later debate targeted the public sphere. Interestingly, it appeared as if the Law of 2004 did not have the effect the legislators assured it would have. In a broader sense, the Law of 2004 sought to regulate the spread of communitarianism and fundamentalism within the heart of the Republic, but the presence of the Muslim woman wearing a full-face veil in the public sphere was taken as the proof of a deep Islamization of France, as if the worst fears expressed during the previous debate had come true. Meanwhile, the legislators asserted that the Law of 2004 was a success. If the republican spokespeople had managed to neutralize and discipline the Muslim-other in schools, a newer and much more profound external-internal threat manifested itself in the public sphere. The Muslim-other was no longer a subject that solemnly threatened national cohesion and the soul of the Republic; now the Muslim-other had become a security threat, explicitly seeking to impose Sharia Law and subvert the Republic.

I structure the chapter through four interrelated questions: What was the rationale for the reasoning underlying the deliberations for the 2010–2011 law? In what ways was the Muslim woman wearing a full-face veil understood to undermine the foundation of the French Republic? What kind of identity was ascribed to her? What kind of politics (identity and technique of governance) did their ascribed identity legitimize?

New Times, Old Threats

During the Second Veil Affair, republican spokespeople understood the full-face veil as a new problem facing the secular Republic. Republican spokespeople once again set out to diagnose the situation. During these deliberations, communitarianism and fundamentalism were still articulated as important moments in the discourse of the Muslim-other, but the other's imagined sectarian and barbaric nature was emphasized. These aspects were beyond the reach of the republican model of integration.

The Return of Religion

According to Éric Besson (UMP) (2010a), the Minister of Integration and National Identity, modernity, globalization, migration, an expanding EU, and a rise in individualism caused individuals to seek meaning and solace in potentially disruptive ideologies and communities such as religious and ethnic communitarianism, which were once again articulated to destabilize and threaten national cohesion. Michèle Alliot-Marie (UMP), Minister of Justice, added that this threat could potentially tear apart the French unity of national cohesion and the will to "live together" (AN 2010a, 5369).

To Sarkozy (2008b), international society was facing two main challenges. These challenges were even more profound than the ones posed by the ideologies of the twentieth century. The first was climate change, which threatened the planet and all of humanity, and the other was the return of religion in the midst of *our* societies. Making a distinction between good and bad Muslims, Sarkozy (2008b) argued that "the return of religion was an incontrovertible reality." Communitarianism was, on the one hand, articulated as the manifestation of a manipulated religion and, on the other, as a religious manipulation of politics. Certain groups, such as Al-Qaida, wanted to impose their intolerant fundamentalism on peaceful worshippers: "The most extreme ones are terrorist networks such as Al-Qaeda. They dream of a confrontation between Islam and the West. Their aim is to dictate law and decide over people who themselves only want to practice their faith in peace (2008b)."[1]

According to Sarkozy (2008a), history revealed the dangers in mixing religion and politics. Religion used for political means had led to barbaric regimes manipulating religion for political ends:

---

1 "Certains groupes veulent imposer leur vision fondamentaliste, hégémonique, intolérante. La forme la plus extrême est celle des réseaux terroristes globaux du type Al Qaeda qui rêvent d'une confrontation Islam contre Occident, pour mieux dicter leur loi à des peuples qui ne demandent pourtant qu'à vivre leur foi dans la paix."

Historically, many crimes have been committed in the name of religion but that in reality had nothing to do with it. This was a denial, a betrayal of religion. The crimes that have been committed in the name of religion were not driven by piety; these crimes were not driven by a religious feeling, these crimes were not driven by faith; they were driven by sectarianism, fanaticism, and by the desire of unrestrained power. Often the religious feeling has been manipulated, often it has served as a pretext to achieve other objectives and to satisfy other interests. And even today, I confirm this to you, it is not the religious feeling that is dangerous, it is its utilization for regressive political ends in the service of a new barbarity.[2]

Here Sarkozy depicts a subverted religion, defined by sectarianism, fanaticism, and a will for power, whereas he links a good religion with faith, piety, and feeling. Sarkozy (2007b) was, however, clear on the point that Islam per se was not incompatible with republican and European values of democracy, free speech, and equality, but *Islamism* was. "Fundamentalism was the negation of Islam," as he liked to put it (Sarkozy 2008a). In the eyes of the President, fundamentalist Islam was understood to be steering France into a veritable clash of civilizations. The Mediterranean was particularly sensitive to cultural and religious quarrels with the potentiality of making the fantasy of the "clash of civilizations" into a "tragic reality" (2007b).[3] According to him, "the biggest problem the world was facing was how to keep fundamentalists and extremists from pushing the world into a war of religions" (Sarkozy 2008d).[4]

The Gerin Report Commission (2010) emphasized ideology and barbarity in the articulation of the Muslim-other. Communitarianism and fundamentalism were "barbaric ideologies" in the sense that they "negated the idea of

---

2 "Beaucoup de crimes dans l'Histoire ont été commis au nom de la religion, qui n'avaient en réalité rien à voir avec elle, qui étaient un reniement, qui étaient une trahison de la religion. Les crimes qui ont été commis au nom de la religion n'étaient pas dictés par la piété, ces crimes n'étaient pas dictés par le sentiment religieux, ces crimes n'étaient pas dictés par la foi; ils étaient dictés par le sectarisme, par le fanatisme, par la volonté de puissance sans limite. Souvent le sentiment religieux a été instrumentalisé, souvent il a servi de prétexte pour atteindre d'autres objectifs et pour satisfaire d'autres intérêts. Et aujourd'hui, encore, je l'affirme devant vous, ce n'est pas le sentiment religieux qui est dangereux, c'est son utilisation à des fins politiques régressives au service d'une nouvelle barbarie."
3 "Dans cette partie du monde où les religions et les traditions culturelles exacerbent souvent les passions, où le choc des civilisations peut rester à l'état de fantasme ou basculer dans la réalité la plus tragique."
4 "Le grand problème du monde, c'est d'éviter que les extrémistes fassent basculer le monde dans une guerre des religions."

progress, civilization, democracy, equality between the sexes" (22).⁵ The Commission liked to talk about communitarianism as a sect or sectarian movement. To subjugate oneself to sectarian movements of this sort had terrible consequences for the subjugated individuals, which according to the Commission, was "well known" (95).

These sorts of anti-republican developments were, said a number of MPS, the result of an over-lenient secularism. MP Éric Diard (UMP) argued that the Law of 2004 was highly ineffective. According to Diard, Salafists in France had doubled since 2004. Today, Diard said, one could count almost ten thousand of them (AN 2010b, 5397).⁶ MP Yves Albarello (UMP) talked about a communitarian melting pot, "a spanish inn," exploiting the French system.⁷ Secularism had lost sight of its objective and the Communitarians were using it to prosper (AN 2010b, 5406). In a similar fashion, MP Julien Dray (SRC) worried that secularism had become too tolerant and had inadvertently helped communitarianism take root. Religious freedom and the right to be different had become manipulative tools, rendering criticism of the full-face veil into "an act of oppression against minorities." This was, according to Dray, dangerous. If the Republic was "perceived as being constructed of a mosaic of minorities and majorities, it would lead to societal cleaveges" (AN 2010b, 5405).⁸

MP André Gerin (GDR) talked about "a French version of the Taliban that were indoctrinating French children" (AN 2010b, 5394).⁹ In addition, just like Sarkozy, he claimed that there was a good version and a bad version of Islam. Through a historical statement, he suggested that "every time a religion

---

5 "[D]es idéologies ou des systèmes de pensée qu'on peut qualifier de 'barbares' au sens où ils nient l'idée de progrès, de civilisation, de démocratie, d'égalité entre les sexes."
6 Empirical facts seemed of no importance to Diard, who, for example, stated that most European countries had prohibited the full-face veil, among them Sweden. This, at the time of writing, was simply not true. No one in Parliament however corrected Diard's false statements.
7 The French term *auberge espagnol* is here to be understood as a pejorative term for a place—tavern, hostel, or inn—where visitors come from near and far, bringing their own things, and which is normally a bit disorderly. The expression might also in this analysis be read as a tacit reference to multiculturalism.
8 "Pour certains, c'est justement au nom de la laïcité et de la liberté religieuse qu'il conviendrait de tolérer le port de la burqa. Ils arguent d'un "droit à la différence" et assimilent toute volonté de limiter le port de ce voile intégral à une volonté oppressive envers des minorités. Je ne crois pas que ce soit une bonne façon de penser, car si nous commençons par concevoir la République comme une mosaïque de majorities [sic] et de minorités, alors nous la concevons comme étant fondamentalement divisée."
9 "ces talibans français qui endoctrinent nos gamins et qui leur bourrent le crane."

had made political claims, the result had been barbarity and war" (AN 2010b, 5394).[10] In this sense, fundamentalism was a threat to Islam. Relying on a medical metaphor, he claimed, "fundamentalism was a gangrene that carried with it the germs of civil war" (AN 2010b, 5395).[11] Supposedly, an intra-Islamic war was on the verge of breaking out in the Republic.

Over T/here
During the Second Islamic Veil Affair, the location of the sectarian and barbaric communitarianism was located in poor metropolitan suburbs. Having made a political affair of the suburbs' re-integration into the Republic in the presidential campaign in 2007 (see Chapter Two), Sarkozy (2008c) stated that the Republic was divided and suggested that one of the reasons for the growing "communitarianism, precarity, and violence" was "all the handicaps that the inhabitants of the suburbs were suffering." He continued, "difficulties, insecurity, violence, suffering, and inequality made these individuals see the surrounding society as a threat." It was this that made "them turn inwards."[12]

The successful integration of the suburbs into the Republic, then, was "not only a question of secularism"; to Sarkozy it concerned "the entire future of the French democracy," "the foundational ideas of the Republic," and "the very idea of the nation."[13] While proposing that some of the reasons for the imagined threat were due to socio-economic factors, and implicitly stating that the Republic's politics of integration was failing, Sarkozy identified the deeper cause of the problem being about identity, culture and morality: "The distress does not come solely from town-planning, it is not only economic or social, it is deeper, it is also about identity, it is cultural, it is moral, in brief, it is human and not only material."[14]

---

10   "Dans notre histoire, chaque fois que le religieux a revendiqué des exigences politiques, il y a eu des barbares et il y a eu la guerre."
11   "C'est la gangrène, qui porte, selon moi, les germes de guerre civile."
12   "Il y a des quartiers en France où il y a tellement de handicaps, tellement de difficultés, tellement de précarité, tellement de violence, tellement de souffrance qu'ils se replient sur eux-mêmes, qu'ils ressentent tout ce qui leur est extérieur comme une menace. Il y a des quartiers dans notre pays, dans notre démocratie, dans notre République où l'on a moins de droits, moins de chances que les autres."
13   "Avec ce qui se passe dans ces quartiers, ce n'est pas seulement l'idée que nous nous faisons de la laïcité, c'est l'avenir de notre démocratie, c'est l'avenir d'une certaine idée de la République qui sont en jeu. C'est l'idée même de nation qui est en cause."
14   "Le malaise ne vient pas seulement de l'urbanisme et de l'architecture, il n'est pas seulement économique ou social, il est plus profond, il est aussi identitaire, il est culturel, il est moral, bref il est humain et pas seulement matériel."

The root cause of communitarianism was articulated as cultural-religious, and while the government and the parliament were using great caution in not making a monolith out of Islam, a large majority nonetheless suggested that a violent suburb was under Islamist control. Some of the most devious results of communalization and the sectarian and fundamentalist presence in the Republic's lost areas were anti-Semitism and racism.

Minister of the Interior Brice Hortefeux (UMP) pointed to an escalation in 2009 in crimes related to racism and anti-Semitism. The reason, according to the Minister, was the events in Gaza (or Israel's Operation Cast Lead) that resulted in 352 anti-Semitic acts (2009). Exactly what these acts were or how they were manifested was not spelt out. Once again, the Israel-Palestine Conflict was playing out in the Republic.[15]

Anti-Semitic acts were particularly problematic, according to Minister of Justice Michèle Alliot-Marie (UMP) (2010a), since they were offensive, not against Jews and Israelis but "against the Republic," every antisemitic act was "an insult to our values and an attack against our country." As such, anti-Semitism was the enemy of national unity since it incarnated hate and a disregard for the other.[16]

The anti-Semitism in the suburbs was thus articulated as anti-republican and as a threat towards national unity, but another sort of racism was also accounted for. MP André Gerin (GDR) explained that a sort of tyranny reigned at the borders of society. He referred to the Imam Bouziane who, in 2004, was working in Vénissieux when he preached in favor of the stoning of women and for a war against the Republic. According to Gerin, "this was an example of the venom of an anti-French, anti-white, and anti-Christian racism" (AN 2010b, 5394).[17] He stated that this supposed war against the Republic reflected itself in violence and criminality in the suburbs as seen in the riots of 2005 and suggested that the legislators ought to keep "a close watch on the relation between

---

15 In January 2009 a massive assault commenced on the Gaza strip where, the UN-appointed fact-finding mission suggested later on that year that the Israeli army had been strategically targeting civilians. This was a claim that the head of the mission, Richard Goldstone, later on withdrew but that was maintained by the other investigators in the mission. See Goldstone, 2009 and 2011. Also see previous discussions about anti-Semitism in France in Chapters 2 and 3.

16 "Il est une offense à la République qui accueille en son sein les Français de toute confession et de toute philosophie, sans jamais leur demander de renoncer à leurs convictions. Tout acte antisémite est une insulte à nos valeurs, une atteinte à notre pays."

17 "[L]a lapidation des femmes, la guerre contre la République, distillant le venin du racisme anti-France, anti-blancs et anti-chrétiens."

the mafia, drug dealers, and fundamentalism" (AN 2010b, 5395).[18] If Gerin geographically located the threat in the outskirts of metropolitan areas, he also added a temporal location, suggesting that pre-modern times reigned. The suburbs appeared as a geographical catalyst for a "medieval" culture, bringing with it racism and anti-Semitism. Fundamentalists supposedly "indoctrinated and brainwashed the minds of the inhabitants in the name of religion" (AN 2010b, 5395). They were especially controlling the minds, wills, and desires of young women—demonstrated in students contesting the biology lessons and refusing to participate in swimming lessons. Gerin stated that "feudalism reigned in the suburbs" and "young women were convicted to a life in hell" (AN 2010b, 5394).[19]

Stigmatization?

During the Second Islamic Veil Affair, space was given to some critical voices. Indeed, scholars heard by the Gerin Commission mostly sought to problematize the topic but when the presented research did not point in the direction the Commission wanted, it discredited the research. For example, the common assumption that devout French Muslims and especially French Salafists were particularly prone to violence is interesting since hearings with experts did not support these claims. According to the scholar Samir Amghar (2009), who the Gerin Commissioned had called in as a specialist during the hearings (AN 2009f, 2–10), Salafism of the early 1990s was a political and revolutionary vision connected with political and economic developments in Algeria. However, according to him, from the mid-1990s Salafism increasingly became an expression of social and political conservatism, distinct from an obsession with the conquest of the state. Amghar concluded that one should describe this movement as a sect since they withdraw from the world in order to bask in the self-assurance of their own personal sanctity and the feeling of being the chosen people. They also hold negative attitudes towards France and its professed values. Nonetheless, he stressed that the path of the Salafists was highly apolitical. The specific form of religiosity professed by the Salafists in France,

---

18 "[N]ous devrions regarder de près ce qui se passe entre les mafias, les trafiquants de drogue et l'intégrisme."

19 "Quand des jeunes filles sont contraintes à une vie d'enfer dans le quartier où elles habitent lorsqu'il s'agit de s'habiller, de vivre leurs rapports amoureux et leur sexualité, c'est le féodalisme. Quand des adolescents de treize ou quatorze ans contestent l'histoire, la biologie, les sciences naturelles, cela s'appelle du bourrage de crâne. Quand des jeunes filles sont exonérées du sport en piscine au nom du religieux, c'est le Moyen Âge contre l'école publique et laïque."

Amghar made clear, is opposed to any form of political engagement in the name of Islam. They defend an apolitical and non-violent vision of Islam. As examples, Amghar noted that they did not partake in demonstrations against the banning of the veil in 2004–2005, nor in demonstrations in relation to the Danish Cartoon Affairs. They also did not take part in the demonstrations in 2009 against the Israeli invasion of Gaza. However, this did not seem to interest the Commission. André Gerin, as the President of the Commission, answered Amghar by questioning how updated his sources were since, according to the Commission, "there was a whole forest of Islamism to discover" (AN 2009f, 8).[20]

Another example of where the Commission discredited researchers was during the hearing with the scholar Jean Baubérot. After the hearing, commissioner Jacques Myard (UMP) commented on Baubérot's input by saying that his "statements were quite disconnected from reality" (AN 2009d, 6). Baubérot had "only been considering the problem of communitarianism from the angle of secularism," ignoring "the attack against personal dignity and moreover neglecting the problem of equality between the sexes." As Baubérot seemed blind to the imagined fact that communitarians were seeking political power, Myard doubted whether Baubérot "had ever visited the field."[21]

Speaking for the Greens in Parliament, MP François de Rugy (GDR) criticized what he argued were the government's way of stigmatizing Muslims. De Rugy argued that there "was no Islamist or fundamentalist threat", that "the image of dangerous extremists lurking in every street corner was false", and "that Muslims in general were not potential extremists" (AN 2010d, 5547).[22]

Rebutting this kind of critique, MP Jacques Myard (UMP) called into question the whole idea of stigmatization of Muslims in France. According to Myard, Muslims were not stigmatized, but he himself. The presence of a veiled woman or the sight of "a man not wanting to shake hands with a woman" were

---

20 "Je ne sais pas si vos données sont parfaitement actualisées car c'est bien toute une forêt que nous découvrons."

21 "Monsieur le Professeur [Baubérot], j'ai écouté avec grand intérêt votre leçon magistrale, mais elle me semble à cent lieues d'une certaine réalité. Vous avez considéré le problème sous le seul angle de la laïcité, ignorant l'atteinte à la dignité de la personne et faisant peu de cas du problème de l'égalité des sexes … Vous ne pouvez nier qu'on soit confronté à un phénomène de communautarisation active, répondant à une volonté politique, ou bien je douterais que vous soyez allé sur le terrain."

22 "Nous ne voyons pas, dans la société française d'aujourd'hui, se lever une menace islamiste ou une menace intégriste; nous ne voyons pas de dangereux extrémistes à tous les coins de rue; nous ne voyons pas en chaque musulman un extrémiste en puissance."

examples of what made Myard feel stigmatized: "It is I who am stigmatized when I meet a veiled woman on the street" (AN 2009d, 7).²³

• • •

Neo-republican discourse on secularism, rather than relying on researchers' comments and writings, used secondhand sources from the media or public speech in general, and personal experiences to create a sort of self-referential articulation of the other. The sense of a state of emergency was created by this discourse. A global threat with its roots in the Islamic world was located inside the Republic, in the suburbs, resulting in barbarity and sectarianism. This articulation of communitarianism and Islamism as barbaric created a dangerous image of an uncontrollable Islam going berserk in the suburbs—a malevolent religion that frequently transgressed the limits of the private and the public by brainwashing its victims into an anti-republican conformity. It also implicitly articulated Christianity as a religion tamed and disciplined by secularism—a *good* religion. Islamism as sectarian created an image of a manipulating force brainwashing its victims into an anti-republican conformity. Whether the Republic was in fact socially and economically divided did not seem to matter. In a circular logic it, was a question of establishing a perception of what the Republic ought to be based on, a perception of what the Republic was, regardless of sociological reality.

The accusation that a minority was practicing racism against the majority established a sense of cultural and civilizational difference. It was a hierarchy creating the emblematic norms of the Republic: white, Christian, French. In addition to the racism and cultural supremacy embedded in this articulation, the conclusion from this logic is that as soon as a non-white-Christian-French—the Arab Muslim—criticized the Republic, it was qualified as a racist statement. Not only did this banalize the analytical category of racism and its relation to power, oppression, and privilege, it also created a censorship of the other's speech, meaning that the other may only speak as long as he or she speaks according to certain republican discursive rules that were implicitly coded as white, Christian, and French. It was argued that republican spokespeople such as André Gerin *were* the Republic embodied. Through this logic the Muslim-other was once again articulated as a post-political other, an enemy to an imagined universal republican French political order. In this sense, the Muslim-other who claimed rights to speak based on secularism,

---

23 "Mais c'est moi qui me sens stigmatisé quand je rencontre des femmes voilées dans la rue, ou que je vois des hommes refuser de serrer la main des femmes."

human rights, or freedom of speech was a manipulator seeking to subvert the true meaning of secularism by using republican and liberal values for illegitimate purposes.

Walking Coffins

An overall sentiment that a perverted religion was slowly eating into the Republic ran throughout the deliberations to the Law of 2010–2011. MP Patrice Calméjane (UMP), for example, stated that the full-face veil was the Salafists' flag (*étendard*) and was a sign of a threat (AN 2010b, 5418). MP André Gerin (GDR) concurred. As he explained to his colleagues in Parliament: "Dear colleagues, the wearing of the full veil challenges us on many levels: the dignity of women, equality between the sexes, and public order. This demonstration of fundamentalism is an indicator to the entire French society, but it is only the tip of the iceberg" (AN 2009b, 2).[24]

What about the Law of 2004? Was it not supposed to put an end to this sort of communitarian deviance? Giving testimony from the field to the Gerin Commission, Philippe Esnol (PS), mayor of Conflans-Sainte-Honorine, stated that the Law of 2004 fortunately slowed down this evolution, in particular by forbidding young girls to wear the veil in schools. Nevertheless, changing times were taken as a manifestation of the inadequacy of the law. The Mayor reported that for a couple of years he had seen two or three women wearing full-face veils and gloves. These women were walking the streets a couple of meters behind what Esnol supposed to be their polygamous husband. If the problem of veiled students in public schools was now seen as regulated (at least partly), the full-face veil was articulated as a broader problem. Esnol stated in a factual manner that the "full-face veil provokes reactions of unease among the population that views it as a provocative display of not wanting to integrate. This comportment can obviously pose problems in the public service, not only to public agencies and marriages, but also in school. How could a teacher know if the woman that presents herself behind a burqa really is the mother of the child she comes to get?" (AN, 2009b, 22).[25]

---

24 "Mes chers collègues, le port du voile intégral nous interroge à différents titres: la dignité de la femme, l'égalité des sexes et l'ordre public. Cette démonstration de fondamentalisme est un révélateur pour l'ensemble de la société française, mais ce n'est que la partie visible de l'iceberg."

25 "provoque des réactions de malaise dans la population, qui ressent cela comme l'affichage provocateur de la volonté de ne pas s'intégrer."

The question I seek to answer here is: What were the problems with the full-face veil that made it intolerable in the secular space, in public institutions, and on republican soil in general? In other words, what did the full-face veil signify beyond being a sign of a communitarian and fundamentalist challenge to the Republic? In Parliament the will to know the essence of the full-face veil took the form of two overarching questions: What did the full-face veil mean? Why do Muslim women wear it? This led the republican spokespeople into a discussion on whether the full-face veil was religious and, if it was religious, whether it negated secularism, a women's dignity or posed a security risk, regardless of its religious or non-religious nature.

A Religious and/or Political Symbol

One question that was discussed quite thoroughly during the deliberations was whether the full-face veil really was a religious symbol. Minister of Justice Michèl Alliot-Marie (UMP) stated in the Senate that the debate was "not a question of religion" (Sénat 2010b, 6731).[26] MP Jean-François Copé (UMP) suggested that wearing the full-face veil was particular in that it was not like any other piece of clothing, "like a red jacket or a pair of white pants," nor was it a religious prescription; it was "the will of extremists to attack the Republic!" (AN 2010b, 5415).[27] MP Jacques Domergue (UMP) similarly concluded that "the burqa was Medieval and archaic"; it was the sign of "Muslim proselytism" (AN 2010b, 5421). Interestingly, according to Domergue, it was "not founded upon religion."[28] From the socialist camp, Mayor Philippe Esnol (PS) proclaimed that Muslims in France had imported the full-face veil from "certain countries" and, according to him, "it did not have anything to do with the Muslim religion" (AN 2009b, 22).[29] Senator Yannick Bodin (S) stated that the wearing of the full-face veil was "not a prescription of the Quran" (Hummel 2010, 30). Rather, it was a prescription by those who wanted to "impose Sharia law and stoning all over the world."[30] MP Jean Glavany (SRC) referred to

---

26 "Ce n'est pas … une question de religion."
27 "porter le voile intégral, ce n'est pas comme choisir une veste rouge ou un pantalon blanc … le port du voile intégral n'est pas une prescription religieuse, mais la volonté des extrémistes de tester la république!"
28 "Au-delà de son caractère archaïque, moyenâgeux, la burqa a une valeur symbolique d'un prosélytisme musulman, non fondée sur la religion."
29 "qui provient de certains pays n'a, pour moi, rien à voir avec la religion musulmane."
30 "Le port du voile intégral n'est pas une prescription du Coran, c'est la prescription de ceux qui veulent que la Charia régisse tous les pays du monde, de ceux qui, implicitement, acceptent aussi la lapidation."

a statement by the CFCM and concluded that "the full-face veil had nothing to do with Islam; that it was not a Quranic prescription" (AN 2010a, 5374).³¹ MP Chantal Robin-Rodrigo (SRC) stated that the full-face veil was an "ambulating prison" ("*prison ambulante*") and unknown to Islam (AN 2010b, 5398). Senator Alima Boumediene-Thiery (S) proclaimed that the government had indadvertedly turned the question of the burqa into a denominational issue. This was wrong and misleading. The burqa had "nothing to do with Islam" or with religion, and to suggest that would only "empower the extremists" (Sénat 2010b, 6747). Boumediene-Thiery emphasized that it was urgent for the legislators to take control of the discussion. If not, the extremists would continue to claim that to prohibit the burqa "was unlawful and contrary to religious liberty."³²

MP Jean Glavany (SRC) equally concluded that invoking liberty of conscience in this case made no sense (AN 2010a, 5374). MP Jean-Christophe Lagarde (NC) accordingly suggested that, since the full-face veil was "a non-existant problem in a number of Muslim countries," it was "a political matter, a question concerning the conception of the human person and of society" (AN 2010b, 5396).³³

MP Jacques Myard (UMP) asked rhetorically if the full-face veil was a simple custom that would die out with time. Myard answered that the full-face veil was "a real political project with its roots in a society that rejects gender equality, diversity, and secularism" (AN 2010b, 5414). The full-face veil was "the first step in an anti-democratic, proselytizing mission based on religious fundamentalism with the aim of imposing religious law in the

---

31 "Tous les responsables du Conseil français du culte musulman nous l'ont dit et ... le port du voile intégral n'a rien à voir avec l'islam, ce n'est pas une prescription du Coran."

32 "Le Gouvernement, qu'il le veuille ou non, a confessionnalisé le débat sur la burqa, laissant croire aux citoyens qu'il fallait expliquer le port de ce vêtement par une radicalisation de l'islam en France. Non, la burqa n'a rien à voir avec l'islam! Merci, madame la ministre, de l'avoir rappelé tout à l'heure. C'est une grave erreur de prétendre le contraire, qui assimile une religion au fanatisme, au sectarisme, et qui nourrit en réalité l'extrémisme. Ne donnons pas aux extrémistes de tous bords l'occasion d'affirmer que l'interdiction de la burqa est une atteinte à la liberté religieuse: non, la burqa n'a rien à voir avec la liberté religieuse, pas plus qu'elle n'a à voir avec la religion! Il faut le rappeler encore et encore: la burqa est étrangère à l'islam. Elle ne saurait découler d'une prescription religieuse."

33 "Le problème du voile intégral est un problème inexistant dans un certain nombre de pays musulmans ... C'est bien l'affirmation politique d'une conception de la personne humaine, de la société, et des relations entre ses membres dont il est question lorsque nous parlons du voile intégral."

Republic." According to Myard, "allowing the full-face veil was to institutionalize intolerance."[34]

To summarize, Senator Marie-Agnès Labarre (SRC), expressing herself on the behalf of senators from CRC-SPG, stated that "the full-face veil was ideological and political, a way to impose Islamic particular law over common law" (Sénat 2010b, 6746).[35]

An Attack on the Republic's Principles and the Dignity of Women

The full-face veil was thus articulated as a manifest sign of a perverted, bad, and religious Islam that transgressed the boundaries of a proper religion. As such, it was understood as a sentimental or a cultural attempt to undermine the Republic rather than a proper judicial matter; it was not contrary to any proper laws but it was against the philosophy, principles, and values imagined to be embodied in the existing legal framework. MP Jean-Philippe Maurer (UMP), for example, declared that the legislators were "united around this question because the burqa was a weapon against liberty, democracy, and women's dignity" (AN 2010b, 5420).[36]

The Gerin Commission (2010) stated that the full-face veil was a threat against secularism in "the philosophical sense more than in a judicial manner" (93).[37] The Commission, however, argued that the full-face veil negated the principle of liberty on many levels and it was said to be an assault against *our* laws, even though no law banning it existed at the time (106). In this sense, Minister of Justice Alliot-Marie concluded that the full-face veil was incompatible with the Republic's "constitutional principles" (Sénat 2010b, 6732). According to MP Yves Albarello (UMP), the full-face veil was a "totalitarian ideology in religious clothes" that was "contesting our three values—liberty, equality, and brotherhood" (AN 2010b, 5406).[38]

---

34 "Le voile intégral va bien au-delà. Il est l'expression d'un réel projet politique d'une société fondée sur une conception rétrograde, qui rejette tout à la fois l'égalité des sexes, la mixité de la société et la laïcité, au nom d'une vision politique d'un intégrisme religieux. Le voile intégral porte la volonté politique d'imposer une loi religieuse personnelle à la République consacrée par le suffrage universel. C'est la négation du vouloir vivre ensemble, la consécration de l'intolérance institutionnalisée."

35 "Le voile intégral a en effet une fonction idéologique et politique. Il est un moyen pour ses promoteurs d'imposer leur loi 'particulière' dans l'espace public à la place de la loi commune."

36 "Nous sommes ici réunis parce que la burqa est une arme contre la liberté, contre la démocratie, contre la dignité de la femme."

37 "Une atteinte à la laïcité au sens philosophique du terme plus qu'au sens juridique."

38 "Il s'agit d'un véritable défi exprimé à l'égard de nos valeurs républicaines, à savoir un refus de celles-ci au nom d'une idéologie à habillage religieux mais en fait d'inspiration totalitaire. Une idéologie contestatrice de nos trois valeurs de liberté, d'égalité et de fraternité."

For Senator Jean-Michel Baylet (RDSE), the full-face veil was simply contrary to reason (AN 2010b, 5406). The Mayor Philippe Esnol (PS) claimed that the full-face veil did "not respect the principle of liberty or the principle of equality, and even less the principle of secularism" (AN 2009b, 22).[39] Echoing President Sarkozy, MP André Gerin (GDR) referred to the full-face veil as an "attack against our public liberties" and continued to argue that it was challenging "the Republic's fundamental principles as well as those of secularism" (AN 2009b, 2). Even if the reasons for this were "socio-economic, they were equally moral, cultural, and spiritual."[40] Gerin concluded that the full-face veil was "the triumph of barbarity over civilization"; in short, the full-face veil, the burqa, was a refusal of the Republic (AN 2010b, 5394). MP Michel Ménard (SRC) similarly advocated that the wearing of the full-face veil "undermined all the principles of the Republic" (AN 2010b, 5407).[41] MP Chantal Robin-Rodrigo (SRC) said that to "us" (the SRC-group), the Republic conceives of itself "with a bare face" (AN 2010b, 5398). The full-face veil was "a practice of a foreign time which is foreign to us." It carried with it "the negation of the French desire to live together, and negated French democratic principles." She concluded that it was "a proselytizing act, a way to affirm to others that one does not recognize oneself in common law, that it was an ostentatious manner in which to display one's rejection of the Republic."[42]

Being the embodied negation of the Republic, according to the republican spokespeople, the full-face veil posed a problem particularly concerning women's dignity. In the proposition for the establishment of the Gerin Commission, it was declared that "the full-face veil was no longer simply a question of a conspicuous religious manifestation but an attempt against women's dignity and the affirmation of femininity" (AN 2009a).[43]

---

39 "Elle ne respecte ni le principe de liberté, ni le principe d'égalité, et encore moins le principe de laïcité."

40 "Il lance un défi à notre civilisation en remettant en cause les principes fondamentaux de la République et celui de laïcité. Le port du voile intégral est une dérive de la société française, sur fond de pauvreté économique, sociale, mais également morale, culturelle et spirituelle."

41 "le port du voile intégral heurte tous les principes républicains."

42 "Pour nous, la République se conçoit à visage découvert ... Cette pratique d'un autre temps nous est étrangère, tant elle porte en elle la négation de notre désir de vivre ensemble et de nos principes démocratiques ... un acte de prosélytisme, une manière d'affirmer aux autres qu'on ne se reconnaît pas dans la loi commune, une manière ostentatoire d'afficher son rejet de la République."

43 "Il ne s'agit plus seulement d'une manifestation religieuse ostentatoire mais d'une atteinte à la dignité de la femme et à l'affirmation de la féminité."

MP Jean-François Copé (UMP) quoted a woman who had been wearing the full-face veil; according to her, Copé concluded, "it was like being imprisoned in a nightmare" (AN 2010b, 5414).[44] MP Jacques Myard (UMP) was more precise about the sartorial complications that the full-face veil posed. According to him, "nature gives everyone a face and the fact that humans have different faces actually helps them to distinguish one from another" (AN 2010b, 5398). "To mask one's face," Myard concluded, "is to not exist for one's fellow humans." It is "to negate what it meant to be a person."[45]

MP André Gerin (GDR) stated that the full-face veil constituted "an attack on public liberties and femininity" (AN, 2009b, p. 2).[46] According to Gerin, the full-face veil was "an ambulating coffin, a human muzzle" (AN 2010b, 5422).[47] MP Pierre Gosnat (GDR) similarly underlined that the full-face veil was "a clothed prison that enchained the body and the soul" (AN 2010a, 5383).[48]

In the Senate, François Fortassin (RDSE) explained that the demand to wear the full-face veil was "the symptom of a retrograde conception of woman's place in society, a symbol of the negation of her dignity" (Sénat 2010b, 6748).[49] Senator Nicole Borvo Cohen-Seat (CRC) declared that "the niqab was a symbol of alienation, of women's imprisonment as well as the negation of their dignity" (Sénat 2010b, 6737).[50] Senator Marie-Agnès Labarre (CRC), expressing herself on the behalf of senators from CRC-SPG, suggested that women wearing the full-face veil did not exist. Wearing it was "an auto-humiliation, a negation of the individual as an autonomous subject and a disruption of public order" (Sénat 2010b, 6746).[51]

While women's dignity and femininity were articulated as being constrained by the full-face veil, it seemed to pose not only a problem to public order, as

---

44   "C'est une prison qui se refermait comme dans un cauchemar."
45   "La nature donne à chacun un visage particulier qui le différencie de son voisin. Autant de visages, autant de personnes, autant de dignités. Masquer son visage, c'est disparaître, ne plus exister pour l'autre. C'est la négation de la personne."
46   "Le port du voile intégral constitue une atteinte à nos libertés publiques et à la féminité."
47   "le voile intégral est un cercueil ambulant, une muselière."
48   "une prison de tissu qui enchaîne les corps et les esprits."
49   "La revendication du port du voile intégral est d'abord le symptôme d'une conception rétrograde de la place de la femme dans la société, un symbole de la négation de sa dignité."
50   "Le port du niqab est le symbole de l'aliénation, de l'emprisonnement des femmes. Il est la négation de leur dignité."
51   "non seulement parce qu'il est impossible de l'identifier, mais aussi parce que, étant consciente de ce fait, elle proclame ainsi qu'elle se nie elle-même en tant que sujet autonome … une telle auto-humiliation est un trouble manifeste à l'ordre public."

suggested by Labarre, it was also offensive to various republican spokesperson's personal sentiments, as seen in the statements made by MP Jacques Myard (UMP), mentioned earlier. Senator Yannick Bodin (PS) told how he "felt shivers down his spine when a heterosexual couple living close to his house walked by, with the woman, like a black silhouette, behind her man and wearing the veil and gloves" (Hummel 2010, 30).[52] Bodin (SOC) added that he "could not imagine" talking to his "neighbor in black"; she simply did not belong to French society, nor did her husband for that matter (Hummel 2010, 30).[53] If it was hard to for Bodin to imagine himself talking to a neighbor in black, MP Patrice Calméjane (UMP) pondered upon what was wrong with "us"—"Westerners, French, and, republicans"—to be treated "as impure and not being given the complicity of a smile" (AN 2010b, 5418).[54] MP Jean-François Lamour (UMP), who had encountered a veiled woman he referred to as a "phantom," recounted that her presence alone was a betrayal of the human being (AN 2010b, 5419). Jean-Paul Garraud (UMP) in the Gerin Commission asked himself how he could not feel "a certain malaise" facing a person who willingly wears a piece of a cloth that, according to Garraud, "completely concealed and isolated her" (AN 2010a, 5369).[55] MP Yves Albarello (UMP) concluded that, "beyond being an offense against women," the integral veil was "an aggression towards everyone crossing its path" (AN 2010b, 5408). The message given out by the veil was clear, according to Albarello: "Western men are impure and sexually obsessed and women not wearting the burqa are prostitutes." Without giving any specific references, Albarello asked, "how anyone could accept this sort of language?"[56]

In the end, it appeared to have made little difference to why the full-face veil was worn. Minister of Justice Michèle Alliot-Marie (UMP) argued that the full-face veil, "whether worn by constraint or through free will, was contrary to

---

52 "Lorsque je les vois se promener, l'homme devant avec ses jeunes enfants, suivi par une silhouette noire intégralement voilée et gantée, j'ai froid dans le dos."

53 "Je ne me vois pas adresser la parole à ma voisine en noir: elle n'appartient pas à notre société; son mari non plus, d'ailleurs."

54 "Renversons la question: sommes-nous, nous, occidentaux, Français, concitoyens républicains, si méprisables et impurs qu'on nous refuse tout contact, toute relation, pas même la connivence d'un sourire?"

55 "Comment ne pas ressentir un malaise face à une personne qui affirme porter librement une tenue qui la dissimule et l'isole entièrement?"

56 "La burqa n'est pas seulement, on l'a dit, une injure faite à la femme; elle agresse tous ceux qui côtoient dans la rue une femme ainsi accoutrée. Pour tous, le message est clair. À l'adresse des hommes, cela veut dire: 'Vous êtes tous des impurs, pour ne pas dire des obsédés sexuels.' Pour les femmes, cela signifie: 'Vous qui ne portez pas la burqa, vous êtes des créatures dévoyées et des prostituées en puissance.' Comment peut-on accepter ce langage?"

public order" (AN 2010a, 5368). Concealing one's face was, according to the Minister, "an attack on human dignity" and "the wearing of a mask or a veil divides the national society and rejects the republican spirit that was founded on the will to live together."[57] MP Patrice Verchère (UMP) sought to be clear on this point: the niqab or the burqa, for whatever the reasons they were worn, were not in accordance with "the principles of the Republic" (AN 2010b, 5418). To MP Chantal Robin-Rodrigo (SRC), it was a matter of common sense. To hide one's face was to say: "You're a threat to me as well as I could be one to you" (AN 2010b, 5399).[58]

In addition to being a threat against republican values and women's dignity, to some MPs the full-face veil was a problematic issue for other reasons. MP Françoise Briand (UMP) referred to a robbery in 2011 involving two people dressed in burqas and sneakers. Briand concluded that the major problem with the robbers' way of dressing was that one could not identify them, since "witnesses could not even distinguish whether the perpetrators were women or men" (AN 2010b, 5413).[59] The full-face veil was not only concealing in terms of gender, it could also hide terrorists and potential child abductors. Senator Jean-Claude Peyronnet (GS) stated that, "in these times of terrorist threats" it was "treacherous to allow a completely veiled person to approach a public building" (Sénat 2010b, 6740). Because of the potential difficulties of identification, it was "a risk to let parents in full-face veils pick up their children after school."[60]

If it was problematic to let a person in a full-face veil approach a building, just walking in this piece of garment was, according to former Minister of Women's Rights (*Ministre des droits de la femme*) Yvette Roudy (PS), equally hard. The burqa, the more complete covering that did not even exist in France, "restrained vision and was an obstacle when trying to cross the street" (AN 2009f, 12). However, primarily, it was "a security issue," since no one could

---

57 "La dissimulation du visage sous un masque ou un voile intégral est contraire à l'ordre public social, qu'elle soit contrainte ou volontaire. Il porte atteinte à la dignité de la personne ... le port d'un masque ou d'un voile intégral revient à se retrancher de la société nationale, à rejeter l'esprit même de la République qui est fondé sur le désir de vivre ensemble."
58 "Rappelons tout de même que cacher son visage, c'est dire: 'Je vous perçois comme une menace.' Et cela signifie encore: 'Je peux en être une pour vous.'"
59 "Rappelez-vous, mes chers collègues, le braquage insolite du 6 février dernier où deux personnes vêtues de burqa et chaussées de baskets ... Ces malfrats n'ont pu être arrêtés, car les témoins croyaient qu'il s'agissait de femmes."
60 "En ces temps de risques terroristes, il est difficile de laisser une personne complètement voilée s'approcher d'un bâtiment public. De même, il est également impossible de lui confier ses enfants à la sortie de l'école, faute de certitude sur l'identification."

know what the veil was hiding: "It erased the identity of the woman wearing it." Such manipulation of the wearer was "Machiavellian."[61] In a similar fashion, Senator Catherine Troendle (UMP) explained the true meaning of the veil by referring to an article published in the weekly Paris-Match. The author of the article had worn a niqab for a day and explained that she felt she "no longer existed;" she had "become a phantom of herself" which caused "a profound muteness and a sense being cut off from the world" (Sénat 2010b, 6743).[62]

Voluntary Submission

Why did women put on full-face veils? MP André Gerin (GDR), as the head of the Gerin Commission, stated that it was the result of a series of negative evolutions (AN 2009d, 16). Arguing along the same lines, Senator François Fortassin (RDSE) stated that women wearing the full-face veil were all victims of a retrograde social environment (Sénat 2010b, 6748). Indeed, to many republican spokespeople, the imagined reality of the social order in the suburbs partly explained the choice of wearing the full-face veil. It was a way to submit to social pressures and a measure to protect oneself against social pressure.

MP Jean-Paul Garraud (UMP) referred to an interview with the student Antoine Sefir to analyze why women wore it. Sefir had told how she put on a piece of cloth, but not a full-face veil, when entering the suburbs. This was to "avoid insults from gangs and from her father" (as cited in AN 2010a, 5371).[63] Garraud, moreover, leaned towards a statement by Sihem Habchi (President of NPNS). According to Garraud, Habchi had declared that by placing oneself in "an ambulating ghetto", one was "respected by all and freed from harassment" (AN 2010a, 5371). Some women in full-face veils even became "more valued as members of their communitarian societies." In this way, the full-face veil became "a solution to escape daily oppression."[64] But if the social environment

---

61 "Essayez de vous promener avec une burqa: cela ne facilite pas la vision et constitue une gêne quand il faut traverser la rue. Par ailleurs, personne ne sait qui se cache sous la burqa—ce qui pose au demeurant un problème de sécurité. L'identité de la femme est gommée, la femme est masquée, elle n'existe pas—et c'est bien le but. Les manipulateurs font preuve d'une habileté machiavélique."

62 "À cet égard, le témoignage d'une journaliste de Paris Match, qui a porté le niqab pendant une journée, est saisissant: 'Je n'existe plus. Je suis le fantôme de moi-même et cette vision me plonge soudain dans un profond mutisme. Je me sens coupée du monde'."

63 "recouvrait ses cheveux d'un fichu afin ... d'échapper aux sarcasmes des bandes, ainsi qu'aux remarques de son père qui craignait le qu'en dira-t-on."

64 "En vous déplaçant dans votre ghetto ambulant, vous avez le respect de tous. Personne ne vous harcèle. On vous valorise même. Ainsi se dessine, petit à petit, pour une partie des filles, une solution pour échapper à l'oppression quotidienne."

in which these women lived prescribed the full-face veil, they, according to this way of reasoning, could hardly be wearing it through free choice. In the Gerin Report (2010), the Commission states that Islamists imposed the wearing of the full-face through "coercion by social or individual pressure," which "clearly" negated women's free choice (95).[65]

For those who did choose to wear it through free will, MP Yvette Roudy (PS) explained they were most often younger women "who believe that they are sincere" (AN 2009f, 12). However, Roudy explained, "we know that manipulation is very easy and that certain slaves come to love their chains." Wearing the full-face veil was thus the result of "a culture of organized submission and domination."[66] According to MP Yves Albarello (UMP), "it could by no means be a matter of free choice," and he emphasized "the importance of not being deceived on this point" (AN 2010b, 5406).[67]

Thus, without any empirical support, numerous MPs draw the conclusion that women who declared that they had chosen the full-face veil out of free will had supposedly been manipulated into doing so.[68] Did this mean that all women wearing the full-face veil were victims? MP Bernard Debré (UMP) concluded that women wearing the niqab or the burqa indeed are "victims of an archaic and sectarian conception of their religion" and, even worse, "victims of a social environment where the fundamental and constitutional principle of equality was unfamiliar" (AN 2010b, 5407).[69]

If women wearing the full-face veil were forced or manipulated to do so, their real desire, following this logic, must be to remove it. In the Hummel Report, senator Yannick Bodin (SOC) came to this conclusion. Referring to an observation of women traveling from Qatar to France, he is cited as saying that

---

65   "Imposé par la contrainte ou par la pression individuelle ou sociale, le voile intégral nie clairement la liberté de choix des femmes."
66   "Certaines femmes déclarent que porter le voile relève de leur liberté. Elles sont en général jeunes et d'allure très libre. Elles nous expliquent qu'il s'agit pour elles d'un choix, et elles sont probablement sincères. Mais nous savons que la manipulation est facile et que certains esclaves aiment leurs chaînes. Enfin, certains conditionnements, qui commencent très tôt, peuvent convaincre ceux qui n'auraient pas pratiqué ou éprouvé leur liberté. C'est donc une affaire de conditionnement, de soumission organisée et de domination."
67   "il ne faut pas s'y tromper. Cette dissimulation ne relève nullement d'un libre choix."
68   On the issue of free will and the veil in France, Egypt, and the US see Borghée 2012; Mahmood 2005; Ahmed 2011.
69   "Les femmes qui se revêtent du niqab ou de la burqa se situent en dehors des préceptes de la religion dont elles se revendiquent. Elles sont des victimes: victimes d'une conception archaïque et sectaire de leur religion ou, ce qui est peut-être encore plus grave, victimes d'un entourage peu conscient du principe fondamental et constitutionnel d'égalité."

these women, "one hour before landing in France, take off their veils and put on jeans and t-shirts" (in Hummel 2010, 30).⁷⁰

The understanding of these veiled women as being manipulated answered to the 2009 DCRI report's conclusion that out of the 367 women wearing the full-face veil in France, only half of them were doing so out of free will. It was also an implicit response to the more problematizing statements about the full-face veil given during the commissions' hearings. Sociologist Samir Amghar explained during the hearings with the Gerin Commission that wearing the full-face veil in France could indeed be a question of an internalized voluntary constraint, but this was not the result of external social pressures exercised by imams, big brothers, or fathers. Amghar's (2009) conclusion was that, for these women, it was a matter of behaving in a manner conforming to their faith, which was a manifestation of belonging to a religious, avant-gardist movement (34). Regardless of the conclusions of the DCRI, Amghar and others, the reigning conclusion was that communitarian pressures were negating any chance of free will, turning women into manipulated and/or consenting victims. They were articulated as mute others with no real possibility of unrestrained agency, since any sign of agency was understood as an expression of manipulation and deceitfulness.

∙ ∙ ∙

Just as with the veil half a decade earlier, the deliberations about the *what* and the *why* of the full-face veil were carried out in relation to how the French majority perceived this symbol. Even if concern was expressed for the women wearing the veils and their personal liberty, the fundamental problem with them wearing the veil was that it negated the idea of the articulated majority's self-image of what it meant to be French. French normality, French womanhood, and how to behave in French public space were implicitly articulated and established in these debates. A *normal* French person was perceived to be honest about themself, by not trying to conceal their face behind a mask. The French normal person smiled if happy and looked sad when sad, and so on. The French woman dressed in white pants or a red jacket, not in a black ghost-costume. She was acknowledging what Commissioner Gerin and others decided her femininity was. In other words, she was free to be feminine as long as she was so in the right way. French public space was a secure, democratic, and gentle agora, where gender and personal identities in general, could be

---

70 "on voit monter dans l'avion des femmes intégralement voilées qui, une heure avant d'atterrir à Paris, enlèvent leur voile pour apparaître en jeans et T-shirts."

easily detectable so as not to confuse fellow citizens and disrupt public order. The entry of the walking coffins disrupted this Republican unity and created a security risk. She was a potential bank-robber, child abductor, and terrorist, while this discursive moment coded public space as white, Christian, and French, as had the debates in 2003 and 2004.

The reasoning underlying these deliberations was in one sense theological. They sought to decide whether the full-face veil was religious and how it related to Islam. But if it was not Islamic, what was it? As I have shown in this chapter, to a large number of republican spokespeople the answer was that the full-face veil was both religious and non-religious at one and the same time. But how could this be? Was this not a conspicuous contradiction in terms? However, by replacing *religious* with *Islamic*, these statements become coherent, at least to a degree. In this logic, Islam, articulated as a potentially perpetual bad religion, since it cannot distinguish the political from the religious, the full-face veil could be articulated as a non-religious sign, but still as an *Islamic* sign—a political or ideological sign. Why political and ideological signs should be prohibited was never discussed in Parliament; it however became clear that the wearing of the Islamic full-face veil, devoid of theological meaning as French Islamic institutions assured, was not protected by the constitutionally assured freedom of conscience, nor by the European Charter on Human Rights (ECHR). In this way, banning Islamic signs or even practices in public could be legitimized since they were not *only* religious. Just as a ban could be legitimized by reference to the articulated political nature of the full-face veil, Islam's presence in France could once again legitimate a state of emergency that needed to be contained through exceptional extra-legal measures.

Here I want to highlight how the culturalized reasoning expressed in the Islamic Veil Affairs managed to inscribe the articulated differences of Islam on the very body of the Muslim-other. The first Islamic Veil Affair was partly a debate about female sexuality, where the woman's right to her own body was overshadowed by a male battle over female bodies; the second Islamic Veil Affair brought this controlling desire into the public space. MP Jacques Myard (UMP) and other MPs claimed that they felt stigmatized by the imagined Islamist expansion in France. When the MP's deliberated on the inner essence of the full-face veil, some referred to their personal discomfort when meeting a veiled woman since she was seen as a sign of this supposed expansion. However, they also desired her since her de-veiling was implicitly articulated as the key to a united France. In this regard the confessed compassion for these supposedly manipulated and controlled Muslim women appears to have been more about the republican self-image than a proper concern for these women. Whatever the articulated reason for banning the full-face veil in public, the assumption that it was legitimate to strip the Muslim woman rested on the presumption that there was a natural or essential female subjectivity imprisoned by the veil. This ideal French womanhood is not only a way of seeking to discipline female comportment, it is a way to control bodies, to create docile subjects. The Republic had no room for those who betrayed their essential true womanhood by still wearing the full-face veil.

Conclusion

In this chapter, I set out to answer the following questions: What was the rationale for the reasoning underlying the deliberations for the Law of 2010–2011? In what ways was the Muslim woman wearing a full-face veil understood to undermine the foundation of the French Republic? What kind of identity was ascribed to her? What kinds of politics (identity and technique of governance) did their ascribed identity legitimize?

Much like the 2003–2004 debates, the Republic was articulated to be on the verge of a communitarian takeover resulting in the collapse of national identity and republican unity. This time, however, the threat level had risen. Islamists were gaining ground and, although the Law of 2004 had been successful in reducing the number of veils in schools, wearing the full-face veil was now a dangerously growing practice. It was the tip of the iceberg of the implantation of Sharia Law, resulting in anti-white racism and an anti-Republican spirit. The Muslim woman wearing a full-face veil was the proof of the success of the communitarian Islamists. She was a subject without a voice. She was manipulated and controlled to the degree that talking with her was useless. Instead, a deeper understanding of her situation had to be crafted on dubious interpretations of Islam and second- and thirdhand sources; that is, on hearsay. The most striking conclusion of her attributed identity was that whilst she was taken to be a Muslim subject, her full-face veil was not. Instead, the full-face veil was articulated to be an ideological-political sign. However, by maintaining this woman's Muslim identity, she became the symbol of a Muslim-other and a political threat. Through racializing techniques, this otherness in the form of religion and race was inscribed onto her body, all of which, as will become clear in the following chapter, were crucial moments in the legitimization of the new laws on the banning the full-face veil in public spaces.

CHAPTER 6

(Re)Inventing Secularism

In the previous chapter, I showed how the Muslim-other was articulated during the deliberations preceding the Law of 2010 prohibiting the full-face veil in public space. In this chapter, I analyze how the republican spokespeople's seemingly neurotic compulsion to articulate national closure through a negative identification with the Muslim-other continued during the Second Islamic Veil Affair, and during Sarkozy's time as president in general. The similarities between the two Veil Affairs are striking in how the republican discourse on secularism was construed by what now should be a familiar reasoning about France's secular history, the content of secularism, and its implementation. However, one difference, and an important one, was that the ambiguity regarding the full-face veil's religious nature came to play a central role in how the Law of 2010 was reasoned. Republican spokespeople discussed whether secularism could actually be a founding principle for a new law. The solution was that the new law was secularist in spirit but not in legal practice.

The structure of the chapter follows the one in Chapter Four. I place emphasis on how republican discourse on secularism—as post-political governmentality as a mode of governance and as a mode of identity—was enforced and allowed to expand through the implementation of illiberal policies and laws. I end the chapter by discussing how secularist morals and values have come to be core precepts in the Republic's newly constructed integration laws and a new integration contract that third country nationals have to sign to obtain a residence permit.

The History of a Christian Civilization

During the deliberations preceding the Law of 2010, a selective reading of history defined the frames in the re-articulation of secularism's history. The President, the MPS, and the commissions all set out to objectively recount and retrace the French Republic's secular history. Taking on the role of teleological interpreters of the secular Republic's telos-spirit, republican spokespeople saw it is a matter of rerouting the Republic to its universal emancipatory path, its ideals and values. According to Sarkozy (2008g), "the Republic had been renewing itself around the same principles, the same values, and the same objectives" for two centuries. This meant that the Republic was "affirming itself in war and in peace, taking different paths, depending on the historical context, but always in search of the same ideals."¹

A Christian Nation

In Chapter Four, I showed how French secularism was constructed as a direct result of the Republic's Christian heritage, at least for the MPS from the UMP. During Sarkozy's presidency and during the second Islamic Veil Affair, this sort of articulation intensified. The Republic's Christian roots were thought to have resulted "in a secular maturity" (2007d). In the eyes of Sarkozy, France had been a great Christian nation since the baptism of Clovis (around year 490), if not *the* Christian Nation. According to him, it was undeniable; Clovis changed the destiny of France and of Europe and, throughout history "French sovereigns have had the chance to manifest their profound attachment to the Church and Saint Peter's successors."²

In 2007, Sarkozy visited the Papal Arch-Basilica of Saint John Lateran to accept *ex officio* the title of Honorary Canon, first attributed to Henri IV. Here Sarkozy (2007d) sought to embrace France's history and "the particular bond that for so long had united the French nation with the Church."³ The President stated that this symbolic act further deepened this bond, and it was "a bond visible in France." According to him, "Christianity had profoundly penetrated French society and culture, its landscape, its way of life, its architecture, and its literature." He concluded by stating that "the roots of France were essentially Christian."⁴

If Christianity was essential to France, religion was essential to civilization. Sarkozy (2008a) proclaimed that he could not think of a country "whose heritage, culture, or civilization did not derive from religion." Nor could he think of "a civilization or morality that did not have a religious origin, regardless of

---

1 "Depuis deux siècles la République, ce sont les mêmes principes, les mêmes valeurs, les mêmes objectifs, mais ce sont des priorités, des procédures, des moyens différents en fonction des époques et naturellement des circonstances … La République s'affirma dans la guerre et dans la paix mais toujours à la poursuite du même idéal."
2 "À de multiples reprises ensuite, tout au long de son histoire, les souverains français ont eu l'occasion de manifester la profondeur de l'attachement qui les liait à l'Église et aux successeurs de Pierre."
3 Other presidents who have been given the title are Général de Gaulle, Valéry Giscard d'Estaing, and Jacques Chirac.
4 "Au-delà de ces faits historiques, c'est surtout parce que la foi chrétienne a pénétré en profondeur la société française, sa culture, ses paysages, sa façon de vivre, son architecture, sa littérature, que la France entretient avec le siège apostolique une relation si particulière … Les racines de la France sont essentiellement chrétiennes."

its philosophical influences." He concluded that "in every civilization there was something religious, something universal that unites all the civilizations."[5]

To Sarkozy (2007d), "a nation that turned a blind eye towards its ethical, spiritual, and religious heritage committed a criminal act." This neglect was equal to "tearing out the roots of the nation, to lose meaning, to weaken national identity."[6] National identity was in need of symbols, and it was the President's "obligation to preserve its history" (Sarkozy 2008a).[7] In this regard, Sarkozy's (2007d) understanding of secularism was that "it should embrace France's Christian roots"; it should even "valorize them." Secularism had tried to tear up these roots, "to negate history," but it should not. A secularism of today, "a secularism that fully assumes its Christian history" was, according to Sarkozy, "a mature secularism."[8]

Historical Emancipation

Another important and additional aspect of secularism's history was the long historical struggle for equality between men and women that, together with secularism, had layed the foundation for an emancipatory path. According to the Hummel Commission (2010), examples of this included: when, in 1881, women were allowed to open a savings account without the authorization of their spouse; when women were allowed in 1965 to open a bank account and work without the authorization of their husbands; and the Algiers Ordinance in 1944 that gave women the right to vote and to be elected. These and other laws were testimony to the emancipatory history of the Republic. This progressive history was, according to the Commission, the result of a "Western humanism" that, throughout the course of history, had "integrated emancipatory demands into concrete and radical realizations of equality" (17).

---

5 "Et je ne connais pas de pays dont l'héritage, dont la culture, dont la civilisation n'aient pas de racines religieuses. Je ne connais pas de culture, pas de civilisation où la morale, même si elle incorpore bien d'autres influences philosophiques, n'ait un tant soit peu une origine religieuse. Dans le fond de chaque civilisation il y a quelque chose de religieux, quelque chose qui vient de la religion. Et dans chaque civilisation il y a aussi quelque chose d'universel, quelque chose qui la relie à toutes les autres civilisations."

6 "une Nation qui ignore l'héritage éthique, spirituel, religieux de son histoire commet un crime ... Arracher la racine, c'est perdre la signification, c'est affaiblir le ciment de l'identité nationale, c'est dessécher davantage encore les rapports sociaux qui ont tant besoin de symboles de mémoire."

7 "j'ai le devoir aussi de préserver [l'histoire]."

8 "[L]a laïcité ne saurait être la négation du passé ... n'a pas le pouvoir de couper la France de ses racines chrétiennes; elle a tenté de le faire: elle n'aurait pas dû. [A mature secularism should] assumer les racines chrétiennes de la France, et même les valoriser."

The moral imperative of history understood the full-face veil as a distressing and regressive symbol, not only a negation of women's liberty and a violation of the sacred secular Republican space but as contrary to a historically solidified Western humanism and equality.

To President Sarkozy, drawing on historical references from the political Right as well as the Left, republican history stretched far back in time and geographically incorporated everything. During Sarkozy's first campaign for president, he set out to reconstruct "a France of cathedrals and crusades, of human rights, and revolution" (quoted in Reuters 2007b).[9] In an account of the French biological lineage, the President stated that Normandie is a land where the blood of the Vikings had mixed with that of the Gauls and the Francs, while the entire time being French land, even the most French of all—according to the President (in De Cock et al. 2008, 16). The importance of properly understanding the diverse history of France was to realize that France had never given into totalitarianism, as the President put it on several occasions (in De Cock et al. 2008, 19). In recounting the true history of the Republic, Sarkozy sought to disassociate the French conservative right from its historical skeletons. The republican right of today, Sarkozy stated, was not heir to the anti-Semitic and reactionary right; instead, he made clear, the right of today was the heir of Gaullism, of Christian democracy, and of liberalism (in Loué 2008, 29). In this articulation of republican history, Sarkozy's answer to the French colonial enterprise in Africa was that, although it was a great mistake, out of it was born an embryo of a common destiny (see De Cock 2008, 32). To critics of his creative take on history, he stated that "there was only one French history because there was only one France" (quoted in Micheau 2008, 65).

⋯

These articulations of history were a way of creating a self-fulfilling, teleological, and evolutionary history of the Republic, as seen during the First Islamic Veil Affair. This was by no means restricted to the Veil Affairs. Suzanne Citron (2008) has for example shown that when republican spokespeople write national history it often turns into a proper catechism of France, a catechism of a perfect Republic (45). However, one particularity with Sarkozy's take on history was the references to all kinds of historical figures and symbolic republican events. It was a way to write a history destined for all French citizens, the creation of a "Dream Team" of republican iconic figures (De Cock et. al. 2008, 14). Françoise Micheau (2008) suggests that in doing so Sarkozy appears to

---

9 "France des cathédrales et des croisades, des droits de l'Homme et de la Révolution."

reconcile two imaginary sides of France: a right-wing, reactionary and Christian identity symbolized by Saint Louis, the Crusades, Pascal, and Cathedrals, and a leftist and secular identity symbolized by Henri IV, the Edict of Nantes, Carnot, Valmy, Voltaire, and Human Rights.

Now, seeking to unify the right block and left block was in itself nothing new; it was, for example, a principle characteristic of Charles de Gaulle's presidency (Gaffney, 2010). Nonetheless, French history recounted in this manner means that it was more than just a battle of particular political struggles, local conflicts, strikes, unions, and resistance and issues like women's right to vote, the right to abortion, and the right to work were signals of the Republic fulfilling itself. The universal thus seemed to need the Republic's particularity to bloom. As Laurence de Cock (2008) has put it, Sarkozy's universalist speech with archaic and racist undertones bears witness to a paternalistic and ethnocentric posture that allowed the president to reactivate the idea of a civilizing mission (32). As such, one can undersand this as a continuation of secularism as post-politics seen in 2003–2004. The political order defended by Sarkozy, implemented, and maintained through the secular Republic, was the natural manifestation of a universal morality and Western humanism. To oppose this historical unfolding was to be against the natural order embodied by the Republic; it was a moral and political crime. This logic thus further strengthened the image of Sarkozy and other republican spokespeople as the administrators of the universal, while a critic of them—the Muslim-other—was an un-natural anomaly who had forsaken their right to partake in society.

The Motor of Limited Tolerance

How were secularism and the purpose of secularism articulated during the Sarkozy era and the Second Islamic Veil Affair? While being an important moment for the legislative debates in 2010–2011, secularism occupied a discursive place that was both unobtrusive and conspicuous. Secularism defined the overall matrix for how to understand the necessity of a new law. But as a secularist law would indadvertedly acknowledge the full-face veil as religious, it could not be used as the legal ground for a new law prohibiting the full-face veil in public space.

Respecting a Value, Respecting a Principle
According to President Sarkozy, secularism was "the value base of France" (quoted in TF1 2007). As such, it was composed of, on the one hand, "the separation between the temporal and the spiritual" and, on the other, "gender

equality."[10] Sarkozy (2008d), moreover, stated that secularism, as "a highly valued state neutrality," respected religion and all citizens, even the non-believers and the atheists."[11]

To Sarkozy (2010a), secularism was therefore not "the negation or rejection of religiosity." He "had no business in expressing preference for any religion"; he needed to "respect them all" (Sarkozy 2008a).[12] As the foundation of French values, he moreover stated that secularism had become a condition for social peace and it was "an essential value of our identity" (Sarkozy 2010a).[13]

The Gerin Commission (2010) followed suit in stating that secularism was a "foundational principle" in the construction of French "peaceful coexistence" (88).[14] The Minister of the Interior, Michèle Alliot-Marie (2007b), referred to secularism as a central component in the "French Pact." This pact referred to the principle of peaceful coexistence, which came with some obligations, especially the active refusal of communitarianism and the will to integrate. In order to live together in a peaceful society it was essential "to accept the gaze of the other," as the Minister put it (Alliot-Marie 2010d). This was "not a question of security," nor was it "a question of religion." Since France was secular, "France assured the respect of all religions."

Diversity, Positive Secularism and Tolerance

Sarkozy often referred to France as a diverse country. Diversity was not only a fact, something that France *was*, it was a practice and a value. Diversity was a result of secularism in that it promoted a plural religious landscape. To Sarkozy (2008a), then, diversity was a "Western value," and a value that "should be shared by all civilizations." According to him, this value was respected in creating the *Conseil français du culte musulman* (CFCM) and it was this value that inspired him in his work to facilitate the construction of mosques to create decent places of worship. Diversity was in his eyes "a civilizational necessity."[15]

---

10 "Nous avons un socle de valeurs: la laïcité, la séparation du temporel et du spirituel, l'égalité entre la femme et l'homme."
11 "Personne ne veut remettre en cause la laïcité. Personne ne veut abîmer ce trésor trop précieux qu'est la neutralité de l'Etat, le respect de toutes les croyances, comme celui de la non-croyance, la liberté de pratiquer comme celle d'être athée."
12 "Je n'ai pas à exprimer ma préférence pour une croyance plutôt que pour une autre. Je dois les respecter toutes."
13 "La laïcité c'est une composante essentielle de notre identité."
14 "Un principe moteur dans la construction de notre vivre-ensemble."
15 "une valeur occidentale … qui doit être commune à toutes les civilisations. C'est une valeur que j'ai voulu faire respecter en France en créant le Conseil du culte musulman. C'est la valeur qui m'inspire quand je veux faciliter la construction de mosquées en France pour

Sarkozy (2008b) stated that he "more than anyone had contributed to the emergence of a French Islam."[16] Moreover, diversity, the "civilizational necessity," sprung out of secularism. Secularism was, according to Sarkozy (2007c), "not a prohibition;" it was "first of all a right, the right to believe or not to believe."[17] But there was more to it; to Sarkozy secularism was also a liberty or, more specifically, as several liberties—a mix of positive and negative liberties. Secularism was "a liberty to not be offended by a fellow citizen's conspicuous religious practice; the liberty for parents to educate their children according to their convictions"; and, finally, "the liberty not to be discriminated against on the basis of one's beliefs" (Sarkozy 2007d).[18] Secularism, then, guaranteed the equilibrium between religion-religion as well as between religion-secularism (Sarkozy 2007e). It was in this sense a "double right," as the he put it, and, in the Republic, religious voices were free to express themselves by the fact that religion was separated from the state (Sarkozy 2007c).

Sarkozy called his take on secularism *positive*. A positive vision of secularism was "the opposite of an aggressive and sectarian secularism" (Sarkozy 2007c). Positive secularism was "not about changing the great equilibrium established by the Law of 1905." This, according to him, was not what the people wanted and not what religion demanded of secularism. It was, rather, "a question about searching for dialogue between the established religions in France and" facilitating "the contemporary life of practitioners."[19] Positive secularism was, according to Sarkozy (2008f), "a secularism that respects, a secularism that unites, a secularism that invites dialogue, and not a secularism that excludes."[20]

---

que les musulmans français puissent prier dans des lieux de culte décents ... La diversité est une nécessité civilisatrice."

16 "Plus qu'aucun autre, j'ai contribué à l'émergence d'un islam de France."

17 "Ce n'est pas une interdiction la laïcité, c'est d'abord un droit. Le droit de ne pas croire et le droit de croire."

18 "La laïcité est aujourd'hui une liberté: la liberté de croire ou de ne pas croire, la liberté de pratiquer une religion et la liberté d'en changer ... la liberté de ne pas être heurté dans sa conscience par des pratiques ostentatoires, la liberté pour les parents de faire donner à leurs enfants une éducation conforme à leurs convictions, la liberté de ne pas être discriminé par l'administration en fonction de sa croyance."

19 "d'une vision agressive et sectaire de la laïcité. Il ne s'agit pas de modifier les grands équilibres de la loi de 1905. Il s'agit en revanche de rechercher le dialogue avec les grandes religions de France et d'avoir pour principe de faciliter la vie quotidienne des grands courants spirituels plutôt que de chercher à le leur compliquer."

20 "[U]ne laïcité qui respecte, une laïcité qui rassemble, une laïcité qui dialogue, et pas une laïcité qui exclut ou qui dénonce."

For these reasons, then, those seeing secularism as something sectarian or ideological were "profoundly mistaken" (Sarkozy 2007c).[21]

Tolerance and inclusion, in their turn, demanded not only respect for other convictions but also the will and desire to take these issues seriously. Thus, for Sarkozy (2008d), "these questions were too important to allow approximations, amalgams, or simplicities." This, he explained, "was why the Republic, by inventing secularism," allowed its citizens to be both profoundly religious and French at the same time (Sarkozy 2008d).[22]

Secularism, invented by the Republic, thus demanded informed citizens to conform, and tolerance was what allowed informed citizens to manage their differences. Secularism as a double right involved a potential destabilization of social cohesion, since the right of one citizen to practice a religion might go against another's right of being free from religious influence. Thus, citizens who wished to practice their religion in the public space were free to do so as long as they respected the rights of and neutrality of others. Sarkozy (2010a) accordingly stated that religions not only needed to conform to "our" laws, they also needed to conform to "our" principles and "our" values.

Following the law is one thing, but how could one ensure that citizens follow the values and principles of the Republic? The answer is found in the access to citizenship, and in secularism's benevolence. For those who were the subject of the debate, access to secularism demanded services in return—principally, respect for it. According to Sarkozy (2007a), here referring to communitarianism, this meant that "no intermediary body, however legitimate it might be, could ever be allowed to create a wall between the citizen and the state."[23] Supposedly, secularism was built on a direct link of trust between the individual and the state, and for an individual to break this trust was to betray the trust of the Republic. This could result in expulsion from the Republic's territory: "Those who do not accept French secularism are not welcome on the territory of the French Republic" (Sarkozy 2007a).[24] Sarkozy (2009b), furthermore,

---

21 In a similar fashion, Minister of the Interior Alliot-Marie accordingly urged for a secularism of tolerance instead of ignorance: "Une laïcité non d'ignorance mais de tolérance" (Alliot-Marie 2007).

22 "respect ... d'autrui, doit conduire chacun ... à porter une réelle attention à l'exactitude des propos ... Ces questions sont d'une importance trop grande, pour que l'on puisse se permettre les approximations, les amalgames, les raccourcis ... cette République qui, en inventant la laïcité, vous permet d'être à la fois profondément juif et Français de tout cœur."

23 "En France, aucun corps intermédiaire, aussi légitime qu'il soit, ne peut faire écran entre le citoyen et l'Etat."

24 "Ceux qui ne respectent pas la laïcité à la française ne sont pas les bienvenus sur le territoire de la République française."

accentuated that the non-acceptance of secularism would result in deportation from France, at least "for those who had come there to incite violence and hate."[25]

The Gerin Commission made similar statements. To them the principle of secularism prohibited anyone "from claiming precedence for religious belief over the common rules" (Gerin 2010, 89). Since the Republic respected all beliefs, citizens also needed to respect the "duty of discretion when practicing their religion publicly."[26]

Faith, Hope, and Unity

The French Republic was supposed to remain neutral with regard to religion. The President, the Gerin Commission, and a large number of MPS proclaimed that "for public servants freedom of expression was more restrained than for the average citizen" (Gerin 2010, 89).[27] How did statements of this kind (stating that public agents were not to carry any religious emblem) match up with the President's and other leading republican spokespeople's obsession with religion, especially with Islam and Christianity? During his political career, Sarkozy had declared himself a devout, practicing Catholic. He was "passionate" about the "spiritual question," as he put it (Sarkozy 2007e). However, to "take the risk of writing about this subject," as he did as Minister of Finance, was not "to insult the principle of secularism," he said (Sarkozy 2007c). Rather, it was "to provide a path to avoid a religious war between Islam and the West" (Sarkozy 2008e).[28]

Sarkozy was not alone in confessing his Christian faith. Minister of the Interior Michèle Alliot-Marie (UMP) confessed that in her "private sphere" she was Catholic (quoted in Guénois 2008 et al). Being Christian was fully compatible with secularism since secularism and Christianity shared the same historical-tolerant lineage. Alliot-Marie recounted how she had seen tolerance at work in

---

25 "seront expulsés tous ceux qui viendront en France pour appeler à la violence et à la haine de l'autre."
26 "le principe de laïcité interdit à quiconque de se prévaloir de ses croyances religieuses pour s'affranchir des règles communes régissant les relations entre collectivités publiques et particuliers. La République respecte bien toutes les croyances mais, en contrepartie, les citoyens doivent aussi respecter un devoir de discrétion dans l'extériorisation de leurs convictions religieuses."
27 "Les agents publics et les usagers se trouvent ainsi dans le cadre de leur service dans une situation juridique différente, la liberté d'expression des agents publics étant beaucoup plus restreinte que celle des usagers."
28 "Pour éviter la guerre des religions entre l'Islam et l'Occident."

her hometown of Saint-Jean-de-Luz. Here, "no one revolted against the priest partaking in republican inaugurations or when the Mayor presided over religious festivals."[29] According to Alliot-Marie, her way of "practicing religion was non-conspicuous." Alliot-Marie was "as against the public display of one's religion as she was against hypocrisy." She did not wish to make her "religion into an element of billposting or reclamation, but neither did she want to hide her religious identity."[30]

This gives rise to the question of whether this is an obvious contradiction in terms—that state officials continuously declared their religious affiliation while at the same time declared that state officials were forbidden to bring religion into the public sphere? The answer to this question is that one kind of religion, an imagined non-conspicuous religion, was not only acceptable; it was, in the words of the President, "profoundly respectable" (Sarkozy 2009b). A respectable religion was a good religion, and, according to a good religion, "it is scandalous to kill or exclude" (Sarkozy 2008e). Sarkozy even said that "not one single word in the Torah, the Bible or the Quran advocated violence, hate, or extremism."[31] If there was no violent kernel inherent in religion, the President said, "religious attachment was no more responsible for fanaticism than the national feeling was the cause of nationalism" (Sarkozy 2008a).[32]

A respectable religion, according to Sakozy (2007d) was a religion promoting faith, hope, and unity. According top him, this "was one of the most important questions of our time" (2007d). To this, he added: "Since the Enlightenment, Europe had experienced many diverse ideologies." However, it "was hope that had led to a better world, hope in human emancipation, democracy, technological progress, the enhancement of economic and social conditions, and in secular morality."[33] Sarkozy (2008d) went on to argue that

---

29 "Cette idée de la tolérance, je l'ai vécue d'abord chez moi à Saint-Jean-de-Luz, où personne ne s'émeut que les grandes cérémonies religieuses soient présidées par le maire et les inaugurations bénies par le cure."

30 "Je suis contre l'affichage mais je suis aussi contre l'hypocrisie. Je ne me cache pas. Je ne souhaite pas non plus en faire un élément d'affichage ou de récupération" (quoted in Guénois 2008 et al)."

31 "qu'il était scandaleux de tuer, d'exclure au nom des religions. J'ai dit qu'il n'y a pas un mot de la Torah, pas un mot de la Bible, pas un mot du Coran qui prône la violence, la haine et l'extrémisme."

32 "Le sentiment religieux n'est pas plus condamnable à cause du fanatisme que le sentiment national ne l'est à cause du nationalisme."

33 "l'espérance est l'une des questions les plus importantes de notre temps. Depuis le siècle des Lumières, l'Europe a expérimenté tant d'idéologies! Elle a mis successivement ses espoirs dans l'émancipation des individus, dans la démocratie, dans le progrès technique, dans l'amélioration des conditions économiques et sociales, dans la morale laïque."

these modernist achievements were "gravely distorted under the rule of Communism and Nazism," primarily due to "a lack of God and religion" since Communism proclaimed that "religion was an instrument in class domination" and Nazism "believed in racial hierarchy." These were "propositions radically incompatible with Judeo-Christian monotheism."[34]

In this crash course in the contemporary history of European ideology, Sarkozy (2007d) stated that "none of these different perspectives have been able to tackle the most profound need of humanity," namely "to find a meaning for life."[35] In the eyes of Sarkozy (2010e), the direct function of religion in the Republic could be to provide consolation for domestic hardships, especially for the "devastating situation" in the suburbs. In the suburbs, "the law of the jungle ruled—the law of the strongest, the smartest, and the most cynical." This was "contrary to liberty, equality, fraternity, and civilization."[36] Today, Sarkozy (2007d) proclaimed, "a progressive dissatisfaction was spreading in the rural parishes." "The suburbs were a spiritual desert marked by the disappearance of patronage, and a shortage of priests." This situation did not make the French happier. The Republic should instead be directed to ensure that "many men and women have hope." On several occasions, he said that "A man of faith was a man of hope."[37]

Sarkozy accentuated the importance of hope by explaining how it could be the foundation and guiding light for France in the twenty-first century—internationally and domestically. According to him, France had been "since time immemorial a generous and intelligent light glowing all over the globe" (2007d). This was why, he suggested, France needed "fully practicing Catholics who could make people realize that the future was not something to fear." People of faith had "a special virtue and an instinctive morality." They "got up every morning to construct a more just and generous world and they could inspire others."[38]

---

34 "Le communisme voyait la religion comme un instrument de domination d'une classe sur une autre, et l'on sait les malheurs auxquels cette théorie a conduit. Le nazisme croyait dans la hiérarchie des races, une proposition radicalement incompatible avec le monothéisme judéo-chrétien."

35 "Aucune de ces différentes perspectives ... n'a été en mesure de combler le besoin profond des hommes et des femmes de trouver un sens à l'existence."

36 "La loi de la jungle, la loi du plus fort, du plus malin, du plus cynique, c'est le contraire de la liberté, de l'égalité, de la fraternité, c'est le contraire de la civilization."

37 "La désaffection progressive des paroisses rurales, le désert spirituel des banlieues, la disparition des patronages, la pénurie de prêtres n'ont pas rendu les Français plus heureux, c'est une evidence... l'intérêt de la République, c'est qu'il y ait beaucoup d'hommes et de femmes qui espèrent... un Homme qui croit, c'est un Homme qui espère."

38 "Depuis toujours, la France rayonne à travers le monde par la générosité et par l'intelligence. C'est pourquoi elle a besoin de catholiques pleinement chrétiens, et de chrétiens

Sarkozy (2010e) seemed to declare a missionary desire—a mission to counteract a decline in faith and hope with "the purpose of giving hope to all those who have lost it to forge a common destiny."[39] He moreover explained that, by having faith in common values and ideals, the French could focus on what they had in common instead of on the difficulties separating them. This had "always been the calling of France as well as the mission of the Church."[40]

When talking about hope and faith in general terms, Sarkozy mostly referred to Christianity and a Judeo-Christian civilization. Islam and Muslims were occasionally included. As he said, "although Christians, Jews, and Muslims do not believe in God in the same manner, they nonetheless address their prayers to the same one" (2008a). It was "the unique God of the books, a transcendent God that occupies the thoughts of every man, a God that does not enslave but liberates, a God that was against self-pride and man's madness, a God who give men a message of humility, of love, of peace, of tolerance, of respect, and of brotherhood." Religion, faith, and hope could be what might unite a France on the verge on entering into a "clash of civilizations."[41]

Sarkozy saw the role of Islam not only as important in the manner stated above (i.e., to provide for personal solace to Muslims), he further ascribed a certain importance in Islamic institutions for maintaining social cohesion. In a speech at the Paris Mosque, Sarkozy (2007b) declared that, thanks to the French Muslims, "France had not seen any escalating tensions between Muslims and non-Muslims." He did not deny that islamophobia existed within the Republic; he was however convinced that "a large majority of the French wanted to counteract it."[42] Furthermore, he stated, "the Paris Mosque had its own

---

pleinement actifs. La France a besoin de croire à nouveau qu'elle n'a pas à subir l'avenir, parce qu'elle a à le construire. C'est pourquoi elle a besoin du témoignage de ceux qui, portés par une espérance qui les dépasse, se remettent en route chaque matin pour construire un monde plus juste et plus généreux."

39 "La rendre à tous ceux qui aujourd'hui l'ont perdue, voilà notre devoir commun."
40 "C'est depuis toujours la vocation de la France. C'est depuis toujours la mission de l'Église."
41 "Sans doute, musulmans, juifs et chrétiens ne croient-ils pas en Dieu de la même façon … c'est bien le même Dieu auquel s'adressent leurs prières … [L]e Dieu unique des religions du Livre, Dieu transcendant qui est dans la pensée et dans le coeur de chaque Homme, Dieu qui n'asservit pas l'Homme mais qui le libère, Dieu qui est le rempart contre l'orgueil démesuré et la folie des Hommes, Dieu qui par-delà toutes les différences ne cesse de délivrer à tous les Hommes un message d'humilité et d'amour, un message de paix et de fraternité, un message de tolérance et de respect."
42 "Grâce à vous, notre pays ne connaît aucune montée de tension dans les rapports entre musulmans et non musulmans. Certes, des cas d'islamophobie existent je ne le nie pas. Mais il y a un très large consensus dans la société française pour les combattre."

way of finding its place within society." The Mosque had shown that France was a country where Islam was compatible with French values such as secularism, tolerance, and the respect for other people: "Islam was a religion that calmly professed a message of love and of peace" (Sarkozy 2007e).[43] Minister of the Interior Brice Hortefeux (UMP) (2010) similarly suggested that the supposed "good relations between French Islam and the Republic did not happen by chance, they were the incarnation of the founding values of peaceful coexistence" made possible by secularism.[44]

If religion, especially in the eyes of President Sarkozy, brought with it faith, hope, and unity, it was also a source for morality and norms. Religion has a traditional, ethical foundation that in modern and secular times could maintain the Republic on a righteous path. This was because a secular morality "deprived of transcendence" was more exposed than religious morality to "historical contingencies and, in the end, decadence" (Sarkozy 2007d).[45] According to Sarkozy, it was in religion that the universal core of all civilizations resided. This was also why "a school teacher could never replace a vicar or a priest in teaching morality, in teaching children to distinguish between good and bad."[46] Sarkozy (2008a) saw a very specific usage of religion in the Republic. Religion could remind humanity what it was to be universal, which was a fact, even a truth. This truth could moreover "be a tool in the fight against barbarity."

To those criticizing him for putting Christianity before secularism and the Republic, Sarkozy (2008d) posed the question of whether "secularism demanded of the President to talk only about highway security, public deficits, spatial politics without talking about essential things, like life, civilization, love, and hope."[47] In a self-evident and pragmatic manner, he set out to prove that the spiritual question was a fundamental one for humanity: "Why else would the

---

43 "un message d'amour, un message de paix."
44 "ces bonnes relations entre l'islam de France et la République ne sont pas le fruit du hasard. Elles sont l'incarnation des valeurs qui fondent notre vivre-ensemble."
45 "Et je veux dire également que, s'il existe incontestablement une morale humaine indépendante de la morale religieuse, la République a intérêt à ce qu'il existe aussi une réflexion morale inspirée de convictions religieuses ... surtout parce qu'une morale dépourvue de liens avec la transcendance est davantage exposée aux contingences historiques et finalement à la facilité."
46 "La transmission des valeurs et dans l'apprentissage de la différence entre le Bien et le Mal, l'instituteur ne pourra jamais remplacer le curé ou le Pasteur."
47 "Le principe de laïcité oblige-t-il le Président de la République à ne parler que de la sécurité routière, des déficits publics, de la politique spatiale, sans jamais parler des choses essentielles, comme la vie, la civilisation, l'amour, l'espérance?"

French have invented secularism to guarantee the right to believe under the same conditions, regardless of religious affiliation?" (Sarkozy 2007c).[48]

* * *

Here, Sarkozy and the Republic appear as bringers of peace between religions. They were peace keepers sanctioned by the Christian God and the universal spirit, in stark contrast to the imagined barbaric and the communitarian Muslims who professed violence and hatred. The good Muslims, those who embraced the Republic and secularism, those who practiced a private and non-conspicuous religion, were free to do so within the constraints of freedom of religion and freedom of speech. In other words, the Muslim citizen was free to practice her or his religion in total freedom as long as it was confined to the boundaries prescribed by the secular Republic. But, since Islam and Muslims had a tendency to fall into extremism, special checks and balances were needed to control and discipline them. The Muslim-other was thus called to testify to his or her desire to participate in the French Republic as if it was an active consent, which surely was not the case for white French natives. In other words, citizenship for the Muslim-other appeared to be conditional; it demanded total obedience, not only of the republican laws but of the republican peaceful coexistence (*vivre-ensemble*).

Secularism became joined with liberty, equality, and brotherhood as the fourth compadre, as it seemed it guaranteed the future well-being of its fellow values. And, as a value that united the French, it not only created possible freedoms and rights, it demanded them. Secularism, then, was understood to be a base layer for moral precepts, something acceptable to all. Sarkozy made this point while referring to a famous anecdote of Jules Ferry. When talking to schoolteachers at the end of the nineteenth century, Ferry stated that "if a family man, one man, was present during class and could not give his approval to what the teachers had said, then the teachers would have to abstain from saying it" (Sarkozy 2009a).[49] This statement seems to clash with the civilizational mission of the Republic—if "no one" is to be hurt by teachings in school, one has to wonder what the school might actually teach. But it might also be read as conforming to the French-white hegemony expressed by the republican spokespeople; that is, if by "honest man" one hears "French man."

---

48 "Si la question spirituelle n'était pas si importante, je me demande bien pourquoi on aurait inventé la laïcité pour garantir le droit de croire dans les mêmes conditions, quelle que soit la religion qui est la sienna."

49 "Demandez-vous si un père de famille, je dis un seul, présent à votre classe et vous écoutant, pourrait de bonne foi refuser son assentiment à ce qu'il nous entendrait dire. Si oui, abstenez-vous de le dire."

Indeed, the only one subjected to the Republic's contemporary civilizational mission was the Muslim-other.

If republican discourse on secularism was articulating a depoliticized and post-political order, the promotion of faith and hope as the solution to the hardships in the suburbs was a depoliticized and post-political calling to the inhabitants of these areas. This further suggested that those seeking solutions to these hardships outside the frame of faith and hope were seeking them outside the "secular morality" avowed by the President, and were therefore potentially amoral beings or enemies of the Republic's teleological progress. This, then, makes legitimate critical political action outside of the hegemonic discursive frames established by the Republic impossible, and could result in the deportation from the Republic, as with the Madame M case in 2008 (see final chapter).

Legislate, Educate!

One question Sarkozy liked to return to during his presidency was how to explain to "those who want to join us, the immigrants," that there were "uncompromisable values, called French identity, that the French could not negotiate" (TF1 2007).[50] In this regard, Minister of Interior Michèle Alliot-Marie (UMP) explained how the prohibition of the full-face veil in public space needed to be dictated by both dissuasive and pedagogic sanctions (AN 2010a, 5367). André Gerin, as the Head of the Gerin Commission, assured that the legislators were ready to take the necessary means to bring back order to the Republic: "We are not in the least afraid of conflict, on the contrary" (AN 2009d, 9).[51]

This pedagogical mission became a matter of proudly reaffirming the Republic's values and principles, of discussing why it was legitimate to do so, why secularism could not in the end be the underlying legal principle legitimating a law, although remaining the all-embracing value, and how the new law would ensure public order.

Reaffirmation

The Gerin Commission made clear that a prohibition of the full-face veil would reaffirm fundamental republican principles and it would be a move towards

---

50   "Si vous n'expliquez pas à ceux qui vont nous rejoindre, les immigrés, qu'il y a des valeurs que nous ne négocierons pas, qui s'appelle l'identité de la France, comment voulez-vous qu'ils s'intègrent?"
51   "nous n'avons pas peur du conflit, au contraire."

"re-establishing secularism in the Republic" (Gerin 2010, 88).[52] It was an occasion to "reaffirm the Parliament's attachment to the great republican principles of liberty, equality, brotherhood, and secularism" (126).[53]

Minister of Justice Michèl Alliot-Marie (UMP) (2010c) declared that the full-face veil was not simply "a challenge to secularism," or "just a question of protecting women against violence;" it was a chance to find "a republican common ground in the fight against the communitarianism that sought to divide our society."[54] Alliot-Marie (2010d), moreover, suggested that the debate was an occasion for the French "to express a unanimous attachment to republican values." In a time when French society was becoming more complex, "the French were asking themselves how to forge the future of the nation." She explained that there was as obligation "to speak with a single voice in expressing a unanimous attachment to the values of the Republic." She encouraged the French to be proud of the model that "founded the French social pact and the French identity." To ratify the law, said Alliot-Marie, "was an honor; it was to show oneself worthy of being French and worthy of the privilege of living in the France."[55]

MP André Gerin (GDR) stressed how important it was that all members of the French society, especially "women's groups," respected secularism and the rules of the Republic" and continued: "Why not also those Muslims who want to live in our country?" (AN 2009c, 2).[56] He declared that it was time for Islam to find its rightful place in the French Republic, and this would take

---

52   "Retour sur le principe de laïcité."
53   "l'occasion de réaffirmer l'attachement du Parlement aux grands principes républicains de liberté, d'égalité, de fraternité et de laïcité."
54   "Ce n'est pas un simple problème de laïcité, ce n'est pas simplement une question de protection des femmes contre les violences, de niqab ou de burqa, c'est un enjeu de rassemblement, de concorde contre toutes les tentatives communautaristes qui visent à fragmenter notre société."
55   "A l'heure de l'internationalisation et de la complexification de nos sociétés, les Français s'interrogent sur le devenir de notre Nation. Notre responsabilité est de faire preuve de vigilance et de réaffirmer les valeurs que nous avons en partage. Notre devoir est de parler d'une seule voix pour exprimer notre attachement unanime aux valeurs de la République ... Soyons fiers de ce modèle qui fonde notre pacte social et forge notre identité. Soyons dignes des exigences attachées à l'honneur d'être Français, au privilège de vivre en France." For similar statements see also Minister of Justice Michèle Alliot-Marie (2010c).
56   "Nous voulons comprendre et surtout déboucher sur des préconisations en souhaitant que la majorité d'entre elles soient partagées par les associations féminines, laïques et—pourquoi pas?—par une partie des musulmans qui veulent vivre dans notre pays dans le respect des règles de la République et de la laïcité."

pedagogical effort. The importance of the law had to be explained to the people subjected to it. Gerin suggested that the legislators had to affirm, "loud and clear," that the wearing of the full-face veil was unacceptable and contrary to the idea of a respectful Islam (AN 2009d, 16). He explained that "a clash of civilizations was about to happen because if we want to pursue the republican emancipatory work, this clash will come" (AN 2009g, 27). Gerin said that Islamic spokespeople had "to publicly take on the question of Islam's place in the Republic, especially in relation to creating an Islam tolerant to secularism and in the fight against alleged barbaric ideologies and fundamentalism."[57]

Beyond explaining what kind of Islam was acceptable in the eyes of the Republic, the pedagogical work was also understood as a means to counteract any untruths about the work of the Commission. According to MP Jean Glavany (SOC), Muslims and journalists spread these untruths on sites like Oumma.com and in the left-wing press, such as in the weekly *Le Nouvel Observateur*. During the hearings of the Gerin Commission, Glavany stressed that "untruths spread about the Commission had to be denounced" and, thus, it was crucial "to communicate with journalists what the commission's work was really about in order to counteract the prejudices that were being spread in the press" (AN 2009c, 3).[58] Senator Sylvie Goy-Chavent (UMP) declared that it was a matter of choosing sides: one was "either for the full-face veil or against it" (Hummel 2010, 32–33).[59]

While the leading voices stressed the pedagogical necessity of implementing the law prohibiting the full-face veil, to some, such as MP Bérengère Poletti (UMP), the case was so self-evident that pedagogy was not even needed. The Republic "now owed it to itself to react and to adopt a law prohibiting the full-face veil but not omitting to explain why it was offensive to the rules of living together and to republican secularism" (Poletti 2010, 7).[60]

---

57 "l'enjeu de civilisation auquel nous sommes confrontés si nous voulons poursuivre l'œuvre républicaine d'émancipation ... [S]i nous devons mener un combat politique contre les idéologies barbares, les responsables du culte musulman doivent, quant à eux, se saisir particulièrement et publiquement de la question de la place de l'islam dans la République française, du respect de la laïcité et de la lutte contre le fondamentalisme."
58 "Nous aurions intérêt à communiquer avec les journalistes pour casser un certain nombre de jugements préétablis qui sont désagréables à lire dans la presse."
59 "Il faut être pour ou contre."
60 "La République se doit de réagir et d'adopter une loi interdisant ce comportement, sans omettre d'expliquer pourquoi il est contraire aux règles du vivre-ensemble et de la laïcité républicaine."

Legitimacy

The application of law was generally justified as a response to an urgent threat posed by anti-republican communitarianism and as a means of establishing an emancipatory politics for the benefit of oppressed Muslim women. Initially, secularism was the principle around which a republican consensus was articulated but, during the course of the debate, the focus shifted to the elements of security and public order.

After the Gerin Commission had handed in their report, President Sarkozy (2010c) stressed the gravity of the situation. For too long the French had been ignoring the assaults against secularism, against gender equality, and to discrimination. This was no longer acceptable. The time had come to act. Since the full-face veil was against women's dignity, it was urgent to prohibit it. Sarkozy declared that "for too long we have been standing idle about the assaults against secularism, against the equality of men and women, against discrimination, and irresponsible parents that do not care for the education of their children. This is no longer acceptable ... The full-face veil is against a woman's dignity. The answer is to prohibit the full-face veil." Sarkozy assured that, based on the Commission's report, the government would submit "a bill in conformity with the general principles of French law."[61]

Minister of Justice Michèle Alliot-Marie (UMP) (2010b) subsequently stated that "the government was determined to give itself the means to get rid of any practices that went against French republican values."[62] Mayor Philippe Esnol (PS) similarly declared that, since the full-face veil "did not respect the principles of liberty, equality, and secularism," it ought to be "prohibited in the territory of the Republic" (AN 2009b, 22).[63]

Sarkozy (2010d) argued that legislating against the full-face veil was the path to a righteous emancipation for the supposedly subjugated women. It was a question of "what society and what Republic one wanted to live in; about

---

61 "Trop longtemps nous avons supporté les atteintes à la laïcité, à l'égalité de l'homme et de la femme, les discriminations, l'irresponsabilité de certains parents qui ne s'occupent pas de l'éducation de leurs enfants. Ce n'est plus supportable ... Le voile intégral est contraire à la dignité de la femme. La réponse c'est l'interdiction du voile intégral. Le gouvernement déposera un projet de loi d'interdiction conforme aux principes généraux de notre droit."

62 "Le Gouvernement est déterminé à se donner tous les moyens de lutter contre des pratiques contraires aux valeurs républicaines."

63 "ne respecte ni le principe de liberté, ni le principe d'égalité, et encore moins le principe de laïcité. Je considère donc qu'elle doit être interdite sur le territoire de la République française."

what kind of human values would be dominant." It was "the political and moral responsibility of the Government and Parliament to act."[64]

To Alliot-Marie (2010d), prohibiting the full-face veil was "a protective mission" and it was an "obligation" to partake in this mission for all members of parliament. She clarified that "the importance of the values that were defended excluded any hesitation and any half measures" (Alliot-Marie 2010c).[65] The Gerin Commission stated that it was important to be clear on one question, namely that the liberty to dress how one wanted was "not an absolute" and, like all liberties, "it could be limited" (Gerin 2010, 95).[66]

Some MPs rasied concerns regarding the fact that the law could be unconstitutional and go against international treaties to which the Republic was bound. In the Garraud Report, Jean-Paul Garraud (UMP), among others, pointed out that France could be convicted in the ECHR if the women wearing the full-face veil were to appeal (2010, 21). One challenge in trying to prohibit the full-face veil was whether the legislators could in fact prohibit a religious garment in public space, as, by law, freedom of conscience was guaranteed and there was no "discrimination against citizens based on their religious belonging." Prime Minister François Fillon (UMP) sought the expertise of the *Conseil d'Etat*. The Council described their mission as seeking an answer to whether "we can envisage a legal ban for particular reasons and within prescribed limits on the wearing of the full-face veil as such," or "are we required to address the more general question of concealment of the face, of which wearing this garment is one form?" (Conseil d'État 2010, 8).[67] Fillon thus formulated the Commission's task not as a question of *whether* the full-face veil ought to be or even could be prohibited, but *how* it would be. Alliot-Marie (2010d) argued that while the full-face veil was indeed religious, the threat it embodied was not. Thus, secularism could not constitute the foundation of a prohibition since a prohibition of the full-face veil on the basis of its religious essence would lead to a ban on all sorts of religious clothes. This was "not imaginable."

---

64 "Dans cette affaire le gouvernement emprunte, en conscience, un chemin exigeant, mais un chemin juste. Chacun est dans son rôle. Quand il s'agit de savoir—car au fond c'est bien de cela qu'il s'agit—dans quelle société, dans quelle République, dans quelle civilisation, avec quelles valeurs humaines nous voulons vivre, il appartient au gouvernement et au Parlement de prendre leur responsabilité politique et morale."
65 "L'importance de ces valeurs que nous défendons tous, sur tous les bancs, exclut toute hésitation et toute demi-mesure."
66 "il faut d'abord évacuer une question: celle de la liberté de se vêtir. Cette liberté n'est pas un absolu et comme toute liberté, elle peut souffrir de limitations."
67 English original.

In the end, the Gerin Commission (2010) came to a similar conclusion. The Comission stated that during the hearings it had become clear to them that "secularism was not a central problem, especially since the full-face veil was not an obligatory prescription by Islam" (87).[68] The Commission argued that should the full-face veil be banned as a religious symbol, all usage of religious clothing symbolizing a religious identity in public needed to be regulated, which, just as for the Minister of Justice, was out of the question (93).

When the law finally passed, it prohibited all forms of concealment of the face in the public space (see Chapter Two). There were, however, exceptions. The Minister of Justice stated that some garments concealing the face were acceptable, such as "concealing one's face for health reasons, professional motives, sports, festivities, or, for artistic and traditional performances, as long as they conformed with republican principles and with the principles of peaceful coexistence" (Alliot-Marie 2010c).[69]

For the critics of the Law and the potential problems it could encounter with the ECHR, the President was clear on the point that "we should not be ashamed of our values, nor should we be afraid of defending them" (Sarkozy 2009a).[70]

Securing Public Order

According to the *Conseil d'Etat,* security and public order were the instances that justified legislation against the full-face veil. This involved a twofold provision:

> First it would stipulate that it is forbidden to wear any garment or accessory that hides the face in such a way as to preclude identification, either where there is a need to safeguard law and order, or where identification seems necessary for access to or movement within certain places, or to

---

68 "au cours des auditions que la question de la laïcité n'était pas tout à fait au cœur de la problématique ... en particulier parce que le port du voile intégral n'est pas une prescription de l'islam."

69 "Certaines activités nécessitent la dissimulation du visage dans l'espace public, sans pour autant porter atteinte à l'ordre public social. Elles peuvent se justifier par des raisons de santé ou des motifs professionnels. Elles s'inscrivent également dans le cadre de pratiques sportives, de fêtes, ou de manifestations artistiques ou traditionnelles. L'interdiction ne s'appliquera pas à l'ensemble de ces situations, dès lors qu'elles sont compatibles avec les principes du vivre ensemble."

70 "[N]ous ne devons pas avoir honte de nos valeurs. Nous ne devons pas avoir peur de les defender."

fulfill certain formalities; second it would strengthen enforcement measures that target persons who force others to hide their faces and thus conceal their identity in the public space. (Conseil d'Etat 2010, 8–9)[71]

Senator François Buffet (UMP) stated that "public order constituted the most incontestable foundation for the law" (Buffet 2010, 15; also see Garraud 2010).[72]

What, then, was meant by public order? Just as with secularism, public order was articulated rather ambiguously. Leaning towards the *Conseil d'Etat*'s report, the Buffet Commission (2010) provided for a discussion on the contents of public order. In their report, the Commission stated that public order was to be understood as either material or immaterial (15). The material public order referred to a "traditional understanding comprising issues of security, tranquility, and public health" (15).[73] A legal foundation, and thus restrictions on rights and liberties based on the material aspect of public order, "would require being justified by existing or potential threats to public order" (15).[74] According to the Commission, whether the full-face veil was actually posing a direct or a potential threat to the material aspect of public order, they concluded that the concept of public order needed to be expanded to its immaterial dimension. In other words, exactly why, how, and where the full-face veil troubled public order was not as self-evident as many of the republican spokespeople implied. Regardless, the Commission treated it as if its meaning was commonsensically objective.

The immaterial dimension of public order first of all aimed at ensuring the public moral code, and wearing a full veil was seen as a threat to this. However, an offense against the moral code alone would not justify a prohibition (Buffet 2010, 16). Quoting a part of the *Conseil d'Etat*'s report headlined "A completely new legal definition of public order," the Commission argued that public order was the minimum requirement needed to ensure life in society. This comprised reciprocal demands and essential guarantees, such as the respect for pluralism. This was of such fundamental importance that these demands and guarantees determined the exercise of other liberties. They could even infringe one

---

71   English original.
72   "que l'ordre public constitue le fondement le plus incontestable de l'interdiction visée par le projet de loi."
73   "L'ordre public dans sa dimension traditionnelle comprend la sécurité, la tranquillité et la salubrité publiques."
74   "les restrictions aux droits et libertés doivent être justifiées par l'existence ou le risque de troubles à l'ordre public."

individual's liberty. To both the *Conseil d'Etat* and the Commission, these fundamental traits of public order, implicit and permanent, were equally fundamental for the social contract and the *vivre ensemble*. In this sense, the full-face veil was articulated as a negation of pluralism since a person entering public space with a hidden face would negate the other non-veiled person's existence:

> From this standpoint, it could be argued that public policy is the minimum requirement for the reciprocal demands and essential guarantees of life in society. These demands and guarantees, like respect for pluralism for example, are of such fundamental importance that they determine the way in which other freedoms are exercised and if necessary require the effects of certain acts of the individual will to be prevented. In our Republic, these fundamental requirements of the social contract, which are both implicit and permanent, could have the following implication: when an individual is in the public space and likely to come across another person quite fortuitously, he may neither renounce his membership of society, nor cause it to be denied by concealing his face from the sight of others to the point of being quite unrecognizable.[75] (Buffet 2010, 16)

The Commission drew the conclusion from this passage that "it was not an exaggeration to transpose the judicial reasoning to the wearing of the full-face veil insofar as a general consensus existed in French society that the face was an essential element of a person's identity," as well as "a component of that person's dignity" (5).[76] Not only was concealing one's face deemed an attack on human dignity, it was "an attack against an individual's social surroundings in general, as well challenging the very possibility of reciprocity in a meeting with another person" (5).[77] To the *Conseil d'Etat* (2010), the safekeeping of public order justified a subversion of public rights, such as freedom of conscience (30).

Shortly before the law came into force in April 2011, the Prime Minister François Fillon (2011) signed a ministerial circular. A pedagogical pamphlet followed to explain the core precepts of the new law. The cover had a full-page

---

75   Original English in *Conseil d'État* (2010, 29–30).
76   "Il ne paraît pas abusif de transposer le raisonnement juridique à la dissimulation du visage dans la mesure où il existe un large consensus dans notre société pour reconnaître dans le visage un élément essentiel de l'identité de la personne laquelle est une composante de sa dignité."
77   "La dissimulation du visage ne porte pas seulement atteinte à la dignité de la personne dont le visage est couvert, elle met aussi en cause la relation à autrui et la possibilité même de la réciprocité d'un échange."

image of a bust of Marianne with flowing hair. The pamphlet bore the headline "The Republic Lives Bare-headed" (*"La République se vit à visage découvert"*) (Government document 2011). Across the white bust of Marianne, here being used as the emblem of the good woman and the docile citizen, was a quotation from the legislative text: "No one in the public space may wear a garment destined to conceal one's face."[78]

Conclusion

The Second Islamic Veil Affair moved from a highly focused debate on secularism, women's dignity, and French and civilizational values to end up with security, public order, morality, honesty, and reciprocity. Here, a French identity was articulated through an imagined warlike situation where good and bad republicans could be distinguished by choosing a side for or against the full-face veil. This sort of unification through war resulted in an aggressive politics of assimilation aimed at the Muslim-other. In addition, it was also a politics seeking to create the sense of a perpetual state of emergency, fear and insecurity where the only solution to the emerging threat was the implementation of a security regime to safeguard the white French against the invasive Islamic barbarians.

These legislative de-veilings invite questions about what these acts were supposed to lead to. And is it not so that the imaginary emancipation led to a construed Republic sketched by a self-avowed heroic male gaze? It was, in others words, another manifestation of the white man's desire to domesticate the brown women away from their brown men, to paraphrase Gayatri Spivak (1988). In the present analysis the veiled woman was caught in this "three man grammatical"—the subject/object whose foreclosed position in the secular space was a subject to be made in the image of "us," but never as one of "us." What we encounter is, as Judith Butler (2009), referring to Michel Schneider, has put it, a paternalist discourse in which Islam and Muslims are portrayed as an infantile o/Other, undeveloped, in need of a nurturing mother and a strong patriarch, where the state apparatus assumed the patriarchal role of the father as the bringer of law, discipline, and punishment (see Schneider 2010). It was, to paraphrase Iris Marion Young (2005), a manner of legitimizing a logic of masculinist protection of women. However, these women were only offered protection insofar as they accepted their predetermined roles as dependent and obedient—a republican, masculine bliss. Republican discourse

---

78 "Nul ne peut, dans l'espace public, porter une tenue destinée à dissimuler son visage."

on secularism thus created an ideal image of the nation as a patriarchal home: "Good men only appear in their goodness if we assume that lurking outside the warm familial walls are aggressors who wish to attack them" (Young 2005, 18).

Other ways of concealing one's face were accepted as they were in accordance with the republican, secular, Christian, and white public sphere. In this fashion, republican discourse on secularism suggests that the French, republican, Western, and Christian society is the antithesis of deceitful or dishonest behavior. In this logic, a bare face becomes the symbol of faithfulness and honesty. Turning to Žižek, one can see the ideological displacement in play here:

> From a Freudian perspective, the face is the ultimate mask that conceals the horror of the Neighbor-Thing: the face is what makes the Neighbor, *le semblable*, a fellow-man with whom we can identify and empathize. (Not to mention the fact that today, many faces are surgically changed and thus deprived of the last vestiges of natural authenticity.) This, then, is why a covered face causes such anxiety: because it confronts us directly with the abyss of the Other-Thing, with the Neighbor in its uncanny dimension. The very covering-up of the face obliterates a protective shield, so that the Other-Thing stares at us directly (recall that the burqa has a narrow slip for the eyes: we don't see the eyes, but we know there is a gaze there) ... We should imagine something similar with the burqa: the opposite of a woman taking off her burqa and revealing her natural face. What if we go a step further and imagine a woman "taking off" the skin of her face itself, so that what we see beneath her face is precisely an anonymous dark smooth burqa-like surface with a narrow slit for the gaze? (Žižek 2010)

The deliberations preceding both of the laws contained contradictory and tautological statements. According to republican spokespeople, the debates never focused on Islam or even secularism. However, as I have shown, they ended up solely focusing on Muslims, Islam, and secularism. This cathexis, this neurotic preoccupation with the the Muslim-other coupled with a narcissistic and secularistic universality created a curious legitimizing logic suggesting "I'm not a racist, because, well, I'm French!" And just like the stone bust of Marianne crowning the pedagogical pamphlet of the Law of 2010—this emblematic icon for the Republic's universal conquest, unable to speak for itself—the women concerned during the second Veil Affair became mere narrative tropes in the Republic's admiration of its own grandiosity.

PART IV
Consequences

CHAPTER 7

Social Contracts, National Borders and Illiberal Governmentality

In this book, I have analyzed the construction of France as a secular Republic in political and legislative speech during the Islamic Veil Affairs (2003–2004 and 2010–2011). As I have tried to show, the republican discourse on secularism's heterogeneity was projected onto the Islamic-other to achieve an imagined homogenous national identity. This discursive technique carried with it a paternalistic and patriarchal gaze that saw a thief in the Islamic-other. The other had stolen the Republic's desired object, its link to fulfillment, which, as is known by now, was the other-woman. In the republican imaginary, the Muslim man became a symbol of an uncontrolled and unreliable libido, whilst the republican and chivalric male gaze showed proof of control and benevolence. The Muslim woman's reluctance to de-veil was taken as a manifestation of the Islamic male-other's successful manipulation of her real desire.

Secularism, here, entered as the tool to retake the stolen object where it was articulated to function as a governmental technique and as a legitimator of an imagined unification of *nation* (France) and *people* (French). This was framed in a post-political republican discourse on secularism, which resulted in the legitimization of illiberal political practices and an extraordinary treatment of the Muslim-other. This was achieved by a selective distribution of rights and freedoms through the construction of meaningful and worthless political subjects. If the Muslim woman did not want to be saved by the Republic, she had no place in the white republican unity.

In this concluding chapter, I discuss some of the political, social, and practical consequences of the republican discourse on secularism beyond the prohibition of veils in schools and full-face veils in the public space. I do this by relating my analysis of reports, laws and decrees produced during the analyzed period to what I have been referring to as discursive displacement, post-political governmentality, and, finally, I end by discussing how the political mainstream's articulation of secularism and Islam has allowed for an expansion of illiberal politics into nationalistic political movements. This chapter is to be read as a proposal for future research more than a proper conclusion of the analysis that has been provided in the previous chapters.

National Frontiers and Social Contracts

In my analysis, I show that secularism was a unifying moment in a French-universal-paternalist signifying discourse on French and republican identity. Secularism was attributed of having the role of both foundation and catalyst of a peaceful, united, and equal society guaranteed by a sort of secularist social contract (i.e., "peaceful coexistence"). This contract, furthermore, was performative in a very material and factual way since it was not only to bind its subjects to republican law, it was also to educate *them*—to elevate *them* from a perpetual state of nature into modernity. Let us return to Rousseau (1987):

> This passage from the state of nature to the civil state produces quite a remarkable change in man, for it substitutes justice for instinct in his behavior and gives his actions moral quality they previously lacked. Only then, when the voice of duty replaces physical impulse and right replaces appetite, does man, who had hitherto taken only himself into account, find himself forced to act upon other principles and to consult his reason before listening to his inclinations. (150)

While the social contract in the writings of Rousseau was an imaginary contract supposedly accepted by all citizens, the sort of secularist social contract encountered in this analysis was taking form in a physically existing one. One can see this formation in two interrelated cases. The first one is the case of Madame M and the other of the integration contract, which was titled *Contrat d'acceuil d'immigration* (CAI).

I have argued that in 2003–2004 the expulsion of the young veiled Muslim woman from her public school was a symbolic expulsion of her from the Republic since the school was articulated as a republican sanctuary, the innermost sacred space of the Republic. During Sarkozy's time as president, the symbolical expulsion was institutionalized into a real one. One case in point is the 2008 Mme M or Madame M case in the *Conseil d'Etat*. "Mme M," as she is called in the legal documents, is a Moroccan citizen who, fulfilling all objective requirements, was denied French citizenship. In the decision made by the *Conseil d'Etat*, dated 27 June 2008, the Council justified the decision primarily because "her radical religious practice was not compatible with essential values of the French community" (Conseil d'Etat 2008).[1] It was Comissioner

---

1 "Elle a cependant adopté une pratique radicale de sa religion, incompatible avec les valeurs essentielles de la communauté française." Although not mentioned in the Council's documents, this case could refer to a circular on nationalization decreed in 2000, see Carrera (2009).

Prada Bordenave's (2008) report on Madame M that provided the background for the Council's decision. In the report, the only interviews accounted for had been conducted with civil servants. There are no interviews with Madame M herself. The application letter Madame M had sent in also played an important part in the sketching out of her portrait.

According to the Commissioner, Madame M lived a "reclusive" and "entrenched" life. The only social encounters she had, besides those with her children, were with men—her husband, father, and father-in-law. If we take this into consideration along with statements such as "she mostly goes to the supermarket in the company of her husband," "she started wearing the veil only in France on the demand of her husband," and "she veils herself as soon as she leaves her apartment," it is tempting to draw the conclusion that patriarchal and controlling men contributed to her isolation. Someone and something was clearly keeping Madame M from being French. Was she then a victim? At first, this seemed to be case. For one thing, the Commissioner reported that Madame M was ignorant of basic democratic rights and of secularism. Considering that Madame M in her letter of application had appealed to the ECHR, the French constitution, and the Republic's secular principles, this was a peculiar conclusion drawn by the commissioner. The appeal should be "regarded with some circumspection," especially since it "without doubt, does not reflect the personal convictions of the person concerned." In other words, Bordenave and the Council deemed Madame M incapable of speaking for herself. She did indeed seem to be a hijacked victim controlled by bearded men programmed by fundamentalist Islam. Since the veil was already perceived as incompatible with any sense of Frenchness and since Madame M was portrayed as a mindless automaton, not only did she become a mute subject, her real identity, was mediated through a constructed Islamic-other to which the fundamentalist man was also subjected. Therefore, according to the Commissioner, Madame M's submission "manifests in her way of dressing as well as in the total organization of her daily life," and what was more, she supposedly found this "normal." This should apparently lead to the conclusion that Madame M's submission to the religious-other not only dictated her whole being, it was a submission based on active consent.

Given the imagined control of the other-man over the other-woman, what reasons were there to talk to Madame M directly if the commissioner knew beforehand that she was a deceptive radical? In this twisted logic, the competing identities or subject positions assigned to Madame M—"victim" and "voluntary submission"—merged into a single, graspable object. This was why the Council understood Madame M's language skills and acceptance of a male gynecologist to be a proof of her deception rather than an indication of the opposite.

This can be seen as yet another example of how a sociological reality was detached from the individual wearing the full-face veil, as if the veil was an external reality and the individual a mute subject. Local conditions were disregarded. Why did the Commissioner not pay attention to the fact that it was in France that Madame M started wearing the full veil? Why were Madame M's visits to a male gynecologist not taken into account? This, of course, further strengthened the picture of submission of the Muslim other-woman to the Muslim other-man and a submission of the Muslim man to the Islamic-other—the woman being manipulated and the man being manipulative, neither of them appear as trustworthy. The only chance of understanding the other was to have a fabricated conceptualization of Islam. By this double privation, Madame M was a subject without voice; a foreclosed, subaltern object only living as a shadow in the light of the men surrounding her.[2] As Spivak explains (1988): "Both as object of colonialist historiography and as subject of insurgency, the ideological construction of gender keeps the male dominant. If, in the context of colonial production, the subaltern has no history and cannot speak, the subaltern as female is even more deeply in a shadow" (287).

Madame M as a subaltern subject is an example of a muted voice, a voice in the shadows. However, in an interview published in *The New York Times*, where Madame M showed remarkable conversational skills, which in Bordenave's conclusion appear non-existent, neither Madame M nor her husband, Monsieur S, referred to themselves as Salafists. Monsieur S even added: "We have nothing to do with them [Muslim fundamentalists]" (Bennhold 2008). This however mattered little to the court ruling.

The case reveals extraordinary treatment of Madame M. As pointed out by legal scholar Danièle Lochak, if we were to pursue this logic to its end, then battered women, for example, would not be worthy of being French (in Van Eeckhout 2008). If the voluntary submission to a patriarchal ideology was what delegitimized a person from citizenship, we could ask if anyone would be viable for citizenship.[3]

The second development of a secularist social contract can be seen in the integration law, the *Code de l'entrée et de séjour des étrangers et du droit d'asile* (CESEDA). Here it is written that an immigrant wishing to integrate into France needs to sign a Contract of Reception and Integration, translated

---

2   I read foreclosure as an absolute denial of the symbolic, making any sort of subject-representation impossible.

3   Another case in point is the Council of State's decision to refuse the Algerian descendent Mustafa Naimi citizenship due to his "hostility" to republican values such as secularism, but also to homosexuals, punk rockers, Buddhists, and Jews (see Bordenave 2008).

into a language that he understands, by which he obliges himself to follow a civic education and, if necessary, a linguistic education (CESEDA, L.311-9). The civic education included a presentation of the Republic's values, especially equality between men and women, and secularism. The CESEDA also stated that non-compliance with the contract will be taken into consideration during the evaluation of a renewal of the visa (*la carte de séjour*). The immigration and integration office, the *Office de français de l'immigration et de l'intégration* (OFII), specifies that the CAI (*Contrat d'accueil et d'intégration*) aims at installing a "relation of confidence and of reciprocal obligation" between "you" and the state (OFII 2011).

The CAI (2007) consists of two pages and bears the headline "Welcome to France." Besides stating the core precepts of the CESEDA law, it explains the pivotal elements of France and French identity in republican speech: "France is a democracy," "France, a country of rights and obligations," "France, a secular country," "France, an equal country," and "Knowing French, a necessity." Of special interest are statements like "everybody is free to have any religious convictions of choice or not to have one as long as it does not disrupt public order" and "equality between men and women is a fundamental principle of French society. Women have the same rights and the same obligations as men." It furthermore states that "this principle applies to all, French and foreigners. Women are not subjected to the authority of their husbands, their fathers or brothers." Finally, it says that "forced marriages and polygamy are prohibited" (CAI 2007).

Together with the CAI came a citizen test to evaluate the foreigner's knowledge of France and its customs.[4] The test comprises true/false statements such as "In France, respecting the law does not apply to everyone"; "French values only apply to the French"; "A job may be refused to you under the pretext that you are a foreigner"; "Women must obey men"; "The head of the family is the man"; "Women do not have the right to adhere to a political party" (Maillot 2008, 136). Thus, the CAI can be understood as a test of the prejudices of foreigners about France, but it can also be understood as laying bare the prejudices the French Republic harbored in regard to immigrants. As Agnès Maillot (2008) has pointed out, the documents silently communicated with an imagined Muslim, North or West African immigrant (137). And how was one to respond to these statements? French history is full of examples of the political elite's juggling with the equal applicability of law, and several public sector jobs *demand* French citizenship.

---

4 See following articles in the Code Civil: 21(4), 21(24), and 21(25). For further analysis see de Groot, Kuipers and Weber 2009, 51.

For the foreigner or immigrant, therefore, it seemed to be a matter of showing one's loyalty to France through secularism and equality—not being conspicuously Muslim. Moreover, if the aforementioned catechism of French religion, as Citron (2008) has put it, created a certain imperative, a fundamentalist morality whose sole law is to die for the Republic (45), one could understand the sacrifice demanded by the Republic not as one of mortal sacrifice, but as one of bodily and mental devotion. This may be understood to apply to all of France and follows Sarkozy's take on economic development. However, in relation to secularist speech, it only applied to those who had not yet accepted the secularist social contract or to those who were thought to reject it. The purpose was to construe subjects whose co-dependence on the Republic required a certain degree of docility so that the Republic's gift to them, the mere belonging to it, demanded their unquestionable loyalty in return. If the imaginary non-acceptance of secularism during the first Veil Affair resulted in expulsion from public schools, during the Sarkozy era the stakes got higher: non-acceptance of secularism resulting in denial of citizenship and, in the worst case, even deportation.

Discursive Displacement and Liberal Faith

Given the conspicuous incongruities in republican discourse on secularism, how can one understand that secularism was articulated to incorporate virtually all and everything valued as progressive in France, past and present? As I have tried to show, one answer to this all-embracing articulation is found in the discursive technique that I have been calling discursive displacement. Žižek (2008) has described this kind of displacement as the core function in liberal faith (82). In this case, this translates to the republican-secularists' way of *really* believing. It is a reasoned un-believing logic found in supposedly secular rituals like Christmas, national holidays, and the cherishing of national saints. While no one believes in Santa, parents dress up as him for the joy of the children, and the children play along so as not to disappoint their parents (and to get presents of course). The French national holiday, *le 14 juillet*, is not just about celebrating the nation and the French Republic; it is really about having a good time with friends and family and watching the fireworks. To cherish the national saint Jean d'Arc is not really giving into religious rituals but, instead, a sound way of keeping tradition alive. It is as if, objectively, all precepts for what is commonly described as the core features in "religious" rituals are there, except that the reasons for why these rituals are played out are not the same.

Thus, while millions of French citizens gather to objectively lend their bodies to nationalistic worship, they may never dream of doing this for the sake of the nation. To connect actions with faith or devotion is reserved for the Muslim-other, the one who really believes. *We* do this for all the right pragmatic, non-conspicuous, and a-ideological reasons, whilst *they* who really believe in what they are doing are ideological dupes. Or, to put it another way, by projecting onto the other one's own contingency and lack, the Muslim-other becomes the carrier of subjective and conspicuous violence while the systemic violence of the self, through displacement, is rendered invisible, neutral, and objective. To quote Marnia Lazreg (1988), this can be understood as a result of the "religious paradigm" that gives "religion a privileged explanatory power" (83; see also Cavenaugh 2009).

The discursive or secularist displacement has been most visible in the will to control women, which, during the Veil Affairs, was one of the significant moments in the discourse of the Muslim and Islamic other—the manipulation by fundamentalists and communitarians to control Muslim women's desires and bodies.

During the analyzed debates, republican spokespeople have used this image as a negative counter image to an imagined French gender-equal society. However, if it is a secular society's desire to publicly strip the Muslim woman of a fundamentalist or communitarian desire, why not, then, as suggested by Alain Gresh, understand Sarkozy's love of the Christian faith as a hidden desire to veil Christian women and wish for their fully-fledged subjugation to men (Gresh 2011). As Paul put it in his first letters to the Corinthians: "I praise you for remembering me in everything and for holding to the traditions just as I passed them on to you. But I want you to realize that the head of every man is Christ, and the head of the woman is man, and the head of Christ is God. Every man who prays or prophesies with his head covered dishonors his head. But every woman who prays or prophesies with her head uncovered dishonors her head—it is the same as having her head shaved" (Corinthians 11, verses 1–6).

Again, how is one to understand the frequent references to the French Revolution? What do we make of the ethnocentric, racist, and exclusionary practices that were inscribed at the very heart of the revolution? On 3 August 1793, Jacques Garnier, a distinguished member of the *Club des Jacobins*, proposed that foreigners "who were to obtain a certificate of hospitality would on their left arm wear a tricolored ribbon on which would be attached the word 'hospitality' and the nation where they were born" (quoted in Wahnich 1997, 10). What about Napoleon Bonaparte's rule? The Napoleonic Civil Code of 1804 broke with the old regime and the revolution in the sense that a French woman marrying a foreigner was forced to take on the husband's nationality and their offspring could only attain nationality from the husband. As Napoleon put it: "The woman belongs to her husband just as the fruit belongs to the gardener" (quoted in Camiscioli 2009, 129). Following the logic of displacement, this could be nothing more than pointing at the esoteric secret of the French political and intellectual elite. Or, it is perhaps nothing more than the realization of Ernest Renan's suggestion for successful nation-building: "Neglect and I would even say historical error are essential factors in the creation of the nation, and it is in this way that historical studies are often a danger to nationality" (quoted in Maillot 2008, 56).

In a similar fashion, Brown (2011) ponders over high heels. High heels are an emblematic symbol in the sexualization of the female body and long-term usage of them causes serious medical problems in the foot. Given the conspicuous non-equality vested in the high-heeled shoe, and the beauty industry in general, how is it that virtually no republican voices are ever heard for their legal banning?

What about sports? In France, demands by a small number of Muslim women for specific opening hours once or twice a week at a municipal pool cause outcry among the secularists. Islamists are dividing the public sphere into a gendered one, we are told. Are not sports generally gender-divided public activities?

A contemporary outlook on French gender equality suffices to problematize the picture of France as the beacon of gender-equality. For example, Mona Cholet (2005) has pointed out that during the time period of this analysis, women who were subjugated to conjugal violence conducted by white-Frenchmen were regularly rendered invisible in the media. These crimes mostly passed as acts of "passion," closing the door to further analysis and problematization of power relations and more visible, structural discriminatory practices such as psychological pressure, manipulation, and control. In 2007 and 2008, 675,000 women were subjugated to conjugal violence and, in 2008, 156 women died because of it (Lafon 2009). One can of course ponder further about how to relate the long-serving Minister Christine Boutin's openly professed attachment to Christianity and her reluctance to accept the most fundamental progressive accomplishments of secularism—for example, her propositions against LGBT adoption and her work for the criminalization of abortion (see Cuneo 2009). To this we can also add a number of measurable statistical social facts, such as unpaid labor and working hours, differences in salaries between men and women, and career opportunities. For example, during the 2000s the difference in salaries between men and women was in general about 25 percent (Meurs and Ponthieux 2006). In terms of unpaid household labor, women contributed 80 percent (Régnier-Loilier 2009; for discrimination of non-French groups on the labor market, prisons, schools, and in housing see Fernando 2014, 13ff).

These examples help us understand that the political function of discursive displacement is not only that it forecloses the other from achieving discursive closure, it also prevents potential dissolution of the articulated frontiers between *us* and *them*. As Alain Badiou (2007) has put it, *our* full identification with the *other*, our complete acceptance and acknowledgment of the other, runs the risk of being too costly since we would open ourselves up to a radical process of change whose outcome we cannot know. Such an identification would make it all too visible that controlling, disciplining, distributing, and managing subjects and bodies are not just reserved for the imagined fundamentalist (76). In Bobby Sayyid's (2003) words, "exercising control over bodies is the function of governmentality itself" (11).

Post-Political Expansion

A couple of days before the implementation of the 2011 law prohibiting any concealment of the face in public space, Rabbi Gabriel Farhi pondered about the then-current situation: "Yesterday one was afraid of Islam practiced in the cellars. Today one is afraid of Islam practiced in the street. Where in the public space is Islam to go?" (France 5 2011). Farhi's question highlights the state apparatus' increasing control of the Muslim-other and Islam through the discourse of secularism. Carl Schmitt's (2005) analysis of early twentieth-century liberalism captures this type of logic: "The essence of liberalism is negotiation, a cautious half measure, in the hope that the definitive dispute, the decisive bloody battle, can be transformed into a parliamentary debate and permit the decision to be suspended forever in an everlasting discussion" (63).

Arjun Appadurai (2006) has used the term "predatory identity" to identify "identities whose social construction and mobilization require the extinction of other, proximate social categories, defined as threats to the very existence of some groups, defined as we" (51). I believe that predatory identity is an accurate description of the logic of expansion in play here. For the parliamentary debate and the everlasting discussion described by Schmitt to continue, increasingly more parts of society must be included in this very debate and discussion. That is, for the universal or natural order to be fully implemented, for *our* and *our people*'s continued existence and purity, the enemy of this natural order must be eradicated. To put it in the words of Appadurai (2006): "No modern nation, however benign its political system and however eloquent its public voices may be about the virtues of tolerance, multiculturalism, and inclusion, is free of the idea that its national sovereignty is built on some sort of ethnic genius" (51). This is the governmental logic in the republican exercise of state power. It leads to a never-ending expanding apparatus aiming to assimilate and/or exclude the other.

Thus, the Republic, the nation, and the state apparatus have been rearticulated and given their *raison d'être* in very specific readings of a teleological-transcendental history. During the Veil Affairs, secularism has been articulated as the emancipatory kernel embedded in the republican spirit, where inequality, prejudice, discrimination, and racism have been not just something the republic sought to overcome but also articulated as essential strangers to the republican telos-spirit. As Sayyid (2009) suggests: "Secularism in the West is not seen as a contingent development arising out of the specific history of the West, but as a necessary condition arising out of the unfolding of history itself" (190). The consequence of this political reasoning is that the foreigner and enemy conflate into one: into an a-moral enemy, an enemy of history's unfolding, and an enemy of universalism. The mere presence of the foreigner taints the imagined reach of the universal.

To be sure, in the wake of the second Veil Affair, republican spokespeople have once again brought Islam and secularism to the agenda. According to Minister of the Interior Claude Guéant (UMP), in 1905, there were few Muslims in France; today, however, he claims there are between five and ten million (in Reuters 2011). Now if, as with recent polls in France, one were to count a Muslim as someone of "Muslim Culture," as someone born in a Muslim country or who has parents born in a Muslim country, around four million Muslims live in France. This includes Christian Pakistanis, Copts from Egypt, Christians from Senegal, and the *pieds-noirs* from Algeria. In studies from 2007 to 2010, the major French institutes for demography and statistics, *Institut National d'Études Démographiques* (INED) and *Institut National de la Statistique et des Études Économiques* (INSEE), have concluded that about two million French citizens have declared themselves to be Muslim, of which 30–40 percent has an occasional and collective practice of their religion (in Fourest, Caroline and Fiammetta Venner 2011, 257).

Notwithstanding, Guéant made clear that, due to uncontrolled immigration, the French sometimes feel that they are no longer at home. They sometimes feel that certain customs are being imposed on them that do not correspond to the rules of *our* common social life (Baubérot 2012, loc., 433). According to Guéant, one step in making the French feel more at home was to regulate two particular cases. These concerned mothers wearing the veil during school field trips and the wearing of the veil in public institutions and private enterprises. Even if the veil was allowed in the public space, Guéant made clear that although the Republic could not legislate, "instructions" were developed from the existing regulations that aimed to "avoid" the wearing of the veil (quoted in AFP 2011). So, then, with an ambiguity reminiscent of the reasoning surrounding the 2004 and 2010 laws, Guéant, together with the *Bureau de Culte*, published a 504-page document entitled *Laïcité et liberté religieuse* (Secularism and Religious Liberty) (see Guéant 2011). The document was, according to Guéant, not a matter of revising the 1905 law but, rather, to "adapt" the law and to provide an "answer" to certain questions (quoted in AFP 2011b). This extensive document once again set out to regulate the veil in the name of secularism, clarifying nothing more and nothing less than that the veil should be prohibited.

Romantic Ideals and Secularist Retaliation

In this book I have analyzed a period when for most of the time the conservative UMP party has dominated political power but, as we have seen, those seated on the right in Parliament and major actors seated on the left were unified around a centrist articulation of secularism to fight off "conspicuous" Islam and Muslims and to create a common destiny for a re-articulated nation. This fight, however, has not been restricted to the republican state apparatus. It seems as if European authors, journalists, artists, and politicians jostle one another to be the most daring in standing up against the imagined Islamist threat. One of the ways in which these figures carry out their daring endeavors is through provocation of Muslims and the prophet Mohammed, ranging from the French and Danish cartoon affairs to Swedish Lars Wilks's roundabout dog (see Gardell 2011). The manifesto *Ensemble contre le novueau totilitarisme* (Together Against the New Totalitarianism) published by *Charlie Hebdo* is yet another example. Among the twelve signatories were Ayaan Hirsi Ali, Caroline Fourest, Bernard-Henri Lévy, and Salman Rushdie. They state that, "having defeated Fascism, Nazism, and Stalinism, the world is facing a new global threat of a totalitarian kind: Islamism" (Hirsi Ali et al. 2006). They then go on to make "a call for resistance against religious totalitarianism" and for "the promotion of liberty, equal opportunity, and of secularism for everyone." They also state that they "refuse to abandon" their "critical spirit for fear of encouraging Islamophobia," which is explained as "an unlucky concept that confounds critique of Islam as a religion with the condemnation of religious Muslims."[5]

---

5 "Après avoir vaincu le fascisme, le nazisme, et le stalinisme, le monde fait face à une nouvelle menace globale de type totalitaire: l'islamisme ... Nous, écrivains, journalistes, intellectuels,

It is as if it is less about secularism than a *modus vivendi*—a reason to exist as public spokespeople, experts, republicans, and truth-tellers. Laborde's (2008) statement about secularists as liberal perfectionists fits well here since they "believe that the state should promote worthwhile forms of life, and that worthwhile forms of life are those that exhibit a high degree of individual autonomy" (102). To paraphrase Gina Gustavsson, this is reminiscent of enlightenment liberals who argue for the interference with individuals' choices that are not the outcome of rational self-reflection (2011, 106). While this does indeed seem to be the case for the republican elite analyzed in this thesis, drawing on the work of Gustavsson, I believe we can further understand the desire to publicly defend the nation against Islam as an expression of liberal romantic ideals. Advocates of romantic ideals focus on particularities as opposed to enlightenment ideals, where they see universality as the foundation for identity. Liberal romantics see humans differently, as essentially bound to culture and religion. Authenticity and truthfulness to oneself are two core foundations in the creation of a heroic liberalism. As Gustavsson (2011) has put it: "The truly heroic individual does not only express her authentic self. She also does so at whatever cost: fearlessly, relentlessly—even in the face of martyrdom" (119). This is an uncompromising heroic ideal where the task of "the good liberal is to be a good warrior, to fight and not surrender, far more so at least than to autonomously reflect upon her own situation, or demand anyone else to reflect on theirs, for that matter" (125). In the fight against the imagined Islamization of Europe, Anders Behring Breivik is perhaps the extreme epitome of the romantic hero.[6] But as I have tried to show in my analysis, the key discursive moments of these ideals have been quite common amongst the political center during the Veil Affairs. And is it not so that the political center's illiberal politics have led to a normalization of enmity against Islam and Muslims, where secularism has become the fundamental element legitimizing political speech that is commonly attributed to radical right wing politics?

---

appelons à la résistance au totalitarisme religieux et à la promotion de la liberté, de l'égalité des chances et de la laïcité pour tous … Nous refusons le "relativisme culturel" consistant à accepter que les hommes et les femmes de culture musulmane soient privés du droit à l'égalité, à la liberté et à la laïcité au nom du respect des cultures et des traditions … Nous refusons de renoncer à l'esprit critique par peur d'encourager l' « islamophobie », concept malheureux qui confond critique de l'islam en tant que religion et stigmatisation des croyants."

6   Apart from Breivik's horrible passage à l'act in Oslo and Utöya in July 2011, killings with similar motives have been carried out in the so-called "Döner Killings" committed by a German Neo-Nazi group killing nine immigrants between 2000 and 2006 and by the serial killer Peter Mangs in Malmö, Sweden.

As Baubérot (2012) has pointed out, the new defender of French secularism on the national political arena is, to many people's surprise, the *Front National*. The FN, historically, has been a political party with a strong Catholic identity and its members have been strong opponents of secularism. With the election of their new, second, leader, Marine Le Pen, in 2011, the FN appeared to be steering in a new direction vis-à-vis secularism. In the words of Jean-Pierre Reveau, elected to the party's Central Committee: "She [Marine] talks about secularism all the time, but her father [Jean-Marie] never spoke about it" (Fourest, Caroline and Fiammetta Venner 2011, 279). According to Marine Le Pen, France is living under an occupation manifested in public prayers and halal food at restaurants. To the critics, she has explained that "by expressing myself in this manner, I have done nothing more than to say what everybody really thinks. It appears as if today, the real defender of the Republic is me and not the enslaved UMPS [UMP and PS]" (2010). In line with this, Marine Le Pen has suggested the creation of a "Ministry of Immigration, National Identity, and Secularism." Secularism is, in other words, a way for Marine Le Pen and the National Front to articulate political speech hostile towards immigrants, and in particular Muslims and Islam, but coated with universal values—yet another example of illiberal political discourse.

As I have tried to show in this book, secularism in France is a contingent and inherently empty category that has come to serve the entire French political spectrum in which Islam and the Muslim-other came to function as a negative counter image of what it meant to be French, as an imaginary mirror of identity. Given its contingency, categorical and general statements of what French secularism is and is not are difficult, if not impossible, to make. Secularism lends itself to a wide variety of regulatory political projects. Secularism has become a nodal point in how France is thought, lived, and institutionalized in political life. Through discursive displacement, it makes possible a narcissistic and post-political imagination where the roots of the evils of our time are always located in the other's many shifting forms.

Bibliography

Abu-Lughod, Lila. 2002. "Do Muslim Women Really Need Saving? Anthropological Reflections on Cultural Relativism and Its Others." *American Anthropologist*, 104(3).

Achi, Raberh. 2007. "Laïcité d'empire: Les débats sur l'application du régime de séparation à l'islam impérial." In *Politiques de la laïcité au XXE siècle*, edited by P. Weil. Paris: PUF.

Agence-France Presse. (AFP). 2003. "Voile: Sarkozy et Raffarin veulent calmer le jeu." *Le Nouvel Observateur*, 5 May. Accessed January 27, 2015. http://tempsreel.nouvelobs.com/societe/20030503.OBS0388/voile-sarkozy-et-raffarin-veulent-calmer-le-jeu.html.

Agence-France Presse. (AFP). 2008. "Mariage annulé: la justice suspend l'inscription de l'annulation du mariage à l'état civil." *Le Monde*, 19 June. Accessed January 27, 2015. http://www.lemonde.fr/societe/article/2008/06/19/mariage-annule-la-justice-suspend-l-inscription-de-l-annulation-du-mariage-a-l-etat-civil_1060558_3224.html.

Agence-France Presse. (AFP). 2009. "Moins de 400 femmes porteraient le voile intégral en France." *Libération*, 29 June. Accessed January 27, 2015. http://www.liberation.fr/societe/2009/07/29/moins-de-400-femmes-porteraient-le-voile-integral-en-france_573216.

Agence-France Presse. (AFP). 2010. "Les trois quarts des décisions de reconduite à la frontière ne sont pas appliquées." *Le Monde*, 8 September. Accessed January 27, 2015. http://www.lemonde.fr/societe/article/2010/09/08/les-trois-quarts-des-decisions-de-reconduite-a-la-frontiere-ne-sont-pas-appliquees_1408620_3224.html.

Agence-France Presse. (AFP). 2011. "Guéant présente un code de la laïcité plus restrictif pour la liberté religieuse." *Le Point*, 21 October. Accessed January 27, 2015. http://www.lepoint.fr/societe/gueant-presente-un-code-de-la-laicite-plus-restrictif-pour-la-liberte-religieuse-21-10-2011-1387645_23.php.

Agamben, Giorgio. 1998. *Homo Sacer. Sovereign Power and Bare Life*. Stanford: Stanford University Press.

Ageron, Charles-Robert. 1993. "Français, juifs et musulmans: l'union impossible." In *L'Algérie des Français*, edited by C. Robert. Paris: Éditions du Seuil.

Ahmed, Leila. 2011. *A Quiet Revolution. The Veil's Resurgence, from the Middle East to America*. New Haven: Yale University Press.

Airiau, Paul. 2005. *Cent ans de laïcité française: 1905–2005*. Paris: Presse de la Renaissance.

Albertini, Dominique. 2009. "Une burqa? Non, je ne sais pas où trouver ça." *Rue 89*, 18 June. Accessed January 27, 2015. http://rue89.nouvelobs.com/2009/06/18/une-burqa-non-je-ne-sais-pas-ou-trouver-ca-107912.

Alduy, Cécile and Stéphane Wahnich. 2015. *Marine Le Pen prise aux mots. Décryptage du nouveau discours frontiste.* Paris: Seuil.

Alliot-Marie, Michèle. 2007. "Consistoire ordinaire public." Allocution de Michèle Alliot-Marie, Ministre de l'Intérieur, de l'Outre-Mer et des Collectivités Territoriales à l'occasion du déjeuner offert à la Villa Bonaparte en l'honneur du Cardinal André Vingt-Trois. *Ministère de l'Intérieur, de l'Outre-Mer et des Collectivités Territoriales,* November 24.

Alliot-Marie, Michèle. 2010a. Discours de Mme Alliot-Marie, ministre d'Etat, garde des Sceaux, ministre de la justice et des libertés. *Ministère de Justice et des Libertés,* 19 February.

Alliot-Marie, Michèle. 2010b. "Attachement au respect des valeurs républicaines." Discours de Mme Alliot-Marie. *Ministère d'Etat, garde des Sceaux, ministre de la justice et des libertés, 11 May.*

Alliot-Marie, Michèle. 2010c. "Projet de loi sur la dissimulation du visage dans l'espace public." Discours de Mme Alliot-Marie, ministre d'Etat, garde des Sceaux, ministre de la justice et des libertés, mardi 6 juillet. *Assemblée Nationale,* 7 July.

Alliot-Marie, Michèle. 2010d. "Projet de loi interdisant la dissimulation du visage." Discours de Mme Alliot-Marie, ministre d'Etat, garde des Sceaux, ministre de la justice et des libertés. *Ministère de la justice,* 15 September.

Allwood, Gill, and Khursheed. Wadia. 2002. "French feminism: National and International Perspectives." *Modern & Contemporary France* 10(2).

Almond, Iian. 2007. *New Orientalists. Postmodern Representations of Islam From Foucault to Baudrillard.* London and New York: I.B Tauris.

Amara, Fadela. 2004. *Ni putes ni soumises.* Paris: La Découverte.

Amiraux, Valérie. 2009. "L'affaire du foulard en France': retour sur une affaire qui n'en est pas encore une." *Sociologie et sociétés* 41(2), 273–298.

Amghar, Samir. 2009. "Foundations of Muslim Radicalism in France." In *Ethno-Religious Conflict in Europe. Typologies of Radicalisation in Europe's Muslim Communities,* edited by M. Emerson. Brussels: CEPS.

Anidjar, Gil. (2003). *The Jew, the Arab. A History of the Enemy.* Stanford: Stanford University Press.

Anthias, Floria and Nira Yuval-Davis. 1992. *Racialized Boundaries. Race, Nation, Gender, Colour and Class and the Anti-Racist Struggle.* London and New York: Routledge.

Appadurai, Arjun. 2006. *Fear of Small Numbers.* Durham and London: Duke University Press.

Ardizzoni, Michela. 2004. "Unveiling the Veil: Gendered Discourses and the (In)Visibility of the Female Body in France." *Women's Studies* 33, 2004.

Asad, Talal. 1993. *Genealogies of Religion: Discipline and Reasons of Power in Christianity and Islam.* New York: The Johns Hopkins University Press.

Asad, Talal. 2003. *Formations of the Secular*. Stanford: Stanford University Press.

Asad, Talal. 2005. "Trying to Understand French Secularism." In *Political Theologies. Public Religions in a Post-Secular World*, edited by H. d. Vries. Fordham University Press: New York.

Assemblée Nationale. 2004a. Session ordinaire de 2003–2004. 148e séance. Compte rendu intégral. 2e séance du mardi 3 février 2004. *Journal officiel de la République française* 15(2), 1272–1307.

Assemblée Nationale. 2004b. Session ordinaire de 2003–2004. 149e séance. Compte rendu intégral. 3e séance du mardi 3 février 2004. *Journal officiel de la République française* 15(3), 1310–1352.

Assemblée Nationale. 2004c. Session ordinaire de 2003–2004. 150e séance. Compte rendu intégral. 1re séance du mercredi 4 février 2004. *Journal officiel de la République française* 16(1), 1356–1391.

Assemblée Nationale. 2004d. Session ordinaire de 2003–2004. 151e séance. Compte rendu intégral. 2e séance du mercredi 4 février 2004. *Journal officiel de la République française* 16(2), 1394–1425.

Assemblée Nationale. 2004e. Session ordinaire de 2003–2004. Compte rendu intégral. 1re séance du jeudi 5 février 2004. *Journal officiel de la République française* 17(1), 1430–1459.

Assemblée Nationale. 2004f. Session ordinaire de 2003–2004 153e séance. Compte rendu intégral. 2e séance du jeudi 5 février 2004. *Journal officiel de la République française* 17(2), 1462–1505.

Assemblée Nationale. 2004g. Analyse du scrutin n° 436. Scrutin public sur l'ensemble du projet de loi relatif à l'application du principe de laïcité dans les écoles, collèges et lycées publiques. *Journal officiel de la République française*.

Assemblée Nationale. 2009a. Proposition de résolution tendant à la création d'une commission d'enquête sur la pratique du port de la burqa ou du niqab sur le territoire national. Enregistré à la Présidence de l'Assemblée nationale le 9 juin 2009. *Assemblée Nationale, 1725*.

Assemblée Nationale. 2009b. Mission information sur la pratique du port de la burqa et du niqab sur le territoire national. Compte rendu n°3.

Assemblée Nationale. 2009c. Mission information sur la pratique du port de la burqa et du niqab sur le territoire national. Compte rendu n°4.

Assemblée Nationale. 2009d. Mission information sur la pratique du port de la burqa et du niqab sur le territoire national. Compte rendu n°9.

Assemblée Nationale. 2009f. Mission information sur la pratique du port de la burqa et du niqab sur le territoire national. Compte rendu n°11.

Assemblée Nationale. 2009g. Mission information sur la pratique du port de la burqa et du niqab sur le territoire national. Compte rendu n°11.

Assemblée Nationale. 2010a. Session extraordinaire de 2009–2010. 10e séance. Compte rendu intégral. 3e séance du mardi 6 juillet 2010. *Journal officiel de la République française* 69(3), 5366–5387.

Assemblée Nationale. 2010b. Session extraordinaire de 2009–2010. Séances du mercredi 7 juillet 2010 Compte rendu intégral. *Journal officiel de la République française 70*, 5392–5433.

Assemblée Nationale. 2010c. Analyse du scrutin. *N°595*.

Assemblée Nationale. 2010d. Session extraordinaire de 2009–2010. 16e séance. Compte rendu intégral 2e séance du mardi 13 juillet 2010. *Journal officiel de la République française 72(2)*, 5536–5551.

Auffrey, Alain. 2015. "'Les Républicains,' un hold-up sémantique." *Libération*, 14 April. Accessed June 16, 2015. http://www.liberation.fr/france/2015/04/14/les-republicains-un-hold-up-semantique_1240905.

Atasoy, Yildiz. 2005. *Turkey, Islamists and Democracy. Transition and Globalization in a Muslim State*. London and New York: I.B. Tauris.

Azar, Michael. 2006. *Den koloniala bumerangen. Från schibbolet till körkort i svenskhe*. Stockholm: Brutus Östlings bokförlag.

Bacchi, Carol-Lee. 1999. *Women, Policy, and Politics. The Construction of Policy Problems*. London: Sage.

Badiou, Aalain. 2007. *Circonstances 4. De quoi Sarkozy est-il le nom?* Paris: Éditions lignes.

Bailly, Lionel. 2009. *Lacan: A Beginner's Guide*. Oxford: Oneworld.

Balibar, Etienne. 1991. "Is there a Neo-Racism?" In *Race-Nation-Class. Ambigious Identities*, edited by E. Balibar and I. Wallerstein. London: Verso.

Bardy, Gérard. 2011. *Charles le Catholique. De Gaulle et l'Église*. Paris: Plon.

Barras, Amelie. 2010. "Contemporary Laïcité: Setting the Terms of a New Social Contract? The Slow Exclusion of Women Wearing Headscarves." *Totalitarian Movements and Political Religions 11(2)*, 229–248.

Baubérot, Jean. 1998. "Two Thresholds of Laïcization." In *Secularism and Its Critics*, edited by R. Bhargava. New York and Oxford: Oxford University Press.

Baubérot, Jean. 2004. *Laïcité 1905–2005, entre passion et raison*. Paris: Editions Seuil.

Baubérot, Jean. 2008. *La laïcité expliquée à M. Sarkozy …: Et à ceux qui écrivent ses discours*. Paris: Editions Albin Michel.

Baubérot, Jean. 2009. "Laïcité and the Challenge of 'Republicanism". Modern & Contemporary France, n°17:2,189–198.

Baubérot, Jean. 2012. *La laïcité falsifiée*. Paris: La Découverte.

Baubérot, Jean, and Jean-Marc Regnault, eds. 2007. *Relations Eglises et autorités outremer. De 1945 à nos jours*. Paris: Les Indes savants.

Baudouin, Jean and Philippe Portier. 2001. "La laïcité française. Approche d'une métamorphose". In La laïcité: Une valeur d'aujourd'hui ? Contestations et renégations du modèle français, edited by J. Baudouin, P. Rennes: Presses universitaires de Rennes.

Bayrou, François. 1994. "Circulaire du 20 septembre 1994 relative au port de signes ostentatoires dans les établissements scolaires." *Bulletin officiel de l'Éducation nationale n°35.*

BBC. 2004. "French Hostage Recalls His Ordeals." *BBC News*, 24 December. Accessed January 27, 2015. http://news.bbc.co.uk/2/hi/europe/4124271.stm.

Bellan, Marie. 2011. "Reconduites à la frontière: Guéant affiche sa détermination." *Les Echos*, 8 August. Accessed January 27, 2015. http://www.lesechos.fr/08/08/2011/LesEchos/20990-029-ECH_reconduites-a-la-frontiere---gueant-affiche-sa-determination.htm.

Bennhold, Katrin. 2008. "A Veil Closes France's Door to Citizenship." *New York Times*, 19 July. Accessed January 27, 2015. http://www.nytimes.com/2008/07/19/world/europe/19france.html?_r=0.

Berezin, Mabel. 2009. *Illiberal Politics in Neo-Liberal Times. Culture, Security and Populism in the New Europe.* New York: Cambridge University Press.

Berger, Peter L. 1967. *The Sacred Canopy.* New York: Garden City.

Bernadette, Sauvagette. 2004. "Le Bureau des cultes." *Le Monde des Religions*. Accessed January 27, 2015. http://www.lemondedesreligions.fr/archives/2004/07/01/le-bureau-des-cultes,5135003.php.

Bernal, Martin. 1991. *Black Athena: The Afroasiatic Roots of Classical Civilization.* Volume 1 *of The Fabrication of Ancient Greece 1785–1985.* New Brunswick: Rutgers University Press.

Bernard, Philippe. 2003. "Foulard à l'école: la réalité cachée derrière les chiffres officiels." *Le Monde*, 11 December. Accessed January 27, 2015. http://www.lemonde.fr/archives/article/2003/12/10/foulard-a-l-ecole-la-realite-cachee-derriere-les-chiffres-officiels_345420_1819218.html.

Besson, Eric. 2010a. Intervention de M. Eric Besson lors du point d'étape du grand débat sur l'identité nationale, le lundi 4 janvier 2010. *Ministère de l'immigration, de l'intégration, de l'identité nationale et du développement solidaire*, 5 January.

Besson, Eeric. 2010b. Discours d'Eric BESSON lors de l'accueil de 93 réfugiés bénéficiaires de la protection internationale à Malte. *Ministère de l'intérieur*, 5 July.

Bidar, Abdennour. 2009. La burqa, une pathologie de la culture musulmane. *Libération*, 29 June. Accessed Januar 27, 2015. http://www.liberation.fr/societe/2009/06/29/la-burqa-une-pathologie-de-la-culture-musulmane_567468.

Bigo, Didier and Anastassia Tsoukala. 2008. *Terror, Insecurity and Liberty. Illiberal practices of liberal regimes after 9/11.* London and New York: Routledge.

Blanchard, Pascal and Sandrine Lemaire. 2006. "La fracture colonial: une crise française." In *La fracture colonial. La société française au prisme de l'héritage colonial*, edited by Nicolas Bancel, Pascal Blanchard and Sandrine Lemaire. Paris: La Découverte.

Bordenave, Prada. 2007. *Conclusions. 2ème et 7ème sous-sections réunies. Séance du 28 novembre 2007. Lecture du 21 décembre. 297355 M. Mutapha Nami*. Paris: Conseil d'État.

Bordenave, Prada. 2008. *Conclusions. N° 286798 Mme M. 2ème et 7ème sous-sections réunies. Séance du 26 mai 2008. Lecture du 27 juin 2008*. Paris: Conseil d'État.

Borghée, Maryam. 2012. *Voile intégral en France. Sociologie d'un paradoxe*. Paris: Michalon Éditions.

Bouamama, Saïd. 2004. *L'affaire du foulard islamique: la production d'un racisme respectable*. Paris: Le Geai Bleu.

Baudouin, Jean and Philippe Portier. 2001. "La laïcité française. Approche d'une métamorphose". In *La laïcité: Une valeur d'aujourd'hui ? Contestations et renégations du modèle français*, edited by J. Baudouin, P. Rennes: Presses universitaires de Rennes.

Baudouin, Jean and Philippe Portier. 2001. "La laïcité française. Approche d'une metamorphose." In *La laïcité. Une valeur d'aujourd'hui? Contestations et négations du modèle français*, Jean Baudouin, and Philippe Portier, 15–34. Paris: PUF.

Bouretz, Pierre. 2000. *La République et l'universel*. Paris: Éditions Gallimard.

Bouzar, Dounia. 2009. La burqa, un signe sectaire et non religieux. *Le Monde*, 22 June. Accessed January 27, 2015. http://www.lemonde.fr/idees/article/2009/06/22/la-burqa-un-signe-sectaire-et-non-religieux-par-dounia-bouzar_1209923_3232.html.

Bowen, John. 2007. *Why the French Don't Like Headscarves. Islam, the State, and Public Space*. Princeton: Princeton University Press.

Bowen, John. 2010. *Can Islam be French?* Princeton: Princeton University Press.

Breuilly, John. 1996. "Approaches to Nationalism." In *Mapping the Nation*, edited by G. Balakrishnan. London: Verso.

Bronner, Luc. 2011. "La place croissante de l'islam en banlieue." *Le Monde,* October 5. Accessed January 27, 2015. http://www.lemonde.fr/societe/article/2011/10/04/banlieues-de-la-republique_1581976_3224.html#ens_id=1574671.

Brown, Wendy. 2008. *Regulating Aversion: Tolerance in the Age of Identity and Empire*. Princeton: Princeton University Press.

Brown, Wendy. 2011. *Lecture: "Civilizational Delusions. Secularism, Tolerance, Equality."* Tankeverket. Stockholm. http://www.tankeverket.com/wordpress/?page_id=11. Accessed December 12, 2012.

Brubaker, Rogers. 1992. *Citizenship and Nationhood in France and Germany*. Cambridge: Harvard University Press.

Buffet, François.-Noël. 2010. *Rapport fait au nom de la commission des lois constitutionnelles, de législation, du suffrage universel, du Règlement et d'administration générale (1) sur le projet de loi, adopté par l'Assemblée nationale, interdisant la dissimulation du visage dans l'espace public* (Vol. 699). Paris: Sénat.

Butler, Judith. 2009. *Frames of War. When Is Life Grievable?* London: Verso.

CAI. 2007. *Contrat d'accueil et d'intégration*. Paris: SIB Imprimerie.
Calhoun, Craig, Mark Juergensmeyer, and Jonathan VanAntwerpen, eds. 2012. *Rethinking Secularism*. London and New York: Oxford University Press.
Camiscioli, Elisa. 2009. *Reproducing the French Race. Immigration, Intimacy, and Embodiment in the Early Twentieth Century*. Durham and London: Duke University Press.
Carrera, Sergio. 2009. "Nationality, Immigration and Republican Integration." In *Illiberal Liberal States Immigration, Citizenship and Integration in the EU*, edited by Sergio Carrera, Kees Groenendijk, and Elspeth Guild. Cornwall: MPG Books.
Carrera, Sergio, Kees Groenendijk, and Elspeth Guild, eds. 2009. *Illiberal Liberal States: Immigration, Citizenship and Integration in the EU*. Cornwall: MPG Books.
Casanova, José. 1994. *Public Religions in the Modern World*. Chicago: The University of Chicago Press.
Casanova, José. 2011. "The Secular, Secularizations, Secularisms." In *Rethinking Secularism*, edited by C. Calhoun, M. Juergensmeyer and J. VanAntwerpen. London and New York: Oxford University Press.
Cavanaugh, William T. 2009. *The Myth of Religious Violence: Secular Ideology and the Roots of Modern Conflict*. New York: Oxford University Press.
Cervulle, Maxime and Nick Rees-Roberts. 2008. "Queering the Orientalist Porn Package: Arab Men in French Gay Pornography." *New Cinemas: Journal of Contemporary Film* 6(3).
Chabal, Emile. 2015. *A Divided Republic. Nation, State and Citizenship in Contemporary France*. Cambridge: Cambridge University Press.
Chadwick, Kay. 1997. "Education in Secular France: (Re)Defining Laïcité." *Modern & Contemporary France* 5(1).
Champenois, Lucien. 1993. "Le conseiller pour les affaires religieuses au Quai d'Orsay." *Administration: l'Etat et les cultes* 116.
Charles, Bénédicte. 2009. "La loi sur la burqa ou la défaite de la laïcité." *Marianne*, 18 June. Accessed August 15, 2012. http://www.marianne.net/La-loi-sur-la-burqa-ou-la-defaite-de-la-laicite_a180925.html.
Chirac, Jacques. 2003a. Allocution de monsieur Jacques Chirac Président de la République à l'occasion de l'installation de la commission de réflexion sur l'application du principe de laïcité. *Palais de l'Elysée, Paris*, 3 July.
Chirac, Jacques. 2003b. Discours prononcé par M. Jacques Chirac, Président de la République, relatif au respect du principe de laïcité dans la République. *Palais de l'Elysée, Paris*, 17 December.
Cholet, Mona. 2005. "Machisme sans frontier (de classes)." *Le Monde diplomatique*, May. Accessed January 27, 2015. https://www.monde-diplomatique.fr/2005/05/CHOLLET/12172.
Chouder, Ismahane, Malika Latrèche, and Pierre Tevanian, (2008). *Les filles voilées parlent*. Paris: La Fabrique.

Citron, Suzanne. 2008. *Le Mythe National: L'histoire de France revisitée*. Paris: Les editions de l'Atelier.
Clément, Pascal. 2004. *Rapport fait au nom de la commission des lois constitutionnelles, de la législation et de l'administration générale de la République sur le projet de loi (n° 1378) relatif à l'application du principe de laïcité dans les écoles, collèges et lycées publics* (Vol. 1381). Paris: Assemblée Nationale.
Clos, Max. 1989. Tchador, exclusion, cannibales. *Le Figaro*, 13 October: 2.
Code de l'éducation. Version en vigueur le 22 juin 2000. Paris: JORF.
Code de l'entrée et du séjour des étrangers et du droit d'asile (CESEDA). 2006. "Code de l'entrée et du séjour des étrangers et du droit d'asile." *Journal officiel de la République française, 170*.
Coller, Ian. 2011. *Arab France: Islam and the Making of Modern Europe*. Berkeley: University of California Press.
Commission nationale consultative des droits de l'homme (CNCDH). 1994. *Rapport annuél de CNCDH*. Paris: La Documentation française.
Commission nationale consultative des droits de l'homme (CNCDH). 2003a. *La lutte contre le racisme et la xénophobie: Rapport d'activité*. Paris: La Documentation française.
Commission nationale consultative des droits de l'homme (CNCDH). 2003b. *La laïcité aujourd'hui: rapport d'étape*. Paris: La Documentation française.
Conklin, Alice L. 1997. *A Mission to Civilize. The Republican Idea of Empire in France and West Africa. 1895–1930*. Stanford: Stanford University Press.
Connolly, Kate. 2010. "Angela Merkel Declares Death of Multiculturalism." *The Guardian*, 17 October. Accessed January 27, 2015. https://www.theguardian.com/world/2010/oct/17/angela-merkel-germany-multiculturalism-failures.
Conseil d'Etat. 1989. "L'avis du Conseil d'Etat." *Le Monde*, 29 November.
Conseil d'Etat. 2008. *Mme M. Section du contentieux, 2 ème et 7 ème sous-sections réunies Séance du 26 mai 2008*. Lecture du 27 juin 2008 (Vol. 286798). Paris.
Conseil d'État. 2010. *Study of possible legal grounds for banning the full veil*. Report adopted by the Plenary General Assembly of the Conseil d'Etat Thursday 25 March 2010. Paris: Conseil d'État.
Cuneo, Louise. 2009. "Christine Boutin : Le débat sur le Pacs a décrispé le tabou de l'homosexualité en France." *Le Point*, 13 October. Accessed January 27, 2015. http://www.lepoint.fr/actualites-societe/2009-10-13/christine-boutin-le-debat-sur-le-pacs-a-decrispe-le-tabou-de-l/920/0/385260.
Dahlstedt, Magnus and Mekonnen Tesfahuney. 2008. *Den bästa av världar. Betraktelser över en postpolitisk samtid*. Stockholm: Tankekraft.
Daughton, James P. 2006. *An Empire Divided. Religion, Republicanism, and the Making of French Colonialism, 1880–1914*. Oxford and New York: Oxford University Press.

Debray, Régis. 2002. *Rapport à Monsieur le Ministre de l'Éducation nationale: L'enseignement du fait religieux dans l'École laïque.* Paris: La Documentation Française.

Debré, Jean-Louis. 2003a. *Rapport fait au nom de la Commission d'information sur la question du port des signes religieux à l'école.* Auditions (Vol. 1275, tome I, 1ère partie). Paris: Assemblée Nationale.

Debré, Jean-Louis. 2003b. *Rapport fait au nom de la Commission d'information sur la question du port des signes religieux à l'école.* Auditions (Vol. 1275, tome II, 2ème partie). Paris: Assemblée Nationale.

Debré, Jean-Louis. 2003c. *Rapport fait au nom de la Commission d'information sur la question du port des signes religieux à l'école.* Auditions (Vol. 1275, tome II, 1ère partie). Paris: Assemblée NationaleDeclaration of the Rights of Man and of the Citizen. (1789). *Conseil constitutionnel,* http://www.conseil-constitutionnel.fr/conseil-constitutionnel/root/bank_mm/anglais/cst2.pdf.

De Cock, Laurence. 2008. "Afrique." In, *Comment Nicolas Sarkozy écrit l'histoire de France,* edited by Laurence De Cock, Fanny Madeleine, Nicolas Offenstadt, and Sophie Wahnich. Marseille: Agone.

De Cock, Laurence, Fanny Madeleine, Nicolas Offenstadt, and Sophie Wahnich, eds. 2008. *Comment Nicolas Sarkozy écrit l'histoire de France.* Marseille: Agone.

De Galembert, Claire. 2008. "Les musulmans de la République ou les paradoxes de la publicisation d'une identité collective islamique en France." In *La laïcité en question. Religion, Etat et société en France et en Allemagne du 18e siècle à nos jours,* edited by Sylvie Le Grand. Villeneuve d'Ascq: Septentrion.

De Groot, Gerard-René, Jan-Jaap Kuipers, and Franziska Weber. 2009. "Passing Citizenship Tests as a Requirement for Naturalisation: A Comparative Perspective." In *Illiberal liberal states. Immigration, citizenship and integration in the EU,* edited by Elspeth Guild, Kees Groenendijk, and Sergio Carrera, 51–77. Farnham: Ashgate.

De Loisy, Anne. 2005. *Bienvenu en France! Six mois d'enquête clandestine dans la zone d'attente de Roissy.* Paris: Le cherche midi.

Délphy, Christine. 2008. *Classer, dominer. Qui sont les autres?* Paris: La Fabrique Editions.

Deltombe, Thomas. 2007. *L'islam imaginaire. La construction médiatique de l'islamophobie en France 1975–2005.* Paris: La Découverte.

Devji, Faisal. 2008. *The Terrorist in Search of Humanity: Militant Islam and Global Politics.* New York: Hurst and Co. and Columbia University Press.

Dornel, Laurent. (2004). *La France hostile. Socio-histoire de la xénophobie (1870–1914).* Paris: Hachette.

Doward, Jamie. 2011. David Cameron's Attack on Multiculturalism Divides the Coalition. *The Guardian,* 6 February. Accessed January 27, 2015. http://www.theguardian.com/politics/2011/feb/05/david-cameron-attack-multiculturalism-coalition.

Dressler, Markus and Arvind-Pal Mandair, eds. (2011). *Secularism and Religion-Making*. Oxford and New York: Oxford University Press.

Dufay, François. 2003. Le coup du foulard. *Le Point*, 5 April. Accessed January 27, 2015. http://www.lepoint.fr/actualites-politique/2003-04-25/le-coup-du-foulard/917/0/119526.

El Guindi, Fadwa. 2003. *Veil, Modesty, Privacy, Resistance*. New York and Oxford: Berg Publishers.

Elmessiri, Abdelwahab. 2000. "Secularism, Immanence, and Deconstruction." In *Islam and Secularism in the Middle East*, edited by John L. Esposito and Azzam Tamimi. New York: New York University Press.

Eldem, Edhem. 2010. *Un orient de consommation*. Istanbul: Ottoman Bank Museum.

Equy, Laure. 2008. "Banlieues. Le plan galère de Fadela Amara." *Libération*, 8 February: 2-4.

Equy, Laure. 2009. "La burqa 'une prison ambulante'." *Libération*, 17 June. Accessed January 27, 2015. http://www.liberation.fr/france/2009/06/17/la-burqa-une-prison-ambulante_565314.

Esposito, John L. and Azzim Tamimi, eds. *Islam and Secularism in the Middle East*. New York University Press: New York.

Europol. 2007. *TE-SAT 2007. EU Terrorism Situation and Trend Report 2007*. https://www.europol.europa.eu/content/publication/te-sat-2007-eu-terrorism-situation-trend-report-1467

Europol. 2011. *TE-SAT 2011. EU* Terrorism Situation and Trend Report 2011. https://www.europol.europa.eu/content/publication/te-sat-2011-eu-terrorism-situation-and-trend-report-1475

Fabre, Rémi. 2007. "L'élaboration de la loi 1905." In *Politiques de la laïcité au XXE siècle*, edited by Patrick Weil. Paris: PUF.

Fernando, Mayanthi L. 2014. *The Republic Unsettled. Muslim French and the Contradictions of Secularism*. Durham and London: Duke University Press.

Ferry, Jules. 2003. "Contre les dérives communautaristes, réaffirmer les principes de la laïcité républicaine." *Conférence de presse*, 27 February. Ministère de l'Education.

Ferry, Jules. 2004a. "Discours de Luc Ferry, ministre de la jeunesse, de l'éducation nationale et de la recherche à l'occasion de l'examen du projet de loi relatif à l'application du principe de laïcité dans les écoles, collèges et lycées publics à l'Assemblée nationale." 4 February. *Ministère de la Jeunesse, de l'Education et de la Recherche*.

Ferry, Jules. 2004b. "L'idée républicaine aujourd'hui Information." 10 March. *Ministère de la Jeunesse, de l'Education et de la Recherche*.

Fillon, François. 2004. "Le Guide republicain, un prolongement pédagogique au débat sur la laïcité. Lettre Flash." 11 June. *Minstère de l'éducation nationale, l'enseignement supérieure et de la recherche*.

Fillon, François. 2011. "Circulaire du 2 mars 2011 relative à la mise en oeuvre de la loi n° 2010-1192 du 11 octobre 2010 interdisant la dissimulation du visage dans l'espace public." *JORF,* n°0052, p. 4128.

Fitzgerald, Timothy. 2007. *Discourse on Civility and Barbarity: A Critical History of Religion and Related Categories.* Oxford: Oxford University Press.

Fitzgerald, Timothy. 2015. "Critical Religion and Critical Research on Religion: Religion and Politics as Modern Fictions." *Critical Research on Religion, 3*(3).

Ford, Caroline. 2005. *Divided Houses. Religion and Gender in Modern France.* New York: Cornell University Press.

Foucault, Michel. 1972. *Archeology of Knowledge.* London and New York: Routledge.

Foucault, Michel. 1984. "Nietzsche, Genealogy, History". In The Foucault Reader, edited by Paul Rabinow. New York: Pantheon Books.

Foucault, Michel. 1991. "Governmentality." In *The Foucault Effect. Studies in Governmentality,* edited by G. Burchell, C. Gordon and P. Miller. Chicago: University of Chicago Press.

Foucault, Michel. 2001a. "Table ronde du 20 mai 1980." In *Michel Foucault. Dits et Ecrits II, 1976–1988,* edited by D. Daniel and F. Edwald. Paris: Gallimard.

Foucault, Michel. 2001b. "Le sujet et le pouvoir." In *Michel Foucault. Dits et Ecrits II, 1976-1988,* edited by D. Daniel and F. Edwald (Eds.),. Paris: Gallimard.

Foucault, Michel. (2001c). "Les mailles du pouvoir." In D. Daniel and F. Edwald (Eds.), *Michel Foucault. Dits et Ecrits II, 1976-1988.* Paris: Gallimard.

Foucault, M. (2004). *Sécurité, territoire, population. Cours au Collège de France, 1977-1978.* Paris: Seuil-Gallimard.

Fourest, Caroline and Fiammetta Venner. 2011. Marine Le Pen. Paris: Éditions Grasset et Fasquelle.

France 2. 2003. "Défense de la laïcité ou rejet de l'islam." *Mots Croisés:* INA.

France 2. 2004. "Dieu, la France et la République." *100 minutes pour comprendre:* INA.

France 5. 2003a. "Menaces sur la laïcité." *Ripostes:* INA.

France 5. 2003b. "Laïcité - le grand débat:" INA.

France 5. 2011. "Laïcité: les religions s'en mèlent:" INA.

Frégosi, Franck. 2008. *Penser l'islam dans la laïcité.* Paris: Fayard.

Gabizon, Cécilia. 2009a. "Qui sont les femmes qui portent la burqa en France?" *Le Figaro,* June 19. Accessed January 27, 2015. http://www.lefigaro.fr/actualite-france/2009/06/19/01016-20090619ARTFIG00011-femmes-voilees-beaucoup-de-francaises-et-de-converties-.php.

Gabizon, Cécilia. 2009b. "Deux mille femmes portent la burqa en France." *Le Figaro,* 9 September.

Gaffney, John. 2010. *Political Leadership in France. From Charels de Gaulle to Nicolas Sarkozy.* New York: Palgrave Macmillan.

Gallerey, Pierre. 1989. "Collège de Creil: Les tchadors de la discorde." *Le Figaro*, 9 October, p. 44.

Gardell, Mattias. 2011. *Islamofobi*. Stockholm: Leopard förlag.

Garraud, Jean-Paul. 2010. *Rapport fait au nom de la commission des lois constitutionnelles, de la législation et de l'administration et de l'administration générale de la République sur le projet de loi (n° 2520), interdisant la dissimulation du visage dans l'espace public* (Vol. 2648). Paris: Assemblée Nationale.

Gaspard, Françoise and Fahrad Khosrokhavar. 1995. *Le foulard et la République*. Paris: La Découverte.

Gauchet, Michel. 1985. *Le Désenchantement du monde. Une histoire politique de la religion*. Paris: Gallimard.

Geisser, Vincent. 2003. *La Nouvelle Islamophobie*. Paris: La Découverte.

Geisser, Vincent and Aziz Zemouri. 2007. *Marianne et Allah*. Paris: La Découverte.

Gentleman, Amelia. 2003. "French Rappers in War of Words with Government." *The Guardian*, 11 November. Accessed January 27, 2015. https://www.theguardian.com/world/2003/nov/11/arts.france.

Gerin, André. 2010. *Rapport d'information n°2262. Fait en application de l'article 145 du Règlement au nom de la mission d'information sur la pratique du port du voile intégral sur le territoire national*. Paris: Assemblée Nationale.

Giry, Stéphanie. 2006. "France and its Muslims." *Foreign Affairs, September/October*. Accessed January 27, 2015. https://www.foreignaffairs.com/articles/france/2006-09-01/france-and-its-muslims.

Goldstone, Richard. 2009. *Human Rights in Palestine and Other Occupied Arab Territories: Report of the United Nations Fact Finding Mission on the Gaza Conflict*. New York: United Nations.

Goldstone, Richard. 2011. Reconsidering the Goldstone Report. *Washington Post*, 1 April. Accessed January 27, 2015. https://www.washingtonpost.com/opinions/reconsidering-the-goldstone-report-on-israel-and-war-crimes/2011/04/01/AFg111JC_story.html.

Göle, Nilüfer. 2010. "Manifestations of the Religious-Secular Divide: Self, State, and the Public Sphere." In *Comparative Secularisms in a Global Age*, edited by E. L. Cady and E. Shakman Hurd. New York: Palgrave Macmillan.

Grenoble, Laurent. 2011. "Tribunal de Bobigny: en France, a-t-on le droit de se dire pour des sanctions à l'égard d'Israël?" *Le Post*, 17 March. Accessed January 27, 2015. http://archives-lepost.huffingtonpost.fr/article/2011/03/16/2436382_17-mars-tribunal-de-bobigny-en-france-a-t-on-le-droit-de-se-dire-pour-des-sanctions-a-l-egard-d-israel.html.

Gresh, Alain. 2011. "Nouvelles d'Orient: Jupe et string obligatoire." *Les blogs du Diplo*, March. Accessed January 27, 2015. http://blog.mondediplo.net/2015-03-27-Une-fabuleuse-decouverte-sur-l-islam.

Grunberg, Anne. 2000. *Les camps de la honte. Les internés juifs des camps français 1939-1944*. Paris: La Découverte.
Guéant, Claude. 2011. *La laïcité et la liberté religieuse. Recueil de textes et de jurisprudence*. Paris: Journaux Officiels.
Guénif-Souilamas, Nacira. 2006. "La république aristocratique et la nouvelle société de cour." In *La république mise à nue par son immigration*, edited by Nacira Guénif-Souilamas. Paris: La Fabrique.
Guénif-Souilamas, Nacira and Éric Macé. 2005. *Les feministes et le garçon arabe*. Paris: L'Aube.
Guénois, Jean-Marie, Anne-Bénédicte Hoffner, and Nicolas Senèze. 2008. "Michèle Alliot-Marie: 'Certains on tune conception archaïque de la laïcité'." *La Croix*, January 24. Accessed January 27, 2015. http://www.la-croix.com/Religion/Actualite/Michele-Alliot-Marie-Certains-ont-une-conception-archaique-de-la-laicite-_NG_-2008-01-24-667720.
Gustavsson, Gina. 2011. "Romantic Liberalism." Essay III in *Trecherous Liberties. Isaiah Berlin's Theory of Positive and Negative Freedom in Contemporary Political Culture*. Uppsala: Acta Universitatis Upsaliensis.
Hale, Dana S. 2008. *Races on Display. French Representations of Colonized Peoples, 1886–1940*. Bloomington: Indiana University Press.
Hargreaves, Alec G. 2007. *Multi-Ethnic France France: Immigration, Politics, Culture and Society*. London and New York: Routledge.
Haski, Pierre. 2011. "Benjmain Stora répond aux critiques des 'Hommes libres'." *Rue 89*, October 4. Accessed January 27, 2015. http://rue89.nouvelobs.com/2011/10/04/lhistorien-benjamin-stora-repond-aux-detracteurs-des-hommes-libres-224831.
Hawley, John C. 2005. "Lavender Ain't White: Emerging Queer Self-Expression in its Broader Context." In *Postcolonial Whiteness. A Critical Reader on Race and Empire*, edited by Alfred J. Lopez. Albany: State University of New York Press.
Hajjat, Abdellali. and Marwan Mohammed. 2013. *Islamophobie. Comment les élites françaises fabriquent le "problem musulman."* Paris: La Découverte [Kindle].
Hazan, Eric. 2006. *LQR. La propagande quotidien*. Paris: Raisons d'agir.
Hazan, Eric and Aalain Badiou. 2011. *L'antisémitisme partout. Aujourd'hui en France*. Paris: La Fabrique.
Hennette-Vauchez, Stéphanie, Marc Pichard, and Diane Roman. 2014. *La loi & le genre. Études critiques de droit français*. Paris: CNRS Éditions.
Hennette-Vauchez, Stéphanie and Vincent Valentin. 2014. *L'affaire Baby Loup ou la nouvelle laïcité*. Paris: LGDJ.
Hirsi Ali, Ayaan, Chahla Chafiq, Caroline Fourest, Bernard-Henry Lévy, Irshad Manji, Mehdi Mozaffari, Maryam Namazie, Taslima Nasreen, Salman Rushdie, Antoine Sfeir, and Ibn Warraq. 2006 "Le manifeste des douze: ensemble contre le

nouveau totalitarisme." *ProChoix*, 1 March. Accessed January 27, 2015. http://www.prochoix.org/cgi/blog/index.php/2006/03/01/412-manifeste-des-douze-ensemble-contre-le-nouveau-totalitarisme.

Homer, Sean. 2005. *Jacques Lacan*. London and New York: Routledge.

Hortefeux, Brice. 2010. Dîner d'iftar de la Grande mosquée. *Ministère de l'Intérieur de l'Outre-mer et des Collectivités Territoriales, 31 August*.

Hosford, Desmond and Chong J. Wojtkowski. eds. 2010. *French Orientalism: Culture, Politics, and the Imagined Other*. Newcastel upon Tyne: Cambridge Scholars Publishing.

Howarth, David. 2000. *Discourse*. Buckingham: Open University Press.

Howarth, David, Aletta J. Norval, and Yannis Stavrakakis. 2000. *Discourse theory and political analysis—Identities, hegemonies, and social change*. Manchester: Manchester University Press.

Howarth, David and Georgios Varouxakis. 2014. *Contemporary France: An Introduction to French Politics and Society*. London and New York: Routledge.

Hulliung, M. 2001. "Rousseau, Voltaire, and the Revenge of Pascal." In *The Cambridge Companion to Rousseau*, edited by P. Riley. Cambridge: Cambridge University Press.

Hulliung, M. 2002. *Citizens and Citoyens: Republicans and Liberals in America and France*. Cambridge: Harvard University Press.

Hummel, C. 2010. *Rapport d'information fait au nom de la délégation aux droits des femmes et à l'égalité des chances entre les hommes et les femmes sur le projet de loi, adopté par l'Assemblée nationale, interdisant la dissimulation du visage dans l'espace public* (n° 675, 2009-2010) (Vol. 698). Paris: Sénat.

IFOP. 2010. Regard croisé France / Allemagne sur l'Islam. *Le Monde*, 13 December. Accessed January 27, 2015. http://www.ifop.com/?option=com_publication&type=poll&id=1365.

India, Xavier J. 2005. "Analytics of the Modern: An Introduction." In *Anthropologies of Modernity: Foucault, Governmentality, and Life Politics*. Oxford: Blackwell Publishing.

Jacoby, Susan. 2004. *Freethinkers. A History of American Secularism*. New York: Metropolitan Books.

Jansen, Yolande. 2013. *Secularism, Assimilation and the Crisis of Multiculturalism. French Modernist Legacies*. Amsterdam: Amsterdam University Press.

Joppke, Christian. 2009. *Veil: Mirror of Identity*. Cambridge: Polity Press.

Jospin, Lionel. 1989. *Circulaire de 12 décembre 1989*. Paris: Journal Officiel.

Kauder, Serge. 2006. Une loi française interdit aux femmes le port du pantalon. *CFO News*, 13 May. Accessed Januart 27, 2015. http://www.finyear.com/Une-loi-francaise-interdit-aux-femmes-le-port-du-pantalon_a438.html.

Keane, John. 2000. "The Limits of Secularism." In *Islam and Secularism in the Middle East*, edited by John L. Esposito, and Azzam Tamimi. New York: New York University Press.

Keaton, Tricia D. 2006. *Muslim Girls and the Other France. Race, Identity Politics, & Social Exclusion.* Bloomington: Indiana University Press.

Kemp, Anna. 2009. "Marianne d'aujourd'hui?: The Figure of the Beurette in Contemporary French Feminist Discourses." *Modern & Contemporary France*, 17(1).

Khiari, Sadri. 2009. *La contre-révolution coloniale en France. De de Gaulle à Sarkozy.* Paris: La fabrique.

Kintzler, Cathérine, Elisabeth de Fontenay, Régis Debray, Aalain Finkelkraut, and Elisabeth Badinter. 1989. "Profs: Ne Capitulons pas!" *Le Novel Observateur*, November 2.

Kuru, Ahmed 2009. *Secularism and State Policies toward Religion: The United States, France, and Turkey.* Cambridge: Cambridge University Press.

Kuru, Ahmed and Alfred Stepan, eds. 2012. *Democracy, Islam, and Secularism in Turkey.* New York: Colombia University Press.

Le Gouvernement de la République Française. 2011. *La République se vit à visage découvert.* Paris. Accessed July 15, 2015. http://www.textes.justice.gouv.fr/art_pix/dep_a5 _visage_20110308.pdf.

La Libération. 1989a. Cover Page. *Libération*, 20 September.

La Libération. 1989b. Cover Page. *Libération*, 21/22 October.

La Libération. 2003. "Des enseignants pour la réintégration des élèves voilées." *Libération*, 30 October. Accessed Januarry 27, 2015. http://www.liberation.fr/ societe/2003/10/30/des-enseignants-pour-la-reintegration-des-eleves-voilees _449964.

La Libération. 2008. "L'essentiel: président." *Libération*, 9 February.

Laborde, Cécile. 2005. "Secular Philosophy and Muslim Headscarves in School." *The Journal of Political Philosophy*, 13(3).

Laborde, Cécile. 2008. *Critical Republicanism. The Hijab Controversy and Political Philosophy.* Oxford and New York: Oxford University Press.

Laclau, Ernesto. 1994. *On Populist Reason.* London and New York: Verso.

Laclau, Ernesto and Chantal Mouffe. 2001. *Hegemony and Socialist Strategy. Towards a Radical Democratic Politics.* London: Verso.

Lafon, Justine. 2009. "Violences faites aux femmes: 'En France, les chiffres sont alarmants'." *Libération*, 24 November. Accessed January 27, 2015. http://www.liberation .fr/societe/2009/11/24/violences-faites-aux-femmes-en-france-les-chiffres-sont -alarmants_595505.

Lazreg, Marnia. 1988. "Feminism and Difference: The Perils of Writing as a Woman on Women in Algeria Author(s)." *Feminist Studies*, 14(1).

Lazreg, Marnia. 1994. *The Eloquence of Silence.* New York: Routledge.

Le Figaro. 1989a. Cover Page. *Le Figaro,* 25 September,
Le Figaro. 1989b. Cover Page. *Le Figaro,* 25 September.
Le Monde. 1989a. Cover Page. *Le Monde,* 7 October.
Le Monde. 1989b. Cover Page. *Le Monde,* 21 October.
Le Monde.1989c. Cover Page. *Le Monde,* 25 October.
Le Monde. 1989d. "Deux des collégiennes de Creil retirent leur foulard." *Le Monde, 5* December: 48.
Le Nouvel Observateur. 2008. "Mariage annulé pour 'non virginité': le parquet va faire appel du jugement." *Le Nouvel Observateur,* 23 June. Accessed January 27, 2015. http://tempsreel.nouvelobs.com/societe/20080602.OBS6619/mariage-annule-pour-non-virginite-le-parquet-va-faire-appel-du-jugement.html.
Le Pen, Marine. 2010. "Nos rues occupées." Conférence de Presse de Marine Le Pen." *Nations Presse,* 14 December. Accessed January 27, 2015. http://www.nationspresse.info/fn/nos-rues-occupees-conference-de-presse-de-marine-le-pen.
Lefort, Claude. 1986. *The Political Forms of Modern Society. Bureaucracy, Democracy, Totalitarianism.* Cambridge: The MIT Press.
Lentin, Alana and Gavin Titley. 2011. *The Crisis of Multiculturalism. Racism in a Neo-Liberal Age.* London: Zed Books.
Lévy, Laurent. 2010. *"La gauche', les Noirs et les Arabes."* Paris: La fabrique.
Liogier, Raphaël. 2006. *"Une Laïcité 'légitime.' La France et ses religions d'etat."* Paris: Médicis Entrelas.
Liogier, Raphaël. 2010. "La distinction sociocognitive et normative entre bonne et mauvaise religion en contexte européen: les cas de l'islam et du bouddhisme." In *Pluralisme religieux et citoyenneté,* edited by M. Milot, P. Portier and J.-P. Willaime. Rennes: PUF de Rennes.
Liogier, Raphaël. 2012. *Le Mythe de l'islamisation, essai sur une obsession collective.* Paris: Seuil.
Loi du 9 décembre 1905 *concernant la séparation des Eglises et de l'Etat.* Paris. Journal Officiel de la République Française, 37e année, n°336, 11 octobre, 1905, p.7205.
Loi n°2004-228 du 15 mars 2004. Version en vigueur le 1er septembre 2004. *Journal Officiel de la République Française, 37e année n°65 du 17 mars,* 2004, p. 5190, texte n° 1.
Loi n°2010-1192 du 11 octobre 2010 interdisant la dissimulation du visage dans l'espace public. Version en vigueur 1er Avril 2011. Journal officiel de la République française, n°0237 du 12 octobre 2010, p. 18344, texte n°1.
Lombard, M.-A. 1989. "Tchador à l'école: deux mois d'un débat qui divise la France." *Le Figaro,* 27 November, p. 10.
Lopez, Alfred J. 2005. "Whiteness after Empire." In *Postcolonial Whiteness. A Critical Reader on Race and Empire,* edited by Alfred J. Lopez. Albany: State University of New York Press.

Lorcin, Patricia. 1999. *Imperial Identities: Stereotyping, Race, and Prejudice in Colonial Algeria*. London and New York: I.B Tauris.

Lorcin, Patricia and Paula Sanders, 2007. "France and Islam: Introduction." *French Historical Studies, 30*(3).

Loubes, Olivier. 2004. "L'interdiction des propagandes politique et confessionnelle dans les établissements scolaires. Deux circulaires de Jean Zay en 1936 et 1937." *Vingtième Siècle. Revue d'histoire, 81.*

Loué, T. 2008. "Affaire Dreyfus." In *Comment Nicolas Sarkozy écrit l'histoire de France*, edited by Laurence De Cock, Fanny Madeleine, Nicolas Offenstadt, and Sophie Wahnich. Marseille: Agone.

Mahmood, Saba. 2005. *Politics of Piety. The Islamic Revival and the Feminist Subejct*. Princeton: Princeton University Press.

Maillot, Agnès. 2008. *Identité nationale et immigration*. Paris: Les carnets de l'info.

Mamdani, Mahmod. 2004. *Good Muslim, Bad Muslim. America and the Cold War, and the Roots of Terror*. New York: Pantheon Books.

Manac'h, Erwan. 2011. "Des militants de la campagne de boycott des produits israéliens" BDS "devant les tribunaux." *Politis*, 18 March. Accessed January 27, 2015. http://www.politis.fr/articles/2011/03/des-militants-de-la-campagne-de-boycott-des-produits-israeliens-bds-devant-les-tribunaux-13474/.

Marelli, Joël. 2006. "Usages et maléfices du thème de l'antisémitisme en France." In *La république mise à nu par son immigration*, edited by Nacira Guénif-Souilamas. Paris: La Fabrique.

Martin, David. 1979. *A General Theory of Secularization*. New York: Harper & Row.

Massad, Joseph. 2015. *Islam in Liberalism*. Chicago: Chicago Universit Press.

Masquet, Brigitte. 2006. "Politique de l'immigration." *Regards sur l'actualité, 326*.

Masuzawa, Tomoko. 2005. *The Invention of World Religions. Or, How European Universalism Was Preserved in the Language of Pluralism*. Chicago: University of Chicago Press.

Masuzawa, Tomoko. 2008. "The Burden of the Great Divide." SSRC. Accessed June 11, 2009. http://blogs.ssrc.org/tif/2008/01/30/the-burden-of-the-great-divide/.

Mathiez, Albert. 2005. "La séparation des Églises et l'État a-t-elle existé réellement sour la Révolution française?" In *1905! La loi de séparation des Églises et de l'État*, edited by Jean-Marc. Schiappa. Paris: Éditions Syllepse.

Mastnak, Tomaz. (2002). *Crusading Peace. Christendom, the Muslim World and Western Political Order*. Berkeley and London: University of California Press.

McCutcheon, Russel T. 2003. *The Discipline of Religion. Structure, meaning, rhetoric*. London and New York: Routledge.

McGoldrick, Dominic. 2006. *Human Rights and Religion: The Islamic Headscarf Debate in Europe*. Oxford: Hart.

McHoul, Alec and Wendy Grace. 1993. *A Foucault Primer. Discourse, Power and the Subject*. London and New York: Routledge.

Meurs, Dominique and Sophie Ponthieux. 2006. "L'écart des salaires entre les femmes et les hommes peut-il encore baisser?" *Economie et statistique*, 398–399.

Miaro, Lucien. 1989. "Les foulards de l'islam au collège: le compromis." *Le Figaro*, 10 October, p. 8.

Micheau, Fanny. 2008. "Croisades." In *Comment Nicolas Sarkozy écrit l'histoire de France*, edited by Laurence De Cock, Fanny Madeleine, Nicolas Offenstadt, and Sophie Wahnich. Marseille: Agone.

Michelet, Jules. 2014. *La Femme*. Paris: Flammarion.

Milner, Jean-Claude. 2009. *De l'école*. Paris: Éditions Verdier.

Ministère d'Éducation nationale. 2011. "Les établissements d'enseignement privé." Paris. Accessed January 27, 2015. http://www.education.gouv.fr/cid251/les-etablissements-d-enseignement-prive.html.

Mission interministérielle de lutte contre les sects (MILS). 2002. *Rapport 2001*. Paris: La Documentation française.

Monod, Jean-Claude. 2007. *Sécularisation et laïcité*. Paris: PUF.

Mouffe, Chantal. 2005. *On the Political*. London and New York: Routledge.

Mouillard, Sylvain and Willy Le Devin. 2013. "Anti-mariage gay: la police évacue les derniers manifestants." *Libération*, 26 May. Accessed January 27, 2015. http://www.liberation.fr/societe/2013/05/26/mariage-pour-tous-dernier-baroud-des-opposants_905765

Mouloud, Laurent. 2003. "Affaire Sniper. Le mauvais cible de Sarkozy." *L'Humanité*, November 11. Accessed January 27, 2015. http://www.humanite.fr/node/486757.

Nilsson, Per-Erik. 2015. "'Secular Retaliation': A Case Study of Integralist Populism, Anti-Muslim Discourse, and Illiberal Discourse on Secularism in Contemporary France." *Politics, Religion & Ideology*, 16:1, 87–106.

Noiriel, Gérard. 1988. *Le creuset français: Histoire de l'immigration, XIXE-XXE siècle*. Paris: Editions de Seuil.

Noiriel, Gérard. 2007. *Immigration, antisémitisme et racisme (Xixe-Xxe Siècle): Discours publics, humiliations privées*. Paris: Fayard.

Nordmann, Christine. 2004. *Le foulard islamique en questions*. Paris: Editions Amsterdam.

Obama, Barack. 2009a. "Remarks by the President on a New Beginning. Cairo University, Cairo, Egypt." *The White House*, June 4.

Obama, Barack. 2009b. "Remarks by President Obama and President Sarkozy of France. Préfecture, Caen, France." *The White House*, 6 June.

OFII. 2011. "Le CAI est il obligatoire?" *Office de l'immigration et de l'intégration*. http://www.ofii.fr/tests_197/le_cai_est_il_obligatoire_1029.html.

Pecqueux, Anthony. 2003. "Les mots de la mésentente entre Sarkozy et Sniper." *Libération*, 13 November. Accessed January 27, 2015. http://www.liberation.fr/tribune/2003/11/13/les-mots-de-la-mesentente-entre-sarkozy-et-sniper_451668.

Poletti, Bérengère. 2010. *Rapport d'information fait au nom de la délégation aux droits des femmes et à l'égalité des chances entre les hommes et les femmes sur le projet de loi interdisant la dissimulation du visage dans l'espace public* (Vol. 2646). Paris: Assemblée Nationale.

Raphelle, R. 1989. "Trois foulards contre la 'sérénité laique'." *Le Monde*, 7 September.

Régnier-Loilier, Arnaud. 2009. "L'arrivée d'un enfant modifie-t-elle la répartition des tâches domestiques au sein du couple?" *Population & sociétés, 461*.

Reuters. 2007. "Identité nationale: Sarkozy insiste." *L'Express*, 14 May.

Reuters. 2008. "Fadela Amara approuve la non-naturalisation d'une femme en burqa." *Libération*, 1 August. Accessed January 27, 2015. http://www.liberation.fr/france/2008/07/15/fadela-amara-approuve-la-non-naturalisation-d-une-femme-en-burqa_18862.

Reuters. 2011. "Guéant : la loi de 1905 'ne sera pas modifiée'." *Le Monde*, 4 April. Accessed January 27, 2015. http://www.lemonde.fr/societe/article/2011/04/04/le-nombre-de-musulmans-en-france-pose-probleme-selon-gueant_1502928_3224.html.

Revel, Jean-François. 2003. "L'intégrisme contre la République." *Le Point*, n°1600, 3 May: 41.

Rigouste, Mathieu. 2005. "L'immigré, mais qui a réussi ... Variantes du discours sur l'intégration." *Le Monde diplomatique,* July, p. 23.

Rigouste, Mathieu. 2009. *L'ennemi inérieur. La généalogi colonial et militaire de l'ordre sécuritaire dans la France contemporaine*. Paris: Editions de la Découverte.

Robine, Joël and Laure Equy. 2009. "Burqa: Gerin installe sa mission parlemantaire (photography)." *Libération*, 1 July. Accessed January 27, 2015. http://www.liberation.fr/france/2009/07/01/burqa-gerin-installe-sa-mission-parlementaire_567989.

Rochefort, Florence. 2007. "Ambivalence laïques et critiques feministes." In *Le pouvoir du genre. Laïcités et religions 1905-2005*, edited by Florence Rochefort. Toulouse: PUM.

Rosanvallon, Pierre. 2001. *Le Sacré du citoyen. Histoire du suffrage universel en France*. Paris: Folio.

Rose, Nikolas. 1999. *Powers of Freedom. Refraiming Political Thought*. Cambridge: Cambridge University Press.

Rouland, Norbert. 1994. "La tradition juridique française et la diversité culturelle." *Droit et Société, 27*.

Rousseau, Jean-Jacques. 1987. "On the Social Contract." In *Jean Jacques Rousseau: The Basic Political Writings*, edited by Donald A. Cress. Indianapolis: Hacket.

Roy, Olivier. 2004. *Globalised Islam. The Search for a New Ummah*. New York: Columbia University Press.

Roy, Olivier. 2005. *L'islam face à la laïcité*. Paris: Hachette.

Rufin, Jean-Christophe. 2004. *Chantier sur la lutte contre le racisme et l'antisemitisme*. Paris: Ministère de l'Intérieur, de la Sécurité Intérieure et des Libertés Locales.

Sanos, Sandrine. 2012. *The Aesthetics of Hate: Far-Right Intellectuals, Antisemitism, and Gender in 1930s France*. Stanford: Stanford University Press.

Said, Edward. 1985. "Orientalism Reconsidered." *Cultural Critique*, 1.

Sarkozy, Nicolas. 2003a. "20éme rassemblement annuel de L'UOIF Intervention de Monsieur Nicolas Sarkozy—Le Bourget." *Ministère de l'intérieur, de la sécurité intérieure et des libertés locales*, 19 April.

Sarkozy, Nicolas. 2003b. "Amélioration de l'exécution des mesures de reconduite à la frontière, October 22." *Ministère de l'intérieur, de la sécurité intérieure et des libertés locales.*

Sarkozy, Nicolas. 2007a. Discours du Président de la République, 12 July. Remise collective de décorations Palais de l'Élysée. *Palais de l'Élysée, Paris.*

Sarkozy, Nicolas. 2007b. Allocution du Président de la République. Rupture du Jeûne Grande Mosquée de Paris - Lundi 1er octobre 2007. *Palais de l'Elysée.*

Sarkozy, Nicolas. 2007c. Allocution du Président de la République à l'Archevêché de Paris en l'honneur de Monseigneur Vingt-Trois, créé Cardinal le 24 novembre 2007 par sa Sainteté le Pape Benoît XVI. *Palais de l'Elysée.*

Sarkozy, Nicolas. 2007d. Allocution de M. le Président de la République française. Salle de la Signature du palais du Latran, Rome (Italie), 20 December. *Palais de l'Elysée.*

Sarkozy, Nicolas. 2007e. Entretien de M. Le Président de la République à l'Osservatore Romano, Centre de Télévision du Vatican et Radio Vatican, 20 December. *Palais de l'Elysée.*

Sarkozy, Nicolas. 2008a. Allocution devant le Conseil consultatif Riyad (Arabie Saoudite). Lundi 14 janvier 2008. *Palais de l'Elysée.*

Sarkozy, Nicolas. 2008b. Allocution de M. le Président de la République française. Vœux aux Corps Diplomatique Palais de l'Élysée. Vendredi 18 janvier 2008. *Palais de l'Elysée.*

Sarkozy, Nicolas. 2008c. Discours de M. le Président de la République Une nouvelle politique pour les banlieues Palais de l'Elysée - Vendredi 8 février 2008. *Palais de l'Elysée.*

Sarkozy, Nicolas. 2008d. Allocution de Monsieur le Président de la République. Diner Annuel du CRIF. Mercredi 13 février 2008. *Palais de l'Elysée.*

Sarkozy, Nicolas. 2008e. Entretien du Président de la République face aux lecteurs du quotidien 'Le Parisien'. Parution mardi 26 février. *Palais de l'Elysée.*

Sarkozy, Nicolas. 2008f. Allocution de M. le Président de la République française. Visite en France de Sa Sainteté le pape Benoît XVI, 12 September. *Palais de l'Elysée.*

Sarkozy, Nicolas. 2008g. Discours de M. le Président de la République. Égalité des chances et diversité. Palaiseau, École polytechnique, 17 December. *Palais de l'Elysée.*

Sarkozy, Nicolas. 2009a. Déclaration de M. le Président de la République devant le parlement réuni en congrès Versailles, 22 June. *Palais de l'Elysée.*

Sarkozy, Nicolas. 2009b. Discours de M. le Président de la République française. La Chapelle-en-Vercors (Drôme), 12 November. *Palais de l'Elysée.*

Sarkozy, Nicolas. 2010a. Allocution de M. le Président de la République Ablain-Saint-Nazaire (Pas-de-Calais). Hommage aux soldats morts pour la France au cimetière national, Notre-Dame de Lorette, 26 January. *Palais de l'Elysée.*
Sarkozy, Nicolas. 2010c. Déclaration de M. le Président de la République, 24 March. *Palais de l'Élysée.*
Sarkozy, Nicolas. 2010d. Intervention de M. le Président de la République lors du Conseil des ministres, 27 May. *Palais de l'Elysée.*
Sarkozy, Nicolas. 2010e. Discours de M. le Président de la République au Vatican, 8 September. *Ambassade de France près le Saint-Siège.*
Sartre, Jean-Paul. 1946. *Réflexions sur la question juive.* Paris: Morihien.
Sayyid, Bobby. 2003. *A Fundamental Fear. Eurocentrism and the Emergence of Islamism.* London and New York: Zed Books.
Sayyid, Bobby. 2009. "Contemporary Politics of Secularism." In *Secularism, Religion and Multicultural Citizenship*, edited by Geoffrey B. Levey and Tariq Modood. Cambridge: Cambridge University Press.
SCEREN. 2004. *Guide républicain. L'idée de la républicaine aujourd'hui.* Paris: Delagrave.
Schiappa, Jean-Marc. 2005. "Note sur l'Algérie colonisée." In *1905! La loi de séparation des Églises et de l'État*, edited by Jean-Marc. Schiappa. Paris: Éditions Syllepse.
Schlegel, Jean-Louis. 2008. "Nicolas Sarkozy, la laïcité et les religions." *Revue ESPRIT: Le gouvernement des villes,* February. Accessed January 27, 2015. http://www.eurozine.com/articles/2008-04-03-schlegel-fr.html.
Schmitt, Carl. 2005. *Political Theologies.* Chicago: University of Chicago Press.
Schmitt, Carl. 2007. *The Concept of the Political.* Chicago: University of Chicago Press.
Schneider, Michel. 2010. *Big Mother: Psychopathologie de la vie politique.* Paris: Odile.
Schwartz, Rémy. 2007. "La jurisprudence de la loi 1905." In *Politiques de la laïcité au XXe siècle*, edited by Patrick Weil. Paris: PUF.
Scott, David and Charles Hirschkind (eds). 2006. Powers of the Secular Modern: Talal Asad and His Interlocutors. Stanford: Stanford University Press.
Scott, Joan W. 2005. *Parité! Sexual Equality and the Crisis of French Universalism.* Chicago: University of Chicago Press.
Scott, Joan W. 2007. *The Politics of the Veil.* Princeton: Princeton University Press.
Scott, Joan W. 2009. "Sexularism." Ursula Hirschmann Annual Lecture on Gender and Europe, EUI, Florence, April 2009. http://cadmus.eui.eu/bitstream/handle/1814/11553/RSCAS_DL_2009_01.pdf?sequence=1.
Selby, Jennifer. 2012. *Questioning French Secularism. Gender Politics and Islam in a French Suburb.* New York: Palgrave McMillan.
Sénat. 2004a. *Séance du 2 mars 2004* (compte rendu intégral des débats). Accessed January 27, 2015. https://www.senat.fr.
Sénat. 2004b. *Scrutin n°155—Laïcité.* Accessed January 27, 2015. https://www.senat.fr.

Sénat. 2004c. *Séance du 3 mars 2004* (compte rendu intégral des débats). Accessed January 27, 2015. https://www.senat.fr.

Sénat. 2010a. *Scrutin (N°276) sur l'ensemble du projet de loi, adopté par l'Assemblée nationale, interdisant la dissimulation du visage dans l'espace public*. Accessed January 27, 2015. https://www.senat.fr.

Sénat. 2010b. 2e session extraordinaire de 2009–2010 compte rendu intégral. *Journal officiel de la République française, 82*, 6708–6769.

Shakman Hurd, Elizabeth. 2008. *The Politics of Secularism in International Relations*. Princeton: Princeton University Press.

Silverman, Max. 2007. "The French Republic Unveiled." *Ethnic and Racial Studies*, 4(30).

Solé, Robert. 1989. "Islam et laïcité: Le port du foulard à l'école pose le problème de l'intégration." *Le Monde*, 21 October: 1 and 13.

Soustelle, Jacques. 1989. "Au-delà des foulards: L'idéntité culturelle de la France." *Le Figaro*, November 2: 2.

Sowerwine, Charles. 2009. *France Since 1870: Culture, Society and the Making of the Republic*. New York: Palgrave Macmilian.

Spivak, Gayatri. 1988. "Can the Subaltern Speak?" In *Marxism and the Interpretation of Culture*, edited by Cary Nelson and Lawrence Grossberg. Basingstoke: Macmillan Education.

Stack, Trevor, Timothy Fitzgerald, and Naomi Goldenberg. 2015. *Religion as Category of Governance and Sovereignty*. Leiden: Brill.

Stasi, Bernard. 2003. *Commission de reflexion sur l'application du principe de laïcité dans la République*. Paris: La Documentation française.

Stavrakakis, Yannis. 1999. *Lacan and the Political*. London and New York: Routledge.

Taguieff, Jean-Pierre. 2005. "Communauté et 'communautarisme' un défi pour la pensée républicaine." *Cahier du CEVIPOF, 43*.

Taira, Temu. 2013. "Making Space for Discursive Study in Religious Studies." *Religion*, 43(1), 26–45.

Tamimi, Azzim. 2000. "Origins of Arab Secularism." In *Islam and Secularism in the Middle East*, edited by John L. Esposito and Azzim Tamimi. New York: New York University Press.

Taylor, Charles. 2007. *A Secular Age*. Harvard: Harvard University Press.

Taylor, Charles. 2008. "What is Secularism." In *Secularism, Religion and Multicultural Citizenship*, edited by Geoffrey Brahm Levey and Tariq Modood. Cambridge: Cambridge University Press.

Taylor, Charles. 2011. "Why we need a Radical Definition of Secularism." In *The Power of Religion in the Public Sphere*, edited by Eduardo Mendieta and Jonathan VanAntwerpen. New York: Columbia University Press.

Telhine, Mohammed. 2010. *L'islam et les musulmans en France: Une histoire de mosquées*. Paris: L'Harmattan.

Tévanian, Pierre. 2005. *Le voile médiatique. Un faux débat: "l'affaire du foulard islamique."* Paris: Raison d'agir.

Tévanian, Pierre. 2014. "A Conservative Revolution within Secularism." *Les mots sont importants*, 15 March. Accessed 27 January, 2015. http://lmsi.net/A-Conservative-Revolution-within.

TF1. 2007. "Interview de Nicolas Sarkozy, président de l'UMP: Rassembler sous une même ambition l'immigration et l'identité nationale." *Journal televisé de 20h*. Paris: INA.

Tincq, Henri. 2003. "La laïcité n'est pas l'adversaire de la religion." *Le monde des religions*, n°1, September-October: 66-69.

Tissot, S. 2008. "Bilan d'un féminisme d'Etat. De Ni putes ni soumises aux lois anti-voile." *Les mots sont importants*, February 1. Accessed January 27, 2015. http://lmsi.net/Bilan-d-un-feminisme-d-Etat.

Tissot, Sylvie. 2012. "Qui a peur du communautarisme?". In *La Cassure: l'état du monde 2013*, edited by Bertrand Badie and Dominique Vidal. Paris: La Découverte.

Torfing, Jacob. 1999. *New Theories of Discourse: Laclau, Mouffe and Zizek*. London: Blackwell Publishers.

Trigano, Shmuel. 2005. "Les non-dits du débat français sur le communautarisme." *Cahier du CEVIPOF, 43*.

Valade, Jean. 2004. *Rapport fait au nom de la commission des Affaires culturelles sur le projet de loi, adopté par l'Assemblée nationale, encadrant, en application du principe de laïcité, le port de signes ou de tenues manifestant une appartenance religieuse dans les écoles, collèges et lycées publics*. Paris: Sénat.

Van Eeckhout, Laetitia. 2008. "Les juges s'appuient sur la soumission de cette femme." *Le Monde*, 27 June. Accessed January 27, 2015. http://www.lemonde.fr/societe/article/2008/07/16/les-juges-s-appuient-sur-la-soumission-de-cette-femme_1072402_3224.html.

Vincent, Elise. 2012. "Le gouvernement affiche une baisse historique des naturalisations en 2012." *Le Monde*, 11 January. Accessed January 27, 2015. http://www.lemonde.fr/a-la-une/article/2012/01/10/le-gouvernement-affiche-une-baisse-historique-des-naturalisations-en-2011_1627783_3208.html.

Wahnich, Sophie. 1997. *L'impossible citoyen. L'étranger dans le discours de la Rèvolution française*. Paris: Albin Michel.

Walby, Sylvia. 1986. *Patriarchy at Work*. Cambridge, UK: Polity Press.

Wieviorka, Michel. 2007. *The Lure of Anti-Semitism. Hatred of Jews in Present-Day France*. Leiden: Brill.

Weil, Patrick. (2007). "La loi de 1905 et son application depuis un siècle." In *Politiques de la laïcité au XXe siècle. PUF, Paris*. Paris: PUF.

Winter, Bronwyn. 2008. *Hijab and the Republic. Undercovering the French Headscarf Debate*. Syracuse: Syracuse University Press.

Yankelevich, Hector. 2004. "Trois fillettes voilées peuvent-elles émouvoir Marianne?" In *La laïcité dévoilée. Quinze années de débat en quarante Rebonds*, edited by Jean-Michel Helvig. Paris: Libération and Éditions de l'Aube.

Young, Iris M. 2005. "The Logic of Masculinist Protection: Reflections on the Current Security State." In *Women and Citizenship*, edited by Marilyn Friedman. Oxford: Oxford University Press.

Žižek, Slavoj. 1989. The Sublime Object of Ideology. London: Verso.

Žižek, Slavoj. 1990. "Eastern Europe's Republics of Gilead." *New Left Review* (183), 51–62.

Žižek, Slavoj. 1999. *The Ticklish Subject: The Absent Cntre of Political Ontology*. London: Verso.

Zizek, Slavoj. 2002. Welcome to the Desert of the Real! Five Essays on September 11 and Related Dates. Verso: London and New York.

Žižek, Slavoj. 2006. "Against the Populist Temptation." *Lacan.com*. http://www.lacan.com/zizpopulism.htm.

Žižek, Slavoj. 2008. *Violence*. London: Verso.

Žižek, Slavoj. 2010. "The Neighbour in Burka." http://www.lacan.com/symptom11/?p=69.

Index

Abbas, Ferhat 27
Agulhon, Maurice 3
Albarello, Yves 140, 149, 152, 155
Alliot-Marie, Michèl 60, 69, 142, 147, 149, 152, 164, 166, 167, 173, 174, 176, 177
Almond, Ian 29
Amara, Fadela 61, 63, 64, 75, 90, 104
Amghar, Samir 143, 156
Andalouci, Siham 64
Anidjar, Gil 13
Anthias, Floria 42, 65
Appadurai, Arjun 193
Asad, Talal 13, 14, 24, 26, 39, 40, 104
Ayrault, Jacques 113, 126

Badinter, Élisabeth 49
Badiou, Alain 68, 193
Bailly, Lionel 134
Balligand, Jean-Pierre 112, 128
Bapt, Gérard 130
Baroin, François 51
Barre, Raymond 73
Barrot, Jacques 92, 102
Baubérot, Jean 17, 22, 23, 26, 27, 46, 55, 112, 119, 123, 144, 194, 197
Bayrou, François 46, 117
Behring Breivik, Anders 196
Benzaine, Kaïna 90, 99
Bertrand, Yves 23, 109
Besson, Éric 1, 2, 138
Biancheri, Gabriel 127
Bodin, Jean 111, 147, 152, 155
Bonaparte, Napoleon 65, 191
Bonnet, Christian 73
Bordenave, Prada 188
Borghée, Maryam 57, 75, 155
Bouamama, Said 53
Boumediene-Thiery, Alima 148
Bouretz, Pierre 5
Bourguignon, Pierre 109, 117
Bousquet, Danielle 93
Boutin, Christine 28, 192
Bowen, John 31–33, 50, 69, 114
Brard, Jean-Pierre 111, 115, 127–129

Brown, Wendy 41, 133, 192
Brunel, Chantal 81
Brunhes, Jacques 111
Buffet, Marie-George 109, 179, 180
Bur, Yves 111, 125, 128

Calméjane, Patrice 146, 152
Cambadélis, Jean-Christophe 83
Cameron, David 3
Camiscioli, Elisa 65, 72, 133, 192
Carayon, Bernard 109
Casanova, José 8, 15–17, 24, 25, 29
Cervulle, Maxime 72
Chabal, Emile 2, 5, 27
Chenière, Ernest 47, 48, 50
Chirac, Jacques 37, 52, 53, 67, 69, 80, 108–110, 114, 115, 118, 119–121, 124–126, 130, 160
Cholet, Mona 192
Citron, Suzanne 162, 190
Clement, Pascal 38, 52, 127
Clement Commission 38
Clos, Max 49
Cohen-Seat, Borvo 151
Coller, Ian 40, 65, 72
Combes, Emile 111
Copé, Jean-François 58, 147, 151
Couanau, René 86

David, Martime 3, 37, 53, 102, 128
d'Estaing, Giscard 73, 160
de Cock, Lauremce 163
de Fontenay, Élisabeth 49
de Galembert, Claire 67
de Gaulle, Charles 28, 160, 163
de Rugy, François 144
Debray, Régis 3, 49, 111
Debré, Jean-Louis 23, 37, 52, 81, 83, 85, 86, 87, 96, 103, 108, 111, 112, 155
Debré Commission 37, 52, 81, 85, 86, 108, 110–112, 123
Délphy, Christine 35
Devji, Faisal 43
Diard, Éric 140

Djavann, Chadhortt 64
Domergue, Jacques 109, 129, 147
Dosière, René 110
Drier, Richard 71
du Séjour, Dionis 120, 127, 130
Durand, Yves 117, 124, 128

Erbakan, Necemettin 20
Erdoğan, Recep Tayip 21
Esnol, Philippe 146, 147, 150, 176

Farhi, Gabriel 193
Feraoun, Mouloud 62
Fernando, Mayanthi 36, 45, 193
Ferry, Jules 5, 48, 83, 107, 109, 111, 116, 124, 128, 129, 172
Ferry, Luc 83, 107, 116, 124, 128, 129
Fillon, François 121
Finkelkraut, Alain 3, 49
Fitzgerald, Timothy 25, 39
Folliot, Philippe 115
Fortassin, François 151, 154
Foucault, Michel 40, 41, 42, 43, 132
Fourest, Caroline 194, 195, 197
Frégosi, Franck 26, 73

Gaffney, John 63, 163
Gambetta, Léon 111
Garraud, Jean-Paul 152, 154, 177, 179
Gautier, Nathalie 126
Geisser, Vincent 13, 53, 67, 70, 72, 94
Gerin, André 38, 46, 56, 58, 59, 60, 120, 126, 128, 130, 140, 142, 143, 145, 146, 150–152, 154–156, 164, 167, 173–178
Gerin Commission 38, 56, 58, 139, 143, 146, 149, 150, 152, 154, 156, 164, 167, 173, 175–178
Glavany, Jean 57, 58, 108, 110–112, 123, 129, 147, 148, 175
Gosnat, Pierre 59, 151
Goy-Chavent, Sylvie 175
Grand, Jean-Pierre 115
Gresh, Alain 61, 191
Guéant, Claude 194
Guénif-Souilamas, Nacira 65
Guibal, Jean-Claude 154
Gustavsson, Gina 196

Habchi, Sihem 154
Hajjat, Abdellali 45
Hargreaves, Alec 47, 73, 74
Hazan, Éric 68
Henri VI 160, 163
Hirsi Ali, Ayan 195
Hobbes, Thomas 111
Hortefeux, Brice 58, 74, 142, 171
Howarth, David 3, 37
Hummel, Christian 38, 147, 152, 155, 161, 175
Hummel Commission 38, 161
Huntington, Samuel 84

India, Xavier 41

Jaurés, Jean 27, 111
Jean d'Arc 190
Joppke, Christian 13
Jospin, Lionel 50
Jung, Armand 123

Keaton, Diane 50, 61, 68, 89
Kemp, Anna 63, 64
Keohane, Robert 14
Kepel, Gilles 89
Khiari, Sadri 67, 71
King Philip IV 109
Kintzler, Catherine 49
Kuru, Ahmet 14, 17, 19–23, 27–29

Labarre, Marie-Agnès 149, 151, 152
Laborde, Cécile 6, 7, 35, 196
Laclau, Ernesto 41, 43
Lacuey, Conchita 126
Lagarde, Jean-Christophe 148
Lamour, Jean-François 152
Lazreg, Marnia 62
Le Bris, Gilbert 93
Le Pen, Jean-Marie 73, 197
Le Pen, Marine 197
Lefort, Jean-Claude 42
Lellouche, Pierre 80
Leroy, Jean-Claude 118
Lévy, Alma 28, 51, 195
Lévy, Bernard-Henri 195
Lévy, Lila 51
Locke, John 111
Lopez, Alfred 71

Madame M   173, 186–188
Maillot, Agnès   189, 192
Mamère, Noël   59
Marelli, Joëlle   88
Mariton, Hervé   120
Massad, Jospeh   13
Masuzawa, Tomoko   13, 25, 30, 39
Maurer, Jean-Philippe   149
Merkel, Angela   3
Micheau, Françoise   65, 162
Mitterand, François   5, 23, 28, 73
Mohammed, Marwan   45, 195
Monod, Jean-Claude   6, 7, 27, 45
Mouffe, Chantal   4, 41, 43
Myard, Jacques   144, 148, 151, 152, 157

Noiriel, Gerard   68, 72, 94
Norval, Aletta   37

Obama, Barack   56

Pasqua, Charles   23, 74
Paul (the Apostle)   108, 152, 154, 177, 191
Perez, Jean-Claude   112
Perruchot, Nicolas   98
Peyronnet, Jean-Claude   153
Poletti, Bérengère   175

Raffarin, Jean-Pierre   51, 108, 109, 115–118, 120, 125, 127
Raoult, Éric   38, 56, 129
Rees-Roberts, Nick   72
Reiss, Frédéric   112
Renan, Ernest   111
Reveau, Jean-Pierre   197
Rigouste, Mathieu   66, 68, 74, 84
Rivière, Jérôme   81
Robin-Rodrigo, Chantal   148, 150, 153
Rocard, Michel   73
Rochefort, Florence   26, 34
Roudinesco, Élisabeth   103
Roudy, Yvette   153, 155
Rousseau, Jean-Jacques   111, 121, 122, 128, 186
Rushdie, Salman   30, 195

Sarkozy, Nicolas   3, 4, 44, 50, 53, 55, 56, 70, 71, 74, 137, 138, 139, 140, 141, 150, 159–173, 176, 178, 186, 190, 191
Sayyid, Bobby   31, 193, 194
Schmitt, Carl   6, 36, 114, 132, 193
Scott, Joan W.   13, 24, 33–36, 50, 62, 72, 75, 133
Selby, Jennifer   36
Shakman Hurd, Elisabeth   26, 28, 39, 65
Solé, Robert   49
Spivak, Gayatri   181, 188
Stasi, Bernard   37, 52, 53, 80, 82, 85, 87, 90, 92, 96, 98, 101, 108, 110–113, 116, 120, 123, 124, 127, 130
Stasi Commission   37, 52, 53, 55, 82, 85, 86, 87, 90, 98, 101, 110–113, 120, 123, 124, 127, 130
Stavrakakis, Yannis   37, 41
Stoléru, Lionel   73

Taguieff, Pierre-André   70
Taylor, Charles   8, 17, 26, 29, 30
Tevanian, Pierre   45
Tissot, Sylvie   63, 69, 70
Torfing, Jacob   37, 41, 44
Troendle, Catherine   154

Vaillant, Daniel   119
Valade Commission   38, 52, 80, 85–87, 96, 98, 100, 108, 111, 119
Vannest, Christian   82
Vivien, Alain   68
Voltaire   111, 163

Wilks, Lars   195
Winter, Bronwyn   32, 33, 49

Yval-Davis, Nira   65

Zemouri, Aziz   53, 72, 94
Zimeray, François   68
Žižek, Slavoj   4, 14, 41, 42, 95, 105, 131, 182, 190

www.ingramcontent.com/pod-product-compliance
Lightning Source LLC
Chambersburg PA
CBHW070134080526
44586CB00015B/1684